Literacy for Sustainable Development in the Age of Information

THE LANGUAGE AND EDUCATION LIBRARY

Series Editor
Professor David Corson, *The Ontario Institute for Studies in Education, 252 Bloor St. West, Toronto, Ontario, Canada M5S 1V6.*

Other Books in the Series
Competing and Consensual Voices
  PATRICK COSTELLO and SALLY MITCHELL (eds)
Computers and Talk in the Primary Classroom
  RUPERT WEGERIF and PETER SCRIMSHAW (eds.)
Critical Theory and Classroom Talk
  ROBERT YOUNG
Language Policies in English-Dominant Countries
  MICHAEL HERRIMAN and BARBARA BURNABY (eds)
Language Policy Across the Curriculum
  DAVID CORSON
Language, Minority Education and Gender
  DAVID CORSON
Learning about Punctuation
  NIGEL HALL and ANNE ROBINSON (eds)
Making Multicultural Education Work
  STEPHEN MAY
School to Work Transition in Japan
  KAORI OKANO
Studies in Immersion Education
  ELAINE M. DAY and STAN M. SHAPSON
Reading Acquisition Processes
  G.B. THOMPSON, W.E. TUNMER and T. NICHOLSON (eds)
Worlds of Literacy
  M. HAMILTON, D. BARTON and R. IVANIC (eds)

Other Books of Interest
The Open University Readers
Language and Literacy in Social Practice
  JANET MAYBIN (ed.)
Language, Literacy and Learning in Educational Practice
  BARRY STIERER and JANET MAYBIN (eds)
Media Texts: Authors and Readers
  DAVID GRADDOL and OLIVER BOYD-BARRETT (eds)
Researching Language and Literacy in Social Context
  DAVID GRADDOL, JANET MAYBIN and BARRY STIERER (eds)

Please contact us for the latest book information:
Multilingual Matters, Frankfurt Lodge, Clevedon Hall,
Victoria Road, Clevedon, BS21 7HH, England
www.multilingual-matters.com

THE LANGUAGE AND EDUCATION LIBRARY 14
Series Editor: Professor David J. Corson,
The Ontario Institute for Studies in Education

Literacy for Sustainable Development in the Age of Information

Naz Rassool

MULTILINGUAL MATTERS LTD
Clevedon • Philadelphia • Toronto • Sydney • Johannesburg

To My Husband, Joe

Library of Congress Cataloging in Publication Data

Rassool, Naz
Literacy for Sustainable Development in the Age of Information/Naz Rassool
The Language and Education Library: 14
Includes bibliographical references and index
1. Literacy–Social aspects. 2. Sociolinguistics. 3. Information technology–Social aspects. 4. Functional literacy. 5. Sustainable development. I. Title. II. Series.
LC149.R37   1999
302.2'244–dc21   98-44259

British Library Cataloguing in Publication Data

A CIP catalogue record for this book is available from the British Library.

ISBN 1-85359-433-4 (hbk)
ISBN 1-85359-432-6 (pbk)

Multilingual Matters Ltd

UK: Frankfurt Lodge, Clevedon Hall, Victoria Road, Clevedon BS21 7HH.
USA: 325 Chestnut Street, Philadelphia, PA 19106, USA.
Canada: 5201 Dufferin Street, North York, Ontario M3H 5T8, Canada.
Australia: P.O. Box 586, Artamon, NSW, Australia.
South Africa: PO Box 1080, Northcliffe 2115, Johannesburg, South Africa.

Typeset by Archetype Information Technology (http://www.archetype-IT.com).
Printed and bound in Great Britain by WBC Book Manufacturers Ltd.

Contents

Acknowledgements

This book would not have been written without the generous support and encouragement of the series editor, David Corson. I am deeply grateful for this and other projects that I have been involved with through his encouragement. I should also like to thank the following people for their help and support whilst writing this book: Paul Croll, my head of department, for the generous reduction of teaching hours to enable me to do some writing during term time; my much valued colleagues Viv Edwards, Alan Rogers, George Hunt and Kevin Brehony for their generous discussion and helpful comments on some of the chapters. I want to thank Louise Morley at the London University Institute of Education for her comments on several chapters in the book, and for her friendship, encouragement and sisterly support always. I am immensely grateful to Stephen May at the University of Bristol for his invaluable comments and suggestions on an earlier draft of the manuscript. I appreciate his encouragement when I particularly needed friendly and collegial support. I am deeply indebted to Tove Skutnabb-Kangas for her enthusiasm, her willingness to share ideas as well as her sisterly support and encouragement. I am especially grateful to her for finding time to read the whole manuscript and making detailed comments, and writing the Foreword in spite of her very busy schedule. I want to thank my husband Joe for his support and encouragement in all my endeavours always.

Foreword

Tove Skutnabb-Kangas

The 'simple literacy' (basic reading, writing, numeracy) and the 'functional literacy' were presented as panaceas in the 1950s and the 1970s, respectively. If everybody learned how to read and write, or learned this selectively, in the work-place, for production-oriented purposes, this would enhance development, both for the individuals themselves, and for their societies. Economic problems would be solved. The first one, with *mass literacy campaigns*, was the quick fix, and the second, the not-so-quick-but-still-imaginable fix, was Universal Primary Education, *UPE before the year 19XX*, XX being constantly postponed.

As UNESCO have recently admitted and as Naz Rassool shows in this book, they have not worked. Literacy, this time possibly also including functional computer literacy, as part of the necessary modernisation package, is still presented by the governments of 'developing countries' and by UNESCO, the World Bank, the IMF and countless 'aid' organisations as a panacea which will solve 'development' problems. What Naz Rassool warns us about in this book is the next, much more sophisticated fix-in-making — which is not going to work either.

Planning for literacies is part of language planning and language policy. Arguments about the necessity of literacy have been sold under a broad umbrella which could be called *human rights and democracy arguments* (which include individual development arguments, cognitive benefits, fulfilling and optimising one's potential, right to information, etc., and arguments about informed participation). Arguments about benefits of literacy have, in addition, been sold as *arguments about economics*: better jobs for the individual, harnessing the mental resources of the population for economic progress and development of the whole society.

A full implementation of this language policy, making the whole world literate in the sense of the simple literacy (basic reading, writing and numeracy skills) would have been perfectly possible already decades ago.

Table 1 Communication (physical or mental) as exchange of commodities or ideas

	Physical communication: exchange of commodities (including physical mobility of people)	*Mental communication: exchange of ideas*
Means of communication	Motorways, roads, railways, airplanes, airports, bridges, tunnels, ships, etc.	Spoken and signed languages, visual and aural images
Tools (vehicles) needed by individuals	Legs, bicycles, motorbikes, cars, lorries, etc.	Physical apparatus for speaking, signing, reading; paper & pen, board & chalk, typewriters, TVs, computers, radios, music instruments, clothes, food, movement, etc.
Cost for material investment by society	Massive (see Means above)	Relatively large (materials for language learning, training of teachers & translators, interpretation equipment etc.)
Cost for material investment by individual	Relatively large for anything above bicycle	Relatively small for most basic tools
Cost for mental investment by society	Massive (research, planning, production, maintenance)	Relatively large (research, planning, interpretation & translation)
Cost for mental investment by individual	Relatively large (time & effort)	Relatively large (time & effort for language learning)
Return on Investment (ROI)	Negative, including environmental side-effects	Positive

This has not happened. Overt arguments against literacy have mostly been about the prohibitive cost.

Literacy is about communication. When discussing the costs in relation to communication, it is important to differentiate between what I call 'physical' and 'mental' aspects, at two levels, in relation to *communication(s)* and in relation to *power and control.*

When people 'communicate' with each other, they can *travel themselves* or *exchange commodities* ('physical communication') or they can *exchange ideas* ('mental communication'). While the costs for physical communica-

Table 2 Exerting power: means, processes and sanctions

Type	Punitive	Remunerative	Ideological
Means	Sticks	Carrots	Ideas
Process	(Physical) force	Bargaining	Persuasion
Sanctions	Negative external (punishment) (shame)	Positive external (rewards, benefits, cooptation)	Internal (guilt; good or bad conscience)

Source: From Skutnabb-Kangas, 1990: 16, mostly based on Galtung, 1980.

tions are enormous, the return on investment (ROI) low and negative, and the rationale for much of the movement of commodities non-existent, except for market capitalism, the costs for mental communications are relatively much lower, the ROI much higher and with few side-effects, and the rationale a positive one for peace and democracy (on this, see, for example, Sachs, 1992 and Galtung, 1996). Languages are our most cost-effective communication tools.

The second aspect has to do with to what extent power and control is exerted via physical or mental means.

When control is exerted through punitive or threatening measures, through a repressive state apparatus and further developments of this, the controller forces the controlled to pay the costs (for the military machinery and the techno-military complex, the police, the prisons, the mercenaries). The costs are again enormous and the ROI questionable for most of the world's population. In addition, the resources are prevented from being used for more positive purposes — all of us can cite figures for how few percent of the world's military budget would solve all the world's problems with clean drinking water, shelter, health services and basic education for all, or how much larger the increases in prison budgets in the USA have been than the increases in education budgets.

Control through carrots gives the controlled a bit more of their share of resources than control through sticks.

Control through ideas is the most important form of control, because the controlled themselves pay for most of the control 'voluntarily', through supporting the consciousness industry: education, mass media, religions. They are being controlled through their own partial consent, through attempts at colonisation of their mind, their consciousness, in a hegemonic way.

But hegemonic control also creates and enables resistance, counter-hegemonies. In earlier hegemonic control where the legitimation came from a god, the controlled did not necessarily need to understand the overt messages in religions — these were often delivered in a 'sacred' language (Latin, classical Arabic, Sanskrit) not understood (at least fully) by the subjects. In 'cuius regio, eius religio' (the one 'owning' the region also decided about the religion for that region) it was enough to accept the legitimacy of the authority of the power-holder — this was the covert message.

In modern hegemonic control we can modify the thesis to: cuius lingua, eius cultura. The one who 'owns' the language also determines the content of the hegemonising message. This is of course the rationale for why the messages of McDonaldisation (see later) come in (simplified) English and why everybody worldwide is supposed (and _wants_) to learn English. This enables global hegemonic control and the homogenisation needed for global markets.

But this control through ideas also means that there is more choice: by whose messages do you want your mind to be colonised?

In order to understand and critically reflect on the messages, to deconstruct them, you need to know the language of those messages well. You also need to appreciate what kind of messages go more often with what language. _Not_ because it would not be possible to express anything in any language; you can certainly talk war — or peace — in any language. But it seems that the users of, e.g., Esperanto, have used the language often for messages of peace, democracy, harmony, conflict resolution, grassroots orientation. It also seems that 'international English' in the consciousness industry is more often used for messages which may support less positive orientations and less reflection on the long-term consequences of a destructive lifestyle, destructive not only for the planet as a whole but also, here, specifically, for linguistic and cultural diversity: Not caring, not knowing.

Thus it is imperative to think of the different types of exertion of power and control and of the different means (including different languages) used for control, in terms of the cost for world peace, environment, biodiversity and linguistic and cultural diversity, the future of humankind on earth.

There are other possible alternatives to the emphasis on literacy. One is: literacy will soon not be needed anymore.

Producing books is too slow, buying them too expensive, storing them too bulky, reading them too linear and boring, and you cannot search in them or even download them in two minutes. Everything is on the Internet anyway. The Book is dead! Libraries will be like dinosaur parks — your greatgreatgrandchild will be taken there to see those funny things that existed in the old days.

True?

Why should people in the 'developing countries' need to become literate anymore? Television has taken over anyway, you just need to listen and watch. Like most youngsters in the West who do not read books (anymore). Like the American cartoon of two young teenagers watching the text which says 'WARNING VIOLENCE' before a film. One asks: 'What's it say?'; the other replies: 'I dunno. I can't read'.

True?

We have for years been able to scan a text and have it outputted from the computer as synthetic speech. Very soon we will have cheap mini-synthesisors which transmit written text as speech. No need to read it yourself.

True?

Soon everybody in the world will know spoken English. We watch and listen to the same things. All of us have access. Then all of us, literate or not, are equal.

True?

NO! What Naz Rassool shows in this book is, in fact, that the literacies we need now and in the future *include* the 'old' literacies — which have not been and are not going to be replaced or are replacable. *In addition* they include multi-faceted new skills and competencies and attitudes; in short, they demand much much more.

She argues that computers and multimedia technology, rather than eradicating reading, have led to 'the omnipresence of textuality, and, relatedly, reading and interpreting texts in our daily lives' and that 'in order to operate effectively within these textual environments, requires a more sophisticated range of knowledges, literacy and communication skills than the linear and functional skills traditionally associated with basic literacy'. She also shows that, despite new curricula and a lot of self-reflection, the literacies attempted today in most countries in the world and including what international agencies like UNESCO do (UNESCO has redefined its literacy targets several times during its lifetime), are nowhere near delivering what they should, or even understanding what literacy means today and what functions it has. Literacy is a 'many meaninged thing'.

At the same time, half the world's population have never made a phone call. The polarisation between 'information-rich' and 'information-poor' societies is sharpening.

My generation in the West may be in the lucky position of having had the best of the 'old' world, and the 'new' that Naz Rassool is writing about. We have full access to the new but have experienced both the old, and the transition, and (some of us) can choose, be critical and selective.

Can the youngsters of today do this? In the West, many have never experienced anything else but the hegemony of the technological 'information' society. In other parts of the world, the hegemony of the images created in the neo-evolutionary neo-liberalist markets discourse, through the consciousness industry, are so strong that there is little choice too.

Instead of the brutality of physical colonisation, what we have now is recolonisation and neo-colonisation, where the means are increasingly cultural and linguistic (that is what the consciousness industry is about). The *Context*, though, is the power relations in which the meanings and images are produced, where legitimate knowledges and social relations are negotiated and validated or invalidated, where hegemonic meanings are challenged and where individuals and groups are disempowered or empowered.

The type of literacy Naz Rassool advocates in this book should not only enable people to 'analyse the representations and significations of multimedia text but also the institutions in which they are produced and, in turn, their relationship with specific ideological, political, economic and cultural interests that underscore the social milieu'. The 'interpretative framework also includes taking account of *structural* inequalities' (those inherent in the social system), and *structured* social inequalities (resulting from policies). Unless literacy leads to a capacity to analyse those power relations it will, once again, reproduce disempowerment.

Promises connected to literacy seem to work like the promises connected to the English language: they are used like carrots to entice powerless groups into letting the exploitation continue. If you only learn X (to read; to speak English), you will be better off, get a better job, develop, become civilised — and people put a lot of effort into learning. When they have succeeded and want the promised benefits, they are being told: X is not quite enough, you need XY and then paradise will descend (to be able to fill out forms and read instructions; to pass these English exams). As an Indian colleague said, after a meeting where a small grant was given to the street sweeper working three jobs to be able to send his child to an English-medium school: 'earlier they were excluded because they did not know English; now they are excluded because of their bad English'.

In the basic literacy discourse, 'development' was claimed to be hampered by the masses of illiterate people in an 'underdeveloped', 'backward', 'traditional' country. It was the development today reflected in the terms 'the developed countries' and 'the developing countries', where the evolutionary paradigm is the set scene ('they are lower than us'), where the norm is clear ('once they become like us . . . ') and where it is only some who still need to develop because they are still (constructed as) deficient in relation to the norm.

The functional literacy targets also promoted the kind of development which demanded structural adjustment programmes to be pressed down on African and other countries by the World Bank and the IMF, programmes which did not work and made the poor still poorer.

The new literacy requirements which include simple computer literacy, again legitimate poverty and structural unemployment, especially in the South but also to some extent in the North, with the hegemonic discourse which, as usual, blames the victim, referring to deficiencies in the victims: positive characteristics, skills, knowledges and attitudes which the victims lack. This time around they lack the technological skills and capacities to function in a postmodern information society.

When some of the world's nuclear waste was about to be sent to Saturn in October 1997, NASA (the American space travel administration) were shocked by the *millions* of protests from many parts of the world (mostly the West) pouring in — the whole campaign was organised in just a few days via the Internet. Individuals getting in contact with other individuals on the other side of the world, finding common ground and acting; a miracle of grassroots organisation, a quick reaction. Freedom of information and expression, direct access to knowledge without censorship, teledemocracy? Learning more about each other, respect and tolerance, PeaceNet, EcoNet, ConflictNet? International understanding, community?

OR

Economic, military and political frameworks, with their concomitant consolidation of information and knowledge hegemonies deciding who gets access to what (hardware, information), the gap between the information-poor and information-rich widening — information increasingly being a commodity to be accumulated for profit. Interacting more in virtual reality than in the family and neighbourhood, losing contact with 'real' reality. Individualised mass-customised information flows — you can choose your news and exclude what you do not want to hear. Except the databanks sell information about you for commercial purposes so that your e-mail fills up with junk mail from advertisers. The diversity that is promoted worldwide is the right of the elites to choose between 600 toothpastes. The lack of symmetry in contemporary processes of globalisation is symbolised by what Cees Hamelink (1994: 112) calls *McDonaldisation*:

> aggressive round-the-clock marketing, the controlled information flows that do not confront people with the long-term effects of an ecologically detrimental lifestyle, the competitive advantage against local cultural providers, the obstruction of local initiative, all converge into a reduction of local cultural space.

The trend in McDonaldisation is towards production for global markets, so that products and information aim at creating 'global customers that want global services by global suppliers' (Hamelink, 1994: 110). The multi-media, including the Net, in fact make McDonaldisation virtual while at the same time glorifying it and creating the images of success in the world to correspond to the McDonaldised personality and lifestyle.

A wrong educational language policy, organised against most scientific evidence about how education should be organised if it is to promote high levels of multilingualism (see articles in Skutnabb-Kangas (ed.) 1995), has been the order of the day in most countries. It has involved linguistic genocide for linguistic minorities and monolingual reductionism for linguistic majorities, coupled with inefficient foreign language teaching, and, in both cases, blaming the victims for the results. Only elites have benefited.

In under-developed countries this wrong policy, in many cases promoted, advocated and partially financed by the West with its experts, is

- the most important *pedagogical* reason for 'illiteracy' in the world.
- the most efficient way of preventing the grassroots from organised resistance to continued neo-colonial exploitation.

Western language policies have, to a large extent, been based on *false either–or thinking* (you need to choose *between* languages, you cannot have both this language and that language and maybe others too). It has also promoted *subtractive* rather than *additive* language learning: the learning of a dominant language has been presented as necessarily happening at the cost of a dominated language, instead of in addition to it.

The West has led and continues to lead the way in irrational language policies, in linguistic and cultural genocide and in prevention of linguistic human rights, and the West is trying to spread the ideas in this irrational language policy to other parts of the world (with a fair success). An interesting issue is the role of language, in general, and the changing conceptions of literacy, in particular, in this process of reproducing unequal power relationships.

In constructing counterhegemonies, several types of analysis are urgent.

Firstly, we have to analyse the role of states and international organisations. Who controls them, and for whose benefit do they work? We cannot rely on the states, controlled by elites, to be nice and rational. The pressure has to come from the grassroots. Literacy is often needed for grassroots movements to grow strong.

Secondly, we have to relativise the question of costs. What are necessary communications? What are necessary costs for these necessary communications? Physical communication costs enormous sums, pollutes the planet, transports often unnecessary things, often unnecessarily. We have to make it cheaper to produce food and commodities locally where it is possible and instead use the moneys for improved mental communication. This includes supporting sophisticated literacies, linguistic and cultural diversity and the learning of additional languages.

Thirdly, the messages in mental communication are important. Whose messages do we want to speak/sign? By which ideas do we want our minds to be colonised globally — by messages of coca-cola and mcdonald or by messages of peace, democracy and sustainable development? We have to analyse the sophisticated means used for control, especially control through ideas, and we have to analyse linguicism (akin to racism and sexism) and other means of hierarchisation and their cooperation and coarticulation.

Fourthly, we who are multilingual must stop being tolerant of the monolingualism of linguistic majority populations in the big dominant countries. *They* are the ones who cause much of the costs — but we pay, because so far we have agreed to learning their languages in order for communication to work, while many of the Brits and North Americans and French and Russians and Chinese have not learned our languages.

Yukio Tsuda (1994) talks about a 'diffusion of English paradigm' (connected with capitalism, science and technology, modernisation, monolingualism, ideological globalisation and internationalisation, transnationalisation, Americanisation and homogenisation of world culture and linguistic, cultural and media imperialism), and an 'ecology of language paradigm' (connected with a human rights perspective, equality in communication, multilingualism, maintenance of languages and cultures, protection of national sovereignties and promotion of foreign language education). We need to stop tolerating both monolingual reductionism and the 'diffusion of English' paradigm and start advocating an 'ecology of languages' paradigm which includes, minimally, bilingualism but hopefully multilingualism for *all*.

Finally, we have to show the controlling elites that the world is NOT a zero-sum game. It is not necessarily so that if we win, they have to lose. Both can win, for instance from a rational languages policy and from the granting of linguistic human rights to everyone, including the sophisticated literacies that Naz Rassool advocates in this brilliant, path-breaking book.

Or, at least: if the irrationality continues, everybody, including the dominant elites, loses.

Bibliography

Galtung, Johan (1980) *The True Worlds. A Transnational Perspective.* New York: The Free Press.

Galtung, Johan (1996) *Peace by Peaceful Means. Peace and Conflict, Development and Civilization.* Oslo: International Peace Research Institute & London/Thousand Oaks/New Delhi: Sage.

Hamelink, Cees J. (1994) *Trends in World Communication: on Disempowerment and Self-empowerment.* Penang: Southbound, and Third World Network.

Phillipson, Robert and Skutnabb-Kangas, Tove (1996) English only worldwide, or language ecology. *TESOL Quarterly,* (Special Topic Issue: Language Planning and Policy, eds Thomas Ricento and Nancy Hornberger), 429–52.

Phillipson, Robert and Skutnabb-Kangas, Tove (1997) Lessons for Europe from language policy in Australia. In Martin Pütz (ed.) *Language Choices. Conditions, Constraints and Consequences* (pp. 115–59). Amsterdam/Philadelphia: John Benjamins.

Sachs, Wolfgang (ed.) (1992) *The Development Dictionary. A Guide to Knowledge as Power.* London & New Jersey: Zed Books.

Skutnabb-Kangas, Tove (1990) *Language, Literacy and Minorities.* London: The Minority Rights Group.

Skutnabb-Kangas, Tove (1996a) Educational language choice — multilingual diversity or monolingual reductionism? In Marlis Hellinger and Ulrich Ammon (eds) *Contrastive Sociolinguistics* (pp. 175–204). Berlin & New York: Mouton de Gruyter.

Skutnabb-Kangas, Tove (1996b) Promotion of linguistic tolerance and development. In Sylvie Legér (ed.) *Vers un agenda linguistique: regard futuriste sur les Nations Unies/Towards a Language Agenda: Futurist Outlook on the United Nations* (pp. 579–629). Ottawa: Canadian Center of Language Rights.

Skutnabb-Kangas, Tove (in press a) Human rights and language wrongs — a future for diversity. *Language Sciences,* Special volume, Phil Benson, Peter Grundy and Tove Skutnabb-Kangas (eds).

Skutnabb-Kangas, Tove (in press b) Language attrition, language death, language murder — different facts or different ideologies? *Proceedings of the Conference 'Strong' and 'Weak' Languages in the European Union: Aspects of Linguistic Hegemonism.* Centre for the Greek Language, Aristotle University of Thessaloniki & Organisation 'Thessaloniki Cultural Capital of Europe 1997'.

Skutnabb-Kangas, Tove (forthcoming) *Linguistic Genocide in Schools: Do Minority Languages Have a Future?* Berlin and New York: Mouton de Gruyter. Contributions to the Sociology of Language Series.

Skutnabb-Kangas, Tove and García, Ofelia (1995) Multilingualism for all — general principles? In Tove Skutnabb-Kangas (ed.) *Multilingualism for All* (pp. 221–56). Lisse: Swets & Zeitlinger.

Skutnabb-Kangas, Tove and Phillipson, Robert (1997) Linguistic human rights and development. In C.J. Hamelink (ed.) *Ethics and Development: On Making Moral Choices in Development Co-operation* (pp. 56–69). Kampen, The Netherlands: Kok.

Tsuda, Yukio (1994) The diffusion of English: Its impact on culture and communication. *Keio Communication Review* 16, 49–61.

Introduction: What is Literacy?

The intention of this book is to explore the complexities that surround the concept of literacy in the contemporary world. This includes a consideration of the role of literacy in the border-less, global 'technoscape' (Appadurai, 1993) of the late 20th century. In particular, it examines the ways in which information technology has changed the ways in which we now need to think about what literacy is, the social, cultural and political purposes that it serves and the value principles that are attached to being literate in the 'information age'.

These issues and concerns are given context by an evaluation of older discourses on literacy within print-based culture. This is in line with Levine's (1994: 114) argument that:

> it is the dynamics of this underlying communication system [print literacy], and the complex interactions between the multiple media and different information technologies on which it relies, that constitutes the key context within which the future forms of literacy and illiteracy will take place. (Information in brackets added)

Many conceptual problems related to print literacy remain unresolved and different views abound as to what literacy is. Similarly, the mass approaches adopted to eradicate world illiteracy during the 1970s, and the role of literacy in the process of societal development, generally, have been called into question (UNESCO, 1997). How do these literacy and development issues relate to a global context within which information and knowledge have become primary cultural and economic resources? What lessons are to be learned from the mass functional literacy campaigns of the 1970s?

Starting with the question, 'What is literacy?', the rest of this chapter seeks to contextualise the issues discussed in the book. It provides a critical overview of some of the debates that surround (a) the way literacy, traditionally, has been conceptualised, theorised and understood; (b) the role that national language has historically played in shaping dominant literacies in society and culture; (c) the links in dominant discourses

1

between literacy levels and social development; and (d) the impact of information technology on the way that literacy is conceptualised and theorised within the context of the 'information society'.

Literacy and Hegemony

Much has been written about the value of literacy from both an individual and societal perspective. And, despite the unresolved debate about definitions and models, a basic consensus surrounds the idea that within a print-dominated culture, a person who can read and write, at whatever level, maintains a position along the 'literate' continuum. At the same time, depending on the context, people are judged to be *illiterate* according to particular emphases placed on different literacy skills and forms of knowledges, and their levels of attainment.

But whilst people may not necessarily all agree about what literacy is, most would probably agree that it is 'good'. We hear about the significance of being literate on the radio and television, read about it in newspapers; we hear about it in school and in everyday conversations between people; it is passed down the generations. These everyday discourses shape our commonsense understandings about the intrinsic value of being literate in the modern world.

We do not usually question these meanings; they exist as self-evident, unquestionable 'truths'. They form part of the natural way in which we approach our everyday world. These subtle, taken-for-granted, everyday commonsense meanings that frame and permeate our individual and collective consciousness, constitute the essence of what Gramsci (1971) describes as *hegemonic* power. The concept of hegemony according to Williams (1989: 57), refers to a taken-for-granted assimilation of selective, dominant values, ideas and beliefs 'to such a depth that the pressures and limits of what can ultimately be seen as a specific economic, political and cultural system seem to most of us the pressures and limits of simple experience and commonsense'.

In reality though, does literacy necessarily empower us as individuals and, at the same time, facilitate societal development as is often claimed? Does literacy develop the intellect and strengthen the power of thought as is maintained by writers such as Goody and Watt (1968), and Oxenham (1980)? Does it 'liberate the mind from the bondage of dependence' and 'contribute toward human fulfilment and liberation' (UNESCO, 1975 quoted in Rogers, 1993 : 159)? Does life expectancy rise at birth as adult literacy rates increase within society (UNESCO, 1997) ?

These are the commonsense, untested and untestable 'truth' claims — the 'hegemony' of literacy as 'cultural capital'. In other words, literacy represents that which we all must have to be able to partake of the 'good life', and contribute to the development of society as a whole. Similar meanings also surround the concept of 'technological literacy'. Nowadays 'technological literacy' has become a necessary requisite for effective functioning as workers and citizens in the information society. Indeed, the impact of information technology on literacy, and relatedly, culture and society has been equated with that of the print revolution during the 19th century. For many writers, like Bolter (1991), it has not only created a new 'writing space', it has fundamentally altered the social and educational status of the conventionally written book. How valid is this view, and what are the implications for the way in which we conceptualise what literacy is?

Are the notions of literacy embedded in these diverse claims equivalent? That is to say, do they tell the same story about literacy, and are they grounded in the same pedagogies? Are they framed by the same sets of knowledge, understanding and skills criteria? If not, why not? Why and how are different views and forms of literacies privileged over others? In a world in which electronic texts play an increasingly important role in everyday life, how realistically can the notion of literacy focused primarily on the reading and writing of conventional print be sustained?

Literacy and Social Policy

Although understanding the literacy process is undoubtedly important in terms of pedagogy, literacy has always been about much more than a set of skills to be learned; it is more than a practical activity. Grounded in broader social and political discourses, it also has potent symbolic value. As a communication practice embedded in society and culture, literacy is deeply implicated in the lives of people, cultural transmission, and cultural reproduction. That is to say, it provides the means, *par excellence*, by which cultures make, and remake themselves. The central role that dominant languages and literary traditions play in this process has been very well-documented in the works of, *inter alia*, Mathieson (1975), Williams (1961) and Graff (1979, 1987). These writers discuss the different ways in which national language policy plays a key role in privileging certain literacies and literary traditions over and against others.

Literacy and national language policy

National language policy provides one of the key means by which control is exercised over the types and forms of literacy that are legitimised in social policy. In a culturally plural society, this becomes important with regard to which different cultural group languages are valued and given social, economic and political status in society. South Africa during the Apartheid era (1948–92) provides a good illustration of the extent to which national language policy formed part of a broader process of defining different groups of people, their cultures, histories and experiences through the systematised exclusion of literacies in different cultural languages. Within that context, literacy only in the official languages, English and Afrikaans, had social and economic currency. The languages of the diverse indigenous South African population groups had no economic exchange value, and social relevance only within their various tribal communities.

Literacy and colonial relations

As will be seen in the following chapters, South Africa pre–1992 was not unique in subjugating minority languages or local cultural literacies. The marginalisation and suppression of the literacies and literature belonging to different peoples have a long history in colonial and neo-colonial domination. The impact of the dominant languages and literary practices that shaped the everyday thinking of people within colonised cultures and societies has been described in the work of writers such as Hall (1993) and Ngugi (1993). Language, these writers argue, provides the frame and terms of reference in which and through which people define themselves as persons, and as citizens. With linguistic imperialism came colonial sociopolitical and cultural systems, practices and processes that positioned disempowered subjects for generations. According to which linguistic criteria were national or different social groups' literacy levels within colonised societies measured, and how accurate was that assessment in terms of the languages that had been subjugated within those societies?

Literacy and postcolonial realities

Language and identity played a central role in the redefinition of postcolonial nations during the 1960s and 1970s. Literacy was to serve an important means to 'emancipate new nations from the cultural alienation and political dependency imposed by colonial rule' (Baumann, 1986: 6). However, the mass literacy programmes that many developing countries embarked on during the postcolonial period have failed to fulfil their promise to raise literacy levels, and to 'empower' people in many 'developing' countries.

The reasons for this are complex and depend on political and social conditions within particular societies. In many instances, as will become evident in the following chapters, it bears out Tollefson's (1991: 202) view that:

though states may fund language programmes and proclaim the importance of language learning, they simultaneously create conditions which make it virtually impossible for some citizens to acquire the language competence they need.

These factors highlight the importance of considering modes of governance, and discursive political interests globally, as influential factors in facilitating or inhibiting the distribution of literacy in different societies.

What are the real and symbolic differences created between those who are literate and those who do not meet the full requirements of 'being literate' in particular societies; between those who live in the modern 'developed' world and others in the 'developing' world? (N.B. Although the terms 'developed' and 'developing countries', for stylistic reasons, will henceforth feature without inverted commas, within the context of the book they should be read essentially as contested and value-laden terms.)

Views and Definitions of Literacy

The issues highlighted here support the sociological perspective that literacy as a social practice is fundamentally grounded in power relations. There are, of course, different views about what literacy is, and what its value is for the individual, culture and society. By referring to *views of literacy*, I mean specific sets of assumptions, values, beliefs and expectations about the impact and effects of literacy on the individual or society.

Similarly, since in a print-based culture, reading and writing provide important means of access to knowledge, *dominant definitions* of what literacy is, can be seen as being instrumental in framing the range of knowledges and skills that are valued and accredited within particular societies. In referring to *definitions* of literacy, I mean simply the statements about what it means to be literate. Thus, a definition will provide a set of criteria to be met before a person can be deemed to be literate, or not, within a particular society at a specific historical moment. Because definitions of literacy serve to underpin particular pedagogic principles, they also influence the range of resources made available in teaching and learning. This, in turn, influences what, and who, can be taught specific forms of literacy skills and knowledges.

How literacy is defined is significant in terms of the framing and selection of particular meanings, emphasising some, whilst screening out others. As such, 'the combination in which words are put together matters, and the order of propositions matters' (Macdonell, 1987: 51). The particular meanings that become attached to different literacies also come from the institutional sites from which they derive their legitimacy. Literacy then is always embedded in a discourse about, for example, knowledge and learning, about working and living in society, about culture, about social development. And, according to Macdonell (1987: 1), 'discourses differ with the kinds of institutions and social practices in which they take shape, and with the positions of those who speak and those whom they address'. Societal literacy discourses can thus be seen as comprising different 'voices', some of which may intersect and overlap, whilst other may contradict, remain indifferent (to other voices and meanings), conflict or are ambiguous in the meanings that they articulate. Institutional voices often overshadow and screen out those of individuals, or minority groups.

Subject disciplines within the academy, national governments and paranational power ensembles such as UNESCO and the OECD constitute important sites in which definitions of literacy are formulated, articulated and provided with educational, political and economic legitimacy. These ideological power positions influence who is allowed to speak, and constitute what Pecheux (1982) refers to as discursive processes through which control over social meaning is exercised. Because notions of 'what is literacy' arise in a variety of defining sites, literacy definitions are subjective and therefore arbitrary. Equally, not all definitions emphasise, or place equivalent value on the same aspects of the literacy process. Literacy then is a socially contested concept (Gee, 1996).

Functional literacy and social development
On the one hand, we have literacy conceptualised as a set of technical skills, representing a quantifiable educational resource to be evaluated against economic outcomes criteria. Within this framework, jobs are matched with 'literacy skills', and skills with 'economic needs'; 'it becomes intertranslatable with time, work, and money, part of the economy' (Gee, 1996: 123). This view of literacy is always linked to discourses about the measurement of societal development. To take a contemporary example, one of the first tasks of the New Labour government in the UK has been to place literacy at the forefront of its strategy 'to raise standards in schools' on the basis that it is 'fundamental to all future learning'. Their rationale for raising educational standards lies in the need 'to meet the challenges from competitors within the international market' (DfEE, 1997b: 11). Within this framework literacy is regarded as having high economic currency and, as such, it serves the interests of a political economy.

As we will see in various discussions in the book, this has been an enduring view in dominant versions of the relationship between literacy and societal development. It became particularly important during the 1970s when *functional literacy* played an important role in UNESCO-funded mass literacy programmes as part of the drive to modernise under-developed economies during the 1970s. *Functional literacy* came to be described as 'the process and content of learning to read and write to the preparation for work and vocational training, as well as a means of increasing the productivity of the individual' (UNESCO, 1960, quoted in Verhoeven, 1994: 6). *Functional illiteracy*, on the other hand, was defined in relation to:

> a person who cannot engage in all those activities in which literacy is required for effective functioning of his [sic] group and his community and also for enabling him to continue to use reading, writing and calculation for his own and the community's development. (UNESCO, 1972)

Basic literacy referred to the acquisition of technical skills involving the decoding of written text and the writing of simple statements within the context of everyday life. As we can see, there is much slippage between UNESCO's definitions.

Compared to the common entitlement meanings inscribed into the notion of *basic literacy*, both *functional literacy* and *functional illiteracy* provided a different perspective of what literacy *is* and also contained different expectations of the levels of functioning that would be required of 'literates'. The latter indicated a relative shift from basic technical skills to more overt concerns about 'coping skills' and 'self-help' skills within the 'community'. *Functional literacy*, on the other hand, signified an ideological shift towards work-based, work-oriented skills learning as a means to increase productivity levels linking literacy with neo-classical views of socioeconomic development. Whereas *basic literacy* and *functional illiteracy* were located in the individual, *functional literacy* had an external means–ends focus. Indeed, the links established between a literate workforce and productivity, and the inferred relationship between this and national economic development contributed to the fact that 'functional literacy' came to denote

> a means by which literacy education was built into a programme of vocational education and training, in which literacy skills and attitudes were taught and developed incidentally, the vocational content itself being central and having clear developmental consequences. (Jones, 1988: 144)

Within the societal modernisation framework of the 1970s, *functional literacy* served primarily as a means to a practical end, namely, to provide workers with the skills necessary to function within the work-place in order to increase productivity levels. This view of literacy was to dominate much of 1970s development discourse, and still features as a social indicator of economic and social development.

The discourse of 'functional' and 'basic' literacy

The UNESCO definitions discussed here derived their hegemonic value to a significant extent from the fact that they essentially presented a neutral, value-free perspective of literacy as a social and personal 'good'. Functional and basic literacy within the UNESCO framework were conceived of as a neutral set of technical decoding skills and functional writing skills existing autonomously outside culture and society. Thus they represented a technique to be learned and then applied. These definitions also presented literacy as value-free because the onus was on the individual to learn to read and write; and, relatedly, her/his ability to learn to read and write. They were deemed to be beneficial and empowering because once acquired, these skills could be applied to other areas of learning; thus they would increase knowledge and develop thinking. They were viewed as contributing to the improvement of life chances because they were useful and could be exchanged for jobs within the labour market; they would enable learners to become employable, good workers.

Literacy as social critique/literacy and empowerment

On the other hand, we have the concept of literacy as a central variable of cultural power which is grounded in the shaping of a reflexive self-identity, self-definition and cultural transformation. This view of literacy derives from the Gramscian perspective of literacy as a social practice which is grounded in a transformative social critique.

The utilitarian–vocational meanings that framed the concept of functional literacy were to be rigorously contested in the critical literacy discourse that emerged in the teaching and writings of Paulo Freire during the 1970s. Freire argued that literacy programmes serving in the interest of economic expediency were ultimately oppressive. They constituted learners as passive subjects locked in a 'culture of silence', the silence of the oppressed. He advocated a critical pedagogy based on 'conscientisation' within which learners would be reconstituted as active participants engaged in a project of social critique as an integral part of their learning. The literacy process within this framework, centred on encouraging critical thinking amongst participants on their lived reality, with the ultimate aim of transforming it.

Freire (1972: 31–2) maintained that 'what is important is that the person learning words be concomitantly engaged in a critical analysis of the social framework in which men exist'. He stressed the importance of intrinsic motivation through the principle of having a self-defining purpose. For Freire, literacy had to arise out of people's own interests which would enable texts to be generated through their own personal and social experiences as opposed to the profit-orientation of functional literacy at the time. This view of literacy was fundamentally 'counter-hegemonic' in that it sought to make people reflect critically upon their lives and the society in which they lived. It challenged the taken-for-granted, everyday view of literacy a neutral set of technical skills. Freire's view of literacy formed the basis of the critique that emerged around the concept of functional literacy at UNESCO's 1975 Persepolis Symposium on Literacy. It subsequently became very influential in developing countries.

Freire's writings were also influential in shaping the overall literacy debate. A sociological reworking of his later concept of 'reading the word and the world' (Freire & Macedo, 1987), which also takes on board the key principles identified by the Kingman Report (DES, 1988), is central to the view of literacy in society and culture developed in this book.

Critical literacy and democratic citizenship

Literacy also has political status in relation to the multiple literacy demands associated with democratic citizenship. This includes having the skills, knowledges and attitudes necessary for exploring, making informed decisions about and exercising responsibilities and rights in a democratic society. For instance, communication skills involving argumentation; formulating, expressing and valuing opinions; understanding bias and omission are central elements of learning how to participate effectively in the democratic process. The Kingman Report published in the UK in 1988 to provide the initial conceptual framework to English as a subject in the National Curriculum, emphasised the important role that *critical literacy* plays in the democratic process. The Kingman Report (1988: 7) stated:

> People need expertise in language to be able to participate effectively in a democracy. There is no point in having access to information that you cannot understand, or having the opportunity to propose policies which you cannot formulate. People receive information and misinfor-mation in varying proportions from, amongst others, family and friends, work mates, advertisers, journalists, priests, politicians and pressure groups. A democratic society needs people who have the linguistic abilities which will enable them to discuss, evaluate and make sense of what they are told, as well as to take effective action on the basis of their understanding. The working of a democracy depends on the discriminating use of language on the part of all its people.

This view of literacy emphasises the integral link between literacy and oracy as well as the importance of being able to read beyond the literal meanings within the text; to engage in social critique. Thus, as is argued in Habermas's (1997) concept of 'communicative action', it allows us to take up positions in relation to the world in a reflective way.

The question is, how equally is this critical literacy distributed within particular societies, and in the world? Censorship and limited access to education are key variables that influence the levels at which people are allowed to participate in the full range of literacy experiences. And thus they serve to demarcate 'knowledge and ways of knowing' (Young, 1971) in the culture.

Mapping a Typology of Literacies

The concept of a unitary and one-dimensional literacy has been contested vigorously in recent years within the framework of what has become known as 'The New Literacy Studies' (Heath, 1983; Street, 1993; Barton & Ivanic, 1991; 1998). It is within this framework that the idea of *multiple literacies* is increasingly gaining ground. Studies in sociolinguistics have also developed around the issue of literacy and discourse (Halliday, 1996; Kress *et al.*, 1997, Veel & Coffin, 1996, Gee, 1996, The New London Group, 1996), and genre-based critical literacies (Carter, 1996), as well as sociological critiques which emphasise the material base of literacy as a social practice (Luke, 1996; Rassool, 1995).

Multiple literacies

Social literacies such as reading the newspaper, writing shopping lists and processing timetable information are regarded as functional to everyday life. Social literacies feature centrally in the OECD definition of literacy. The International Adult Literacy Survey (IALS) conducted by the Organisation for Economic and Cultural Development (OECD,1995: 14) defined literacy in terms of the following criteria:

(1) *Prose literacy*: the knowledge and skills needed to understand and use information from texts including editorials, news stories, poems and fiction.
(2) *Document literacy*: the knowledge and skills required to locate and use information contained in various formats, including job applications, payroll forms, transportation schedules, maps, tables and graphics.
(3) *Quantitative literacy*: the knowledge and skills required to apply arithmetic operations, either alone or sequentially, to numbers embedded in printed materials, such as balancing a cheque book, figuring out a tip, completing an order form or determining the amount of interest on a loan from an advertisement. (OECD, 1995: 14)

This view of literacy incorporates transactional-functional literacy and different social literacies, and thus it acknowledges the different social and personal purposes that reading and writing serve in everyday life. It also supports the view that *different literacies* are essential to the classification of 'being literate' in OECD countries. In addition, *prose literacy* as defined here, includes some of the skills and knowledges associated with the 'formal' literacy in the democratic society discussed later. In linking with sociocultural knowledges, the OECD definition frames a view of literacy which has at its centre the ability to function within a modern society.

Cultural literacies, on the other hand, are embedded in, for example, religious and ethnic-group-based cultural practices and may have high personal value associated with issues of group and self-identity. These forms of cultural literacies have been discussed in significant detail in social anthropological studies (cf. Cole & Scribner, 1981; Parry, 1982; Street, 1984; Scribner, 1984;). The value principles associated with everyday social and cultural literacies, may derive from existing patterns of cultural relations and would traditionally be agreed by social or group consensus. Thus they form part of the 'social character' (Williams, 1961).

However, cultural literacies defined within the framework of cultural 'norms' refer to the acquisition of 'a knowledge of selected works of literature and historical information necessary for informed participation in the political and cultural life of the nation' (McLaren, 1988: 213). Thus, they have high status associated with literary canons and form part of the 'selective tradition' described by Williams (1961), as the process by which certain meanings and practices are emphasised over others (see *formal literacies*).

Vernacular, local or community literacies are generally associated with different subcultures, communities, age and gender groups and obtain their relative value within particular, usually informal, contexts of interaction. Examples of vernacular literacies and their relationship with multiple identities are discussed in more detail later.

In contrast, what I shall call *formal* literacies, have historically been associated with the languages, knowledges, discourses and registers of, for example, education, law, medicine, politics and are embedded in institutions associated with economic, cultural and political power. 'Formal' literacies are embedded in different, formalised, genres. Reading within this paradigm would generally rely on significantly more than the ability to decode first-order textual meanings. It involves different levels of reading proficiency including the ability to interpret and analyse textual and meta-textual meanings. Writing associated with formal literacies, similarly, also extends beyond technical and functional skills to include, *inter alia*, systematised discourse styles and subject registers. 'Formal' literacies have traditionally had more social status and economic currency within a stratified labour market.

Definitions of literacy also change over time as societies undergo transition from one sociohistorical or ideological or technological milieu to another, creating different sets of literacy needs and priorities. In turn they obtain meaning within the pedagogical framework in which they are grounded, and the specific value principles that are attached to them.

The concept of *computer literacy* emerged as a policy consideration during the late1970s and early 1980s. In the UK, the Further Education Unit (FEU) played a significant role in supporting the view that computer literacy involved the development of functional competencies. The FEU definition made a distinction between information technology (IT) and Computer Assisted Learning (CAL). IT skills were seen as involving additional basic skills in electronics, that is, knowledge about computers and systems. CAL, on the other hand, was viewed as being facilitated by a functional computer literacy which placed emphasis on technical skill and the use potential of the computer in business and industry. Students were therefore to be taught a wide and not necessarily in-depth range of computer skills. CAL was seen as forming part of 'the common core of basic skills' in vocational education (FEU, 1983: 6), and became the practical FEU view of computer literacy.

The pedagogical meanings that underpinned the concept of CAL underscored the need to induct learners into a functional computer literacy which comprised basic keyboard skills, and generic practical skills that would yield relatively immediate benefits to the individual within the job-market. In other words, as was the case with UNESCO's functional literacy discussed earlier, CAL also became a means–ends variable in the vocational training curriculum. It became a 'life skill' as essential to individual development as are 'other forms of literacy'. As a set of neutral and value-free technical skills, it became part of 'cultural capital', an individual asset to be exchanged within the job-market.

The broader significance of the FEU's concept of computer literacy lies in its linking of literacy with computers. Despite its functional orientation, computer literacy demanded users' ability to deal with on-screen information as opposed to conventional reading and writing skills involving the handling of books. The representation of written-text had altered. As is indicated earlier, this factor has gained in importance in the current phase of technological development. This notion of computer literacy is subjected to further critique in Chapter 7.

Multiple Literacies, Discourse and Multiidentities

Gee's (1996: ix) argument that each of the literacies discussed here is linked with 'different social languages and are in different 'Discourses'', provides a useful way of looking at the shaping of complex multiple identities within and through different literacy practices — and the power relations in which they are embedded. Discourse here derives from sociolinguistics and refers to socially accepted ways of 'behaving, interacting, valuing, thinking, believing, speaking and often reading and writing' (Gee, 1996: viii) that are associated with particular social roles. The different identities that we inhabit as students, workers, parents, citizens, community members each rely on our tacit, and discursive knowledges (Giddens, 1984) of the specific contexts in which we operate as well as our interaction with the wider social world.

Contested literacies and contesting identities

According to Gee (1996), these discourses do not necessarily 'represent consistent and compatible values'. Vernacular literacies grounded in minority ethnic group cultures and in youth subcultures, for instance, very often exist in conflict and struggle with dominant institutionalised meanings. Some of the tension may revolve around issues related to inclusion/exclusion, 'normal'/'deviant', standardised/non-standardised languages, and gendered discourses (Gee, 1996). How these issues are resolved would depend, to a large extent, on the social position of the users of these literacies, the value attached to their languages and cultures as well as the importance attached to them as people or citizens within society. Barton and Hamilton (1998: 10) underline the fact that 'vernacular literacies which exist in people's everyday lives are less visible and less supported'. They argue further that 'literacy practices are patterned by social institutions and power relationships, and some literacies become more dominant, visible and influential than others' (Barton & Hamilton, 1998: 11).

At the same time, the fact that these literacies may not all share the same status does not necessarily mean that they all are disempowered or disempowering. Some may serve specific purposes for the individual or group, for example, as would be the case for subway graffiti-artists or Cyberpunks. Gee suggests that 'each of us is a member of many Discourses, and each Discourse represents one of our multiple identities' (Gee, 1996: ix). As such, the Cyberpunk may be one of the multiple identities inhabited by, *inter alia*, the lawyer, physicist or judge. This concept of 'multiidentities' is underscored in the New London Group's (1996: 71, henceforth referred to as NLG) argument:

As people are simultaneously members of multiple lifeworlds, so their identities have multiple layers that are in complex relation to each other. No person is a member of a singular community. Rather, they are members of multiple and overlapping communities — communities of work, of interest and affiliation, of ethnicity, of sexual identity...

The pluralistic view of literacy advocated by Gee (1996), and the NLG), goes a considerable way towards describing a multifaceted literacy process and, as such, also overcoming the absolutism of the literate/illiterate dichotomy that has traditionally framed the debate about the measurement of literacy. In this instance, 'being literate' would depend on the context of interaction, and the identity inhabited at any particular moment. Looked at in this way, being literate then is not only about 'getting it right' with regard to reading and writing. It is also about knowing the rules of particular discourses, different language registers, and understanding the literacy conventions of different forms of text.

For example, whilst 'formal', social and some cultural literacies may demand a strict adherence to standardised orthographic conventions, some vernacular literacies may invent their own. The trademark logos of graffiti artists operating on the subway, and the language of advertising provide good examples of how new conventions are created and, indeed, become integrated into the craft of artists belonging to particular subcultures, and those involved in producing the messages and meanings of consumer culture.

Multiliteracies and multimodal texts

Gee's notions of multiliteracies and 'Discourse' also provide a very useful means of interpreting the multiple identities and realities that now form an integral part of multimodal computer text. Information technology has allowed us to communication across time and space and to participate in a variety of new communication genres. These represent a collage of textual information comprising print, image and multisensory experiences. Kress *et al.* (1997: 257) point out:

> Not only is written language less in the centre of this new landscape, and less central as a means of communication, but the change is producing texts which are strongly *multimodal*. That is, producers of texts are making greater and more deliberate use of *a range of representational and communicational modes* which co-occur within one text. (Original emphases)

These require different modes of reading involving different ways of engaging with a composite text. The new multimodal textual environments have also altered the literacy process itself. We now rely on a variety of skills, knowledges, behaviours, multisensory 'experiences' and 'personae' to access, retrieve and process information and to produce knowledge.

Multimodal computer technologies such as virtual reality textual environments and the Internet enable us to participate in different realities, and to communicate across time and space.

Taking account of the complex changes taking place in the world the NLG (1996: 63) focuses on the concept of 'multiliteracies' which they address, first, in terms of the emergence of a 'multiplicity of communications channels and media'. This refers to the 'increasing multiplicity and integration of significant modes of meaning-making, where the textual is also related to the visual, the audio, the spatial, the behavioural' (1996: 64, see also Kress , 1997). Second, their concept of 'multiliteracies' addresses 'the increasing saliency of cultural and linguistic diversity'(1996: 63). This refers to increasing levels of communicative competence in different languages, dialects and registers needed to function as workers and citizens in the global cultural economy. In addition, McLaren (1988: 214) advances a view of critical literacy which involves 'decoding the ideological dimensions of texts, institutions, social practices, and cultural forms such as television and film, in order to reveal their selective interests'.

These developments suggest that the whole terrain of communication has been altered, shifting the literacy goal-posts increasingly into areas concerned with knowledge, information, context and content. In a world suffused by information we need to be not only literate in terms of reading and writing and having functional technical skills but also to be able to participate in a range of discourses and as, is suggested by the NLG, and McLaren, also different languages, registers and dialects. Within the multiple reading worlds created by information technology, the literacy goal-posts have already been shifted.

If this is the case, then how adequately are multiple and multimodal literacies catered for in dominant views of literacy in the contemporary world? How are these literacies, and the technologies in which they are embedded, distributed in the world? How do we read, interpret and interact with, and within, this rich textual and information dominated world? How equitably is access to technology and information distributed in the world? What is 'information'? What are the literacy disparities that exist between information-rich and information-poor societies? What does 'technological literacy' mean in relation to the concept of 'sustainable development' in the information age? What is the role of the citizen in this process?

Multiple literacies and sustainable development in the age of information

Whilst the technological progress that I have described here has undoubtedly transformed ways of living and, in the process, improved the quality of life within many social contexts, it has also raised important ethical and moral questions on a global level. For example, we live with the awareness that vast sections of the world's population continue to live in poverty. Many countries lack a basic infrastructure to support an adequate standard of living for the majority of their population. A large proportion of the population within these countries is still trying to meet the literacy and technical skills demands of the first industrial revolution. As a result, their technological, economic and social development rely to a significant extent on imported knowledge and expertise.

As is argued earlier, important political questions are raised by the fact that that this is the case after at least two decades of UNESCO-funded mass literacy campaigns geared to eradicate illiteracy worldwide. It also raises questions about the views of functional literacy that framed mass literacy campaigns and national literacy programmes during that period, the value ascribed to particular forms of literacy, and the relationship between these and broader social and political factors that support, or inhibit social and individual development. This factor is particularly pertinent in a world in which the production, circulation and access to information have become important with regard to those who have power to define, and those who do not.

Moreover, we have become increasingly aware of the fact that unlimited and unregulated economic growth grounded in an unfettered consumer culture can have detrimental social, cultural and environmental consequences. Many developing countries rely on the export of raw materials as their main source of national income. However, in many instances, limited national policies on the protection of natural resources, combined with increasing demands for raw materials from the developed world, have contributed to the fact that many natural resources are depleted after a few years leaving in their wake de-forestation and pollution.

But these issues cannot be discussed adequately without also addressing the effects of the International Monetary Fund's Structural Adjustment Programme (SAP) on developing countries' economies. Emphasis in the SAP on the need to exercise cuts in public expenditure impacts directly on the availability of education and, relatedly, the types and range of literacies that can be made available to people living in 'developing' countries. Asymmetries of power within different societies and, as is evident here, also between 'developed' and 'under-developed' countries create long-term political, economic and social disparities and imbalances locally, regionally and globally. As these concerns have entered public discourse we have gradually become more aware of the fact that we are living in an increasingly inter-dependent world.

On the eve of the 21st century literacy has re-emerged as a major variable in the drive for 'sustainable development' on a global scale. The Brundtland

Report, *Our Common Future*, defined the concept of sustainable development as 'development that meets the needs of the present without compromising the ability of future generations to meet their own needs' (UNCED, 1987: 43). Central to this view of development is the responsibility that we all share in shaping the world of the future. If we accept this proposition then we must acknowledge that the ways and means by which societal choices and decisions are made about the nature of development, have greater chances of success if they are informed by the people whose lives will be affected now and in the future. Some of these meanings featured centrally in UNESCO's Project 2000+: *Scientific and Technological Literacy For All* (1993) the aim of which is to encourage everyone to become informed citizens and to be part of an enlightened society for sustainable development. Furthermore, all citizens need to be provided with the opportunity to develop scientific and technological literacy, including the ability to apply scientific and technological knowledge and understanding for social benefits, and in everyday life, and to be part of a scientific and technological culture (Chewpechra, 1997).

However, the notion of sustainable development described here relies on much more than this; it requires the active involvement of citizens in policy decision-making. This, in turn, relies on citizens who are knowledgeable about the complex modern world and how it works. The argument for basic literacy skills as the primary means by which personal efficacy is measured, and a means–ends functional literacy can no longer be sustained in the modern world.

The Aims of the Book

This book has three overarching aims. First, it seeks to evaluate the theoretical frameworks that have traditionally framed discussions about literacy. In order to address the discursive way in which literacy meanings are produced at the interface of society and culture, it positions literacy as a dynamically inter-related social, educational, ideological and cultural practice.

Second, it argues that literacy and its historical links with societal development cannot be analysed without taking account of the dynamic and multilayered interactions between history, culture, politics and ideology. Thus it seeks to examine historical discourses on literacy and development and the definitions, models of development and policy frameworks that have supported different national literacy programmes during the past three decades. Drawing on key concepts across disciplinary boundaries, it discusses the important role that literacy has played in the management of both hegemonic and economic relations during periods when society changes from one milieu to another.

Third, the book aims to contextualise literacy within the 'information' society, and to identify the range of skills, knowledges, awarenesses and levels of 'communicative competence' needed to participate effectively as active 'citizens' in the democratic process within the global cultural economy. This discussion is located within the theoretical framework of 'critical literacy discourses' and Giroux's concept of 'border pedagogies'. Counter-hegemonic or critical literacy discourses articulated within arenas of struggle against dominant literacy and social meanings, have traditionally emphasised agency through individual empowerment.

The argument that debates about societal literacy levels generally play an important role in maintaining hegemony, but especially so during periods of sustained social, cultural and political change, is a recurring theme throughout the book. The book also explores the view that dominant meanings exist in tension, that they often provide a powerful site of struggle and contestation, and that they are therefore inherently subject to change as policy priorities change as societies transfer from one social, technological and ideological milieu to another. As such, it explores the potent symbolic power of literacy within specific hegemonic and political projects within the framework of national governments.

How the Book is Organised

In order to contextualise theoretical and political issues that have historically surrounded the concept of literacy, and also to address contemporary issues and concerns, the book is divided into three parts that are organised around the three aims identified earlier.

Part 1: Theoretical Frameworks

This section of the book examines the theorisation of literacy and highlights the disparate nature of the literacy debate in academic discourse. It seeks to provide a cross-disciplinary framework in which the multifaceted nature of literacy discussed in this book can be addressed.

Chapter 1: 'Literacy: In Search of a Paradigm' examines the disparate nature of the way in which literacy has featured in academic discourse. In order to highlight the differences and ambiguities inherent in academic literacy discourse the chapter, schematically, explores the construction of literacy meanings within a variety of subject-disciplines. This is juxtaposed with theoretical perspectives emerging within a range of inter-disciplinary frameworks and the range of meanings, and analytical possibilities that can thus become available.

Part 2: Literacy and Development Issues

Part 2 examines older literacy discourses and practices within the framework of the nation-state. In particular, it focuses on the unequal distribution of literacy within different sociohistorical periods as an outcome of the particular national language policies pursued at the time. It also provides an overview of literacy and development issues during the past three decades.

Chapter 2: 'Literacy and the Nation-State' examines literacy as a social practice in terms of its relationship with institutions, political systems, structures and processes within the nation-state. Emphasis is placed on the importance of addressing literacy within the context of language-state relations. The chapter draws on examples within a variety of sociohistorical contexts and highlights the tension that exists between literacy defined for societal development, and the literacy needs identified by individuals and minority interest groups for personal and cultural development.

Chapter 3: 'Literacy and Social Development' retains the focus on the nation-state and examines, critically, the links made historically between literacy and social development. This discussion looks at different theories that have underpinned models of social development and identifies the literacy meanings legitimated within these frameworks. Placing emphasis on the role of governance, the chapter discusses prevailing arguments for an increased role for non-government organisations in societal literacy programmes in developing countries.

Drawing on key motifs identified earlier, Chapter 4: 'Mass Literacy Campaigns — Some Lessons from the Past' discusses mass literacy campaigns that featured as part of the drive for modernisation during the 1970s, in terms of their effectiveness in securing sustained social and economic development. Providing an overview of a selection of mass literacy campaigns in relation to the particular social, political and economic conditions in which they arose, what they set out to achieve, and what their real and symbolic outcomes were, it identifies lessons to be learned from experiences in different societies to inform future approaches aimed at addressing levels of societal literacy.

Part 3: Globalisation: The Implications of Technological Development, Social and Cultural Change for Concepts and Definitions of Literacy

Whilst many of the tensions within the debate about literacy and its links with social development have remained unresolved, they have been made more complex by broader developments within the global terrain. A central argument is that the complex ways in which information technology intersects and interacts with social life necessitate the re-examination of the ways in which literacy, and the notion of 'text' are conceptualised in the 'information' society.

Highlighting the dynamic inter-relationship between literacy as a social and cultural practice, Chapter 5: 'Technological and Cultural Transformations' examines the dynamic relationship between technological change, social and economic development, and their collective impact on shaping the economic, social and cultural value attached to particular forms of literacy during periods of sustained social and cultural change. In order to provide a brief historical overview it starts by examining the construction of literacy meanings during the first and second industrial revolutions. It then focuses more particularly on the current period of technological change. It explores the ways in which information technology has re-defined the work process and work experience creating new labour skills demands and worker awarenesses, placing different emphases on particular forms of literacy and knowledge. Examining the nature of the changes taking place, it identifies key worker competencies and awarenesses demanded within the re-structured labour market, and the implications of this for the identification of educational priorities.

Chapter 6: 'Changing Definitions of "Text" within the Information Society' centres on literacy as an ideological practice, and explores the view that information technology has fundamentally altered the literacy experience, and that it identifies new areas to be considered in terms of societal literacy, and relatedly, knowledge needs. Examining the argument expressed by Bolter (1991) and others, that information technology texts will ultimately impact on the usefulness and the value attached to books and print literacy, the first part of the chapter discusses the evolution of different conceptions of text in relation to the technologies in which they are embedded. This includes conventional written/print text; photography; multimedia texts such as television, film and video texts; computer texts including hypertext and hypermedia, the Internet, Computer Bulletin Boards, e-mail and Virtual Reality textual environments. These texts are analysed in terms of the type and range of information made available, levels of interpretation involved and the effects of the technologies in which they are embedded on social life. The second part of the chapter provides a critical evaluation of the information society, and examines the social construction of 'information' as cultural capital.

Chapter 7: 'Conceptualising Literacy, Knowledge and Power' in the Technological Society addresses literacy as an educational practice and problematises common conceptions of literacy within the broader context of new communication challenges within an increasingly global cultural economy. It examines the social construction of 'technological' literacy as cultural capital, that is, the knowledge that we all must have in order to function in the 'information' society. Drawing on key motifs in Chapter 6, it discusses the re-defined literacy demands of the 'information' society as well as the organic nature of the interactions taking place on a global basis. It examines the implications of these for the way in which we conceptualise, 'read' and interpret meaning within the re-defined 'writing space' (Bolter, 1991) — and the ways in which we interact with the changing cultural landscape in which we live. The chapter provides a schematic set of guidelines to frame a re-conceptualised view of 'technological literacy/capability' that includes the different communicative skills needed to (a) operate effectively in the information-based global cultural economy, and (b) the skills needed to participate meaningfully in the democratic process in the 'information' society.

Chapter 8: 'Towards a 'Communicative Competence' for Democratic Participation in the Information Society' returns to some of the key issues discussed throughout the book and, in particular, those related to the changing literacy and communication needs of the information society discussed in the previous two chapters. Locating the material basis of the 'information' society, it concretises the social and cultural knowledges identified earlier as central to being 'literate' in the 'information' society. Defining the concept of participatory democracy as the basis for sustainable social development within the an information-based social environment, it explores the range of skills and communicative competence, knowledges and awarenesses to function effectively in the democratic process, within the flexible parameters of the information society.

Disparities, inequalities and contradictions between information-rich and information poor societies are highlighted throughout the book as a whole. It is hoped that the broad area of literacy and development covered in the book, its international perspective and its emphasis on information technology textual environments will contribute to the ongoing discussion about different ways of conceptualising literacy within the technological global cultural economy. It is also hoped that that it will contribute to a more textured and dynamic discourse on the role of literacy in societal and individual development.

Part 1:
Theoretical Frameworks

Underpinning the discussion in this part of the book is Stubbs' (1980) argument that a major weakness in the overall academic literacy discourse has been its discreteness. This lack of integration, it is suggested, has led to a range of views concerning what literacy is, what it is for, what its value is to the individual and society and, by the same token, what its limits are with regard to empowering individuals and transforming social life. Foregrounding changing realities within the global cultural economy, it seeks to identify analytical categories through which the discussion of literacy in this book can be integrated into a coherent framework in relation to the systems, structures and processes in which literacy practices are constituted — and their relationship with people living in different social contexts.

Chapter 1

Literacy: In Search of a Paradigm

Literacy in Academic Discourse

Considerable developments have taken place in the broad area of literacy studies during the past two decades. Within this ongoing debate, the idea that literacy cannot be regarded as an autonomous set of technical skills is gaining support amongst many critical theorists. Literacy is now more generally regarded as a social practice that is integrally linked with ideology, culture, knowledge and power. Moreover, as is discussed in the previous chapter, reference is being made increasingly to different literacies or, as Gee (1996) and the NLG (1996) put it, 'multiliteracies' suited to a range of context-related situations. In consequence, the concept of literacy has lost much of the rigidity and linearity associated with it in the traditional, decontextualised, skills-oriented framework.

Instead literacy is perceived to be *organic* because it is seen as a cultural activity that involves people in conscious and reflexive action within a variety of situations in everyday life. Much of this has been reflected in various interpretations of Freire's approach to critical literacy, and its impact on adult literacy programmes internationally. Barton and Hamilton's (1998) description of community literacies provides another excellent account of the ways in which literacy practices shape people's lives. Community literacies as described by Barton and Hamilton (1998) illustrate the self-defining principles of literacy. They show how, through participating in literacy events, people can interrogate the narrative of everyday life and, in the process, redefine themselves in relation to the social world. Barton and Hamilton's ethnographic documentation of individual 'literacy histories and literacy lives', provides evidence of the ways in which people can change things in their everyday lives, and also transform the consciousness of others. Within this framework, emphasis shifts from concerns about *process*, or individual behaviours during reading, to that of *agency*, or active involvement, within a defined context.

Literacy is regarded also as being *multidimensional* because it is seen as serving a variety of social, economic, ideological and political purposes.

25

The *social purposes*, referred to here, derive from the literacy practices that feature in everyday life such as reading for information, learning, pleasure, recreation and religion. *Economic purposes* can be seen in relation to the literacy skills and knowledge demands made on people in the work-place. People seek to enhance their capabilities as workers as those who are literate are perceived to have better job opportunities in the labour market, and thus literacy obtains an exchange value. In this sense literacy is regarded as an investment in 'human capital'. Human capital theory emphasises the direct relationship between education, worker productivity and the economy, and is underscored by the principle that people need to invest in themselves in the acquisition of skills to make them more employable. As will be seen in Chapters 3 and 4, this view of literacy has occupied a pivotal position in the discourse on societal development. Economic purposes can also be seen as relating to the specific value attached to 'formal' literacies associated with different professions and social roles.

Political purposes refer to the literacy practices in which people engage in their multiple roles as citizens, activists or community members allowing them to take up positions in relation to the social world. At the same time, they also describe the broader relationship between literacy and specific interests in society. These revolve around social structure and different power interests that shape definitions of literacy, and influence levels of access to the types and forms of literacy for different groups of people in society. *Ideological purposes* relate to the values, assumptions, beliefs and expectations that frame dominant literacy discourse within particular social contexts. Together, these different aspects and the criteria that define them, frame the 'normal' levels of literacy 'competence' for everyday living, and thus they influence our commonsense understandings of 'personal efficacy'.

Literacy as a Site of Struggle over Meaning/Literacy Wars in Education

Alongside this dynamic debate we have had an ongoing critique within the educational terrain, from within the framework of experimental behavioural psychology (henceforth referred to as experimental psychology). Experimental psychology provides a view of literacy that is primarily concerned with the de-coding of texts involving the perceptual process (phonological and graphic), word structure (morphological) and technical writing (spelling) skills. Of significance to this perspective are the *cognitive processes that underlie skilled reading and learning how to read* (Stanovich, 1986; Goswami & Bryant, 1990). For these writers 'teaching literacy is about teaching the skills of reading and writing' *per se* (Oakhill & Beard, 1995: 69).

That is, teaching children 'how to analyse the sounds in words [one word at a time] and how alphabetic letters symbolise these sounds' (Bryant, 1994), otherwise referred to as sound–symbol correspondences, or graphic–phoneme correspondences. Providing a 'scientific' approach to literacy, this approach presents literacy as a neutral technology. As Gough (1995: 80) puts it:

> I confess to subscribing to the autonomous model, 'a literacy narrowly conceived as individual, psychological skills'. I believe that literacy is a single thing' . . . that texts have independent meanings. . . that readers can be separated from the society that gives meaning to their uses of literacy, and that their cognitive skills, importantly including their ability to read and write, can be assessed, and thus abstracted from social persons and cultural locations.

Experimental psychology represents the subject-discipline which, at least until the 1970s, influenced the dominant literacy meanings incorporated into educational policy frameworks. It is also the subject-discipline that has contributed greatly to discussions about literacy within the social terrain. When literacy is discussed in, for example, the media or in political rhetoric, reference is often made to the learning of 'basic' literacy skills or the 'three Rs', direct instruction and rote learning.

Literacy outcomes are measured in terms of skills acquisition, and the personal and social benefits derived from being literate. Being able to read and write is viewed as central to increasing or enhancing individuals' 'life chances'. Again, Gough (1995: 80) underlines this in his statement that, 'I believe that learning to read and write does contribute to social progress, to personal improvement and mobility, perhaps to better health, almost certainly to cognitive development'. This is in line with the views expressed by cognitive and social psychologists such as Goody and Watt (1968) and Ong (1982), regarding the intrinsic value of literacy to the development of the intellect and, relatedly, the development of society. Views of literacy as an 'autonomous' set of skills decontextualised from society and culture have been critiqued in considerable detail elsewhere (Street, 1984; 1993).

Experimental psychology versus psycholinguistics

What has been referred to polemically as the 'literacy wars' (Stanovich & Stanovich, 1995) first started as an attack by experimental psychologists on the orthodoxy that evolved during the 1970s around the emphasis placed by psycholinguists on the reading *process* and the production of meaning through the use of contextual cues. Psycholinguists hold the view that:

three language systems interact in written language: the graphophonic [sound and letter patterns], the syntactic [sentence patterns], and the semantic [meanings]. We can study how each one works in reading, and writing, but they can't be isolated for instruction without creating non-language abstractions. (Goodman, 1986: 38–9)

Readers construct meaning during reading by drawing on their prior learning and knowledge in order to make sense of texts (Goodman, 1986). As such, literacy is defined in terms of the range of meanings produced at the interface of person and text, and the linguistic strategies and cultural knowledges used to 'cue' into the meanings embedded in the text. I will return to this discussion later in the chapter.

A further critique was subsequently mounted against advocates of the 'whole language' and 'real book' approach who argue that children *learn to read by reading* (Goodman, 1976, 1986; Smith, 1971, 1979). The 'whole language' approach draws on key elements in the psycholinguistic perspective of reading discussed here, and research on writing within the broader framework of applied linguistics, notably the work of Britton (1975), Wells (1986) and Wilkinson (1965). Of significance is the 'language experience' approach that emerged within the Schools Council Initial Literacy Project, *Breakthrough to Literacy* (Mackay *et al.*, 1978), and the writing process. The 'language experience approach' and 'process writing' emphasise learners' active involvement in the construction of texts, as opposed to placing a reliance on textbooks. Overall emphasis is placed on the *meaning* that learners want to communicate.

This approach represents to a top-down model of literacy development, that is, it is seen to develop 'from whole to part [meaningful units of language], from vague to precise, from gross to fine, from highly concrete and contextualised to more abstract' (Goodman, 1986: 39, information in brackets added). Goodman (1986: 26) summarises the principles of this approach in the argument that:

language development is empowering: the learner 'owns' the process, makes the decisions about when to use it, what for and with what results . . . literacy is empowering too, if the learner is in control with what's done with it . . . language learning is learning how to mean: how to make sense of the world in the context of how our parents, families, and cultures make sense of it. (Quoted in Weaver, 1990: 5)

This philosophical approach to literacy, which involves both text and context, has been criticised within experimental psychology as operating on broad assumptions and not having sufficient empirical data. As such, it is viewed as lacking scientific validity (Stanovich & Stanovich, 1995).

A comparative analysis

Although the *foci* are different within the psycholinguistics and experimental psychology paradigms, they do share some similarities. For instance, their overall analyses are located within the individual child and developmental processes in which 'the child is seen as progressing through successively more complex stages, each building on the other, each characterised by a particular structuring of component cognitive and affective capabilities' (Cole & Scribner, 1981: 12). Similarly, literacy within both paradigms has an exclusively individual, child-focused, pedagogic orientation. Much of the emphasis in the psycholinguistic approach to literacy also centres on perceptual skills and orthographic knowledge although this is approached from a different perspective.

But there are also differences. The one emphasises context and meaning, whilst the other stresses individual skills in isolation. Experimental psychologists have as their central goal:

> that children should learn how their writing system works. This means, for alphabetic writing systems, making sure [that] they learn the alphabetic principle, something that requires some attention to fostering students' phonemic awareness. (Perfetti, 1995: 112).

This involves a significant measure of direct teaching and skills reinforcement. It is only once basic literacy skills have been acquired that they can be 'applied and extended in a wealth of ways which might come within the remit of the broader definitions of reading' (Oakhill & Beard, 1995: 69). For psycholinguists, on the other hand:

> language learning is easy when it's whole, real, and relevant; when it makes sense and is functional; when it's encountered in the context of its use; when the learner chooses to use it . . . language is learned as pupils learn through language and about language, all simultaneously in the context of authentic speech and literacy events . . . . (Goodman, 1986: 29)

Risk-taking involving readers in predicting and guessing as part of the meaning-making process, and writers in clarifying ideas and experimenting in spelling and punctuation, is seen as an essential part of the literacy process in this paradigm.

Stanovich and Stanovich (1995: 98) summarise the basis of the disagreement between the two camps as being:

> selectively focused around the necessity of explicit analytic instruction in word decoding in the early years of schooling. The current differences between the camps are all traceable to differing underlying

assumptions about the process of reading that were present in the debates about top-down versus bottom-up models of reading that began over twenty years ago. Two decades of empirical research have largely resolved these debates in favour of bottom-up models.

Bottom-up models lay stress on the need for children to build 'word knowledge' proceeding from part-to-the-whole and thus would emphasise the need for children to know common letter-strings, initial sound blendings, phonics and to have phonological awareness as an integral part of learning to read and write.

This one-dimensional skills-based view is problematised by Hasan (1996) who, arguing from an applied linguistics perspective, suggests that reading and writing constitute complex processes that fundamentally involve the ability to grasp the principle of representation. She argues that:

> becoming literate in the sense of being able to read/write presupposes the ability to 'see' a phenomenon as 'standing for' something other than itself . . . the fundamental attribute for the onset of literacy is the ability to engage in acts of meaning: to be an initiate in literacy is to be able to make sense. (Hasan, 1996: 379)

In other words, children learn that words represent actions, emotions and concrete elements in the social world; they stand for something other than themselves. Literacy is integrally linked with a semiotic system that is grounded in language, culture and society. Signification is important in relation to making sense of any representational text, and will be discussed further in the evaluation of literacy and different types of texts in Chapter 6.

Experimental psychology versus the New Literacy Studies

Recently criticisms from experimental psychologists have also extended to the views expressed by adherents of the 'New Literacy Studies' (NLS) whose focus is on the *sociocultural aspects of literacy* (Street, 1993; Barton *et al.*, 1994; Barton & Ivanic, 1991; Barton & Padmore, 1991). This paradigm argues against a universal concept of literacy and proposes an acceptance of different 'literacies' within various social and cultural contexts. The NLS draws on a range of conceptual-analytic frameworks including social anthropology, sociology, critical linguistics and discourse theory.

Of these, social anthropology has been very influential historically in shaping the overall literacy discourse. Social anthropology draws on key motifs in cognitive psychology but interpretations of the intellectual and social 'consequences' of literacy are related to large groups of people within particular societies. Thus they will include 'the study of kinship organisation, conceptual systems, political structures, economic processes' (Street,

1993: 14). Since literacy issues are discussed in relation to social and cultural practices within the context of social change, some anthropological analyses draw also on sociological concepts and sociolinguistics as well as historical relations. In this regard, the NLS draw on a range of research traditions and build on previous critical discussions on literacy. This includes the writings of Cole and Scribner (1981), Brice Heath (1983) and Scollon and Scollon (1981) whose work has challenged previous theories based on superficial and biased assumptions about literate and oral cultures. These writers stress the need to take account of the different ways of making sense of the world reflected within different cultures and communities.

To give an example, the approach advocated in the psycholinguistic paradigm is not applicable to the acquisition of Quranic literacy in non-Arabic speaking societies as described by Cole and Scribner (1981) in their study of the Vai in West Africa. Quranic literacy is learned initially 'by rote-memorisation since the students can neither decode the written passages nor understand the sounds they produce. But students who persevere, learn to read [that is, sing out] the text and to write passages — still with no understanding of the language' (Scribner & Cole, 1988: 246). As a student of Quranic literacy myself in my early years, I recall that whilst we did not know the language (classical Arabic) we, nevertheless, did learn sound–symbol correspondence, we did learn to decode and we also learned about the rules and conventions of classical Arabic script. Technically then we *did* learn to read as described by experimental psychologists. But we learned really only to 'bark' at print. Our reading purpose (prayer) did not necessitate comprehension as textual interpretation is traditionally performed by the Ulamah (learned scholars) (see Rassool, 1995). This bears out Cole and Scribner's (1981) view that specific uses of literacy have specific implications, and that particular practices promote particular skills.

A comparative analysis

Many of the differences between the NLS and experimental psychology paradigms relate to the particular *focus* of the disciplines in which literacy is articulated. The latter's concern about the teaching of reading and writing skills relates to a significant extent to their primary involvement with the diagnosis of reading ability and the remediation of specific literacy problems amongst individual children in schools. Oakhill and Beard (1995: 72) summarise the differences in research approach between the subject-disciplines in their argument that:

> experimental research by psychologists adopts 'stipulative' [or 'operationalised] definitions, in order to facilitate 'controlled and circumscribed'

studies. Ethnographic and other sociological studies tend to adopt or seek to establish 'descriptive' [or 'essentialist'] definitions, advancing particular constructs to enable them to discuss different 'literacies'. Thus the New Literacy Studies can be said to be developing new philosophical lines of enquiry, rather than seeking to replace 'old' notions of literacy.

There is some validity in this view and I return to this discussion again later in the chapter.

Literacy as a Bounded Discourse

Other subject-disciplines involved with theorisation and research into literacy include *cognitive psychology* which is concerned mainly with the impact of literacy on intellectual development — and, particularly, abstract thinking skills. Although there is some congruence with the views held in experimental psychology, the overall focus of research is different. Whilst emphasis within the latter is mainly on decoding skills, the former is concerned with the development of higher order reading skills and cognitive processes.

Social psychology, on the other hand, draws on elements of cognitive psychology, namely, the relationship between language and thought but locates its arguments within particular environments, cultures and societies. A variety of views of literacy prevail within this framework. Most influential has been the level of importance attached to the 'great divide' between literate and oral cultures by writers such as Goody and Watt, (1968), Ong, (1982) and Hildyard and Olson, (1978). Others including Vygotsky (1962) and Luria (1979) emphasised the development of cognition and consciousness in relation to 'the social relations with the external world' (Luria, 1979: 43). Their emphasis was particularly on the cognitive consequences and the political and ideological dimensions of literacy acquisition during a period of social change in the USSR. This included the economic transition from a predominantly agrarian society to post-revolutionary industrialism as well as the sociocultural and ideological transition from the semi-feudalism of Tsarist Russia towards the modernist ideals of the new 'socialist' milieu. The underlying thesis was that 'sociocultural changes formed the basis for the development of higher memory and thinking processes and more complex psychological organisation' (Cole & Scribner, 1981: 10).

Overall, social psychology is primarily concerned with educational and cultural practices and the 'impact and 'effects' of literacy on larger groups of people, and much emphasis is placed on the transference of cognitive literacy skills to the process of living in society. More recently social psychology has also focused on the uses to which basic literacy knowledges are applied and, accordingly, centres on '_what_ people read, the _amount_ of reading that is done, the _purposes_ and _effects_ of reading' (Edwards, 1997: 119, original emphases).

Literacy theorised within _sociolinguistics_ generally takes account of the different forms and functions of written and spoken language within a variety of social and cultural contexts. Emphasis is placed on the communicative functions of speech and written language within different language communities. With regard to literacy, it also considers the communicative functions of 'text' including different textual forms and conventions, and their embeddedness in different language and cultural systems. As is the case with psycholinguistics, both readers and writers bring meaning to the text in terms of their knowledge of the language system as well as the sociocultural context. Stubbs (1980: 15) states that in order to:

> make sense of written material we need to know more than simply the 'linguistic' characteristics of the text: in addition to these characteristics we need to recognise that any writing system is deeply embedded in attitudinal, cultural, economic and technological constraints... People speak, listen, read and write in different social situations for different purposes.

Its focus on appropriateness in relation to context incorporates a consideration of 'communicative competence' in oral discourse. 'Communicative competence' is defined as:

> a synthesis of knowledge of basic grammatical principles, knowledge of how language is used in social settings to perform communicative functions, and knowledge of how utterances and communicative functions can be combined according to the principles of discourse (Canale & Swain, 1980; quoted in Verhoeven, 1994: 8)

Verhoeven (1994: 6) incorporated this notion of 'communicative competence' into the concept of 'functional literacy' which he appropriated from the UNESCO framework, reinterpreted and redefined in terms of 'the demands of literacy in the complex world'.

This redefined notion of functional literacy involves the development of different levels of competence including 'grammatical competence' relating to phonological, lexical and morpho-syntactic abilities, 'discourse competence' relating to cohesion and coherence within the text; 'de-coding competence' involving code conventions and automisation, that is, 'grasping the essentials of the written language code itself'; 'strategic competence' centring on the meta-cognitive abilities involved in the planning, execution and evaluation of written texts; and 'sociolinguistic' competence revolving around understanding of literacy conventions, and cultural background knowledge (Verhoeven, 1994: 9).

The notion of 'grammatical competence' described here by Verhoeven shares similarities with the overall emphasis in the experimental psychology paradigm, on developing linguistic awareness/competence as part of the process of learning to read. The model of communicative competence that he advances overall also includes knowledge of discourse and subject register. Discourse here refers to appropriate language use within a specific communicative event and thus involves role relationships, cultural norms and values, different textual conventions including content, form (schemata) and style as well as knowledge and understanding of the context. Subject register describes the language categories and forms of description particular to certain subjects or genre, for example, the language of science, history, music or art. The notion of 'communicative competence' will be addressed again in Chapters 7 and 8.

On a different level, although multilingualism and issues of bi-literacy have been discussed within sociolinguistics, analysis has been limited to language policy and language programmes within particular societies. Issues related to local and subjugated literacies have not generally been theorised in this paradigm. Hymes (1973) and Labov (1972), concentrating mostly on speech communities, foregrounded the importance of going beyond the linguistic perspective in order to transcend inequalities between language and competence. These writers argued that linguistic inequalities needed to be analysed in relation to people and their location within the social structure. This perspective has been incorporated into the work of, *inter alia*, Kress *et al.* (1997), Fairclough (1992), Gee (1996), Halliday (1996) and Hasan (1996).

Research Approaches

Within a macro-perspective, the research approaches adopted in social anthropology and sociolinguistics employ a variety of measurement instruments including descriptive interpretive approaches, participant observation, field notes and taped transcripts in ethnographic case studies and, in the instance of sociolinguistics, also textual analysis. In contrast, in the micro-perspective adopted by psycholinguistics and experimental psychology, the measurement of literacy include, largely, psychometric testing, checklists, reading inventories, analysis of writing samples, observation quantification, interviewing and the classification of behaviour. Important emphases are reading diagnosis, instructional techniques and strategies, although these derive from very different views of the literacy process.

Definitions and models of literacy

Definitions of literacy relevant to teaching contexts tend to be implied rather than stated in the macro-perspective adopted in some of the paradigms. As is already highlighted in the UNESCO discourse discussed in the previous chapter, the issue of definition extends beyond the rhetorical. Indeed, Scribner (1984: 6) suggests that definitional problems have more than academic significance. She argues that:

> each formulation of an answer to the question 'What is literacy?' leads to a different evaluation of the scope of the problem (i.e. the extent of *il*literacy) and to different objectives for programs aimed at the formation of a literate citizenry . . . A chorus of clashing answers also creates problems for literacy planners and educators. (Original emphasis)

Account needs to be taken also of the fact that research paradigms or theoretical frameworks that take the individual as the unit of analysis, argue outside a consideration of the fact that literacy is a primary means of cultural transmission, which is essentially a social achievement (Scribner, 1984). Although the literacy act in itself is often a private experience as is suggested by experimental psychologists (Gough, 1995), it obtains its meaning ultimately within society and culture; it is a means of social communication; of knowledges, thoughts and ideas. As is argued by Hasan (1996: 378), 'the goals of literacy can hardly have a value in and of themselves: they need to be seen in the context of the wider social environment which is at once the enabling condition and the enabled product of literacy pedagogy'.

With the exception of psycholinguistics, and the Freirean approach discussed in the previous chapter, *models of literacy* are not clarified; they are understood at the level of commonsense, that is to say, they tend to feature as taken-for-granted variables in literacy analysis. Models of literacy refer to pedagogic frameworks in which theories about the literacy process are generated. They would therefore include the range of meanings produced in literacy practices as well as conceptions of how and what meanings can be obtained in texts — and contexts. Thus, models of literacy make explicit the range of knowledges or literacies that they frame — and the process through which they are accessed. Models of literacy do not constitute instructional techniques, although they may frame them. If we are to assess the value of literacy, we cannot do so effectively without taking account of the knowledges that they make available, and the contexts in which they are situated.

Many of these views also originate within different ideological frameworks. For example, literacy theorised as a sociocultural practice emphasises ideology, politics and power. In contrast, literacy theorised within the cognitive and behavioural psychology framework regards literacy as a value-free, autonomous set of skills, a neutral technology that can be applied to different literacy demands in everyday life. Similarly, literacy theorised within psycholinguistics makes a variety of assumptions about what literacy *is* (e.g. print-text based). Its primary focus on the literacy *process* also implicitly underscores a de-ideologised view of literacy. According to Luke (1996 : 311), in psycholinguistics:

> language and literacy are theorised by reference to the internal states of human subjects — for example, . . . models of language acquisition, developmental stage theories, schema theory, and humanist models of personal response and expression.

In other words, each perspective brings with it not only its own particular view of what literacy is and what it is for, but also a particular worldview.

Table 1.1 provides a brief and schematic outline of a selection of *subject-disciplines* in order to highlight the distinct nature of the literacy meanings produced within each framework.

What I am concerned with here are not the substantive or methodological differences between these perspectives *per se*. Rather, the point that I want to make is that because the *foci* are different within these subject-disciplines, and because their research approaches differ they yield a wide variety of information on literacy within a broad context. This discreteness supports Stubbs' view that each subject-discipline advances a particular analytical and research framework yielding different views on what constitutes important knowledge about literacy.

Boundaries, Knowledge and Power

With the exception of the integrated approach adopted by the New Literacy Studies and social anthropology, the divergent views on literacy discussed here lend support to Stubbs' contention that the field of literacy studies is marked by a lack of integration. The theorisation of literacy in different subject disciplines, he argues, has resulted in the development of a variety of conceptual-analytic frameworks. Stubbs (1980: 3) identified this problem in his argument that:

> one reason why the literature on reading is so vast and unintegrated is that topics have been approached from different directions from within disciplines, including psychology, education and linguistics. Often these approaches have been largely self-contained, making little reference to work within other approaches, and, in fact, putting forward contradictory definitions of *reading* and *literacy*. (Original emphases)

Table 1.1 Literacy as a bounded discourse

Subject-discipline	Literacy foci
Experimental behavioural psychology	Focus on the individual Perceptual process Logographic knowledge Phonological awareness Technical writing skills Decoding of texts Functional literacy Methods of instruction
Cognitive psychology	Focus on individuals and groups Impact of literacy on intellectual development Abstract thinking skills
Social psychology	Focus on groups Variety of positions taken: (a) great-divide theory — differences between oral and literate cultures (e.g. Goody & Watt; Hildyard & Olson) (b) emphasis on development of cognition and consciousness in relation to social relations within external world — ideological and political aspects of literacy (e.g. Luria; Vygotsky) (c) emphasis on need to understand various ways in which different societies and cultures make sense of their world — challenge great-divide theory (Scribner; Cole & Scribner)
Psycholinguistics	Focus on the individual Reading and writing *process* Internal relations between perceptual processes, orthographic systems and reader's knowledge of language Meaning production at interface of person and text
Sociolinguistics	Focus on individuals and groups Different forms and functions of written and spoken language within variety of social contexts Bilingualism and multilingualism Discourse and subject registers Communicative competence
Social anthropology	Focus on groups Interpretations of social consequences of literacy related to groups of people within their sociocultural contexts Social change

Whilst the sociocultural approach (NLS) and social anthropology derive their terms of reference across disciplinary boundaries, the rest of the views discussed here, to a large extent, rely on the frame and terms of reference of specific subject-disciplines as the basis of their interpretation and analysis.

Bernstein (1990: 156) defines a discipline as 'a specialised, discrete discourse, with its own intellectual field of texts, practices, rules of entry, modes of examination and principles of distributing success and privileges'; they are 'oriented to their own development rather than to applications outside themselves'. Each subject-discipline frames 'a domain of objects, a set of methods, a corpus of propositions considered to be true, a play of rules and definitions, of techniques and instruments' (Foucault 1970: 59). And, as we could see in the different research approaches discussed earlier, each subject-discipline projects a particular view of what constitutes research, and different sets of variables operate within each frame of reference to define selected aspects of literacy as foci for research. As a result, different sets of data emerge that are analysed using subject-specific terms of reference and arguments to arrive often at conclusions that, generally, are not integrated in a meaningful way within the educational terrain. This bears out Scribner's (1984) argument regarding difficulties in educational planning. It also bears out the views expressed by Oakhill and Beard (1995, referred to earlier), regarding the nature of the differences in the conceptual-analytic frameworks of NLS and experimental psychology.

Conceptual-analytical frameworks derive from the subject-discipline that provides the frame and terms of reference to the analysis. This includes subject-specific terminology, relational concepts as well as the range of assumptions, questions and problematics that can be engendered within this context. They refer also, at meta-level, to the ways in which discourses are structured as well as how meanings are produced and reproduced.

Conceptual-analytical frameworks grounded in subject-disciplines, according to Bernstein (1990), are not neutral; they are constituted in 'self interest' with their own subject-specific views of the 'truth' — which implicitly support a particular view of the world. Thus they constitute what Foucault (1980: 133) refers to as 'regimes of truth':

> 'truth' is to be understood as a system of ordered procedures for the production, regulation, distribution, circulation and operation of statements . . . [and] is linked in a circular relation with systems of power which produce and sustain it, and to effects of power which it induces and which extend it. A 'regime' of truth.

Together these frame what are legitimate knowledges and ways of knowing in research. Some of this professional interest is expressed in Oakhill and Beard's (1995: 69) argument that:

[w]hilst acknowledging the undoubted contribution of language, motivation and cultural factors to literacy acquisition, *we should not forget the contribution of scientific experimental research to our understanding of reading and its development.* (Emphasis added)

Oakhill and Beard sought to reinforce the scientific validity of their 'language-as-system' and empirical research paradigm over and against the ethnographic and theoretical-analytical approaches adopted in what they term as 'sociological perspectives on literacy' (1995: 72), and the broad assumptions that they associate with psycholinguistic research.

Conceptual-analytic frameworks are ultimately embedded in particular ideologies and, as such, each represents a distinctive view of 'what is legitimate knowledge'. Without acknowledging the ideology with which their own perspective of literacy (reading) is imbued, Oakhill and Beard (1995: 72) call for counter-critiques of the 'ideological influences on how misplaced orthodoxies become so widely accepted', and why it takes so long for them to 'receive critical scrutiny'.

Literacy discourses in society

In addition to hierarchies constructed between subject-knowledges, different levels of importance are also attached to selected forms of knowledge within the social and political terrain. This relates, to a large extent, to prevailing (dominant) ideologies that underscore policy frameworks as well as particular hegemonic projects pursued by political and economic interest groups. Thus it is that some literacy knowledges are chosen for inclusion in educational policy frameworks, whilst others are marginalised, excluded or derided in social and political debate at specific moments in societal development.

For instance, the argument for *basic skills* and *rote learning* derives its scientific legitimacy largely from the positivism of behavioural psychology and, for a long time, constituted (and in many instances continue to be) the dominant view of 'what literacy is' in education. Moreover, as we could see in the discussion in the previous chapter of literacy relations in South Africa during the Apartheid years, 'official' literacies are inscribed into national language policy. In Foucauldian terms, 'knowledge and power are inseparable, . . . forms of power are imbued within knowledge, and forms of knowledge are permeated by power relations' (Ball, 1990: 17). Ideologically, definitions of literacy can then be seen as constituting 'power/ knowledge' discourses (Foucault, 1980). According to Foucault, discourse defined in terms of power/knowledge constitutes the means by which power is exercised through relations of dominance established within the social terrain. This is a recurring theme in the rest of the book.

Border crossings

Some critiques of the unitary subject-discipline approach have come from what has become known as *critical literacy discourse* and include a diverse range of research approaches and conceptual frameworks.

Street (1984, 1993), one of the most significant contributors to the debate about adult literacy research in the UK during the past two decades, has made important inputs towards a re-conceptualisation of literacy within an inter-disciplinary framework. In his research conducted in Iran during the 1970s, Street analysed literate behaviours and the way meanings are produced in the reading process amongst the peasants of the village of Chesmeh. He identified two different forms of literacy that prevailed in Iran at the time, namely 'commercial' literacy (economic) and 'Maktab' (religious) literacy. Of major importance was the fact that Street was identifying different forms of literacy for specific social and economic purposes. Moreover, his critique of the 'autonomous' model of literacy adhered to by Goody (1968), and his identification of the 'ideological' model of literacy were major contributions to the way in which literacy has been theorised during the past decade.

The significance of this research in both methodological and conceptual terms was the way in which micro-social processes were linked with broader developments within society — whilst taking account also of historical relations. In his critique of the 'psychologistic' paradigm, Street (1984, 1993) challenges the claims made of the role of literacy in fostering rationality and abstract-thinking capabilities. Instead, he argues that literacy should be understood as a social practice in which there is an interplay of different ideologies. Street also stresses the importance of analysing literacy within its institutional as well as the wider sociopolitical and economic context. As such, it is argued that

> the uses, consequences and meanings of literacy; the differences and similarities between written and spoken registers and inter-register variation with spoken and written modes; and the problem of what is culture specific and what [is] universal in literacy practices — must be answered with reference to close descriptions of the actual uses and conceptions of literacy in specific cultural contexts. (Street, 1993: 3)

Street's views on the theorisation of literacy have been central to the development of the New Literacy Studies discussed earlier. In pedagogical terms, this paradigm supports the development of different literacies, the centrality of the learner to the teaching and learning context, 'the politicisation of content in literacy instruction, and the integration of the voices and experiences of learners with critical social analysis' (Auerbach, 1992, quoted in Verhoeven, 1994: 7). This framework also takes account of the often neglected complex issue of literacy within multilingual social settings — the disappearance of minority languages, subjugated literacies and the importance of maintaining local literacies.

Critical linguists such as Skutnabb-Kangas and Phillipson (1995), similarly, carry this thread through their analysis of linguistic imperialism which refers to the imposition of colonial languages historically. These writers address the issue of linguistic human rights within which the concept of local literacies is grounded. Writers within this broad framework identify the inter-relationship between literacy, national language planning policies and power processes.

Social historians such as Graff (1979, 1987) and Williams (1961), analysing the political economy of literacy programmes, explore the importance attached in social policy to specific ideologies during different historical periods. Within a macro-perspective, these writers draw on sociological concepts in their emphasis on the sociocultural, political and structural variables that contribute to literacy inequalities and, *de facto*, sociocultural and economic inequalities. Significant contributions have come also from writers who focus on the political economy of textbooks and texts (De Castell *et al.*, 1989; Apple, 1982, 1986, 1993). In addition, important new developments have come from writers who locate their analyses within a *'postmodern' analytical framework*.

Border pedagogies

Drawing on Gramscian cultural theory centred on the role of language in maintaining hegemonic relations — and the contestation and resistance that this intrinsically generates, writers such as Giroux (1987, 1993) and McLaren (1995) emphasise the links between knowledge, ideology and power. These writers extend the concept of 'conscientisation' advanced within the Freirean framework and propose concepts that they term *'critical pedagogy'* and *'border pedagogies'*. Outlining a 'postmodern' framework which borrows concepts from feminist research and cultural theory, Giroux (1993: 75) stresses the need for a language:

> that allows for competing solidarities and political vocabularies that do not reduce the issues of power, justice, struggle, and inequality to a single script, a master narrative that suppresses the contingent, the historical, and the everyday as serious objects of study.

This approach emphasises agency, difference, contestation and the relationship between these and social structures and ideological forces. Giroux argues further that 'critical pedagogy needs to create new forms of knowledge through its emphasis on breaking down disciplinary boundaries and creating new spheres in which knowledge can be produced' (Giroux, 1993: 76).

Critical pedagogies or 'border' pedagogies draw on aspects of feminist theory, cultural studies and the sociology of knowledge and, in this sense, constitute politicised discourses. Most of the writers within the cross-disciplinary paradigm ground their analyses in the 'specificities of peoples' lives, communities, and cultures' (Giroux, 1993: 67) and place relative emphasis on the time–space dimensions of specific literacy knowledges. Significantly though, only a few (McLaren, 1995; Giroux, 1993) embed their analyses in an exposition of the complexity of social theory that incorporates the variables of gender, 'race' and social position as analytic categories.

As was the case with the discussion on subject-disciplines earlier, at the level of practice, the views of literacy highlighted in the critical literacy paradigm continue to raise qualitative questions about: (a) definitions of literacy, (b) models of literacy, (c) criteria for and, relatedly, the level of importance attached to local variables in the measurement of societal literacy levels, (d) what literacy in relation to human rights means in concrete terms and (e) the real and symbolic impact and effects of particular forms of literacy on individual 'empowerment' and social development. Account also needs to be taken of the fact that literacy meanings are in a constant state of flux — and thus are subject to alteration within different social milieux. Scribner (1984: 8) underlines this point in her argument that

> since social literacy practices vary in time and space, what qualifies as individual literacy varies with them. At one time, ability to write one's own name was the hallmark of literacy; today in some parts of the world, the ability to memorise a sacred text remains the modal literacy act. Literacy has neither a static nor a universal essence.

This issue is highly pertinent at the moment as new technologies and, relatedly, new ways of living evolve within society. I discuss this issue in more detail later in the chapter, and again in Part 3 of the book.

Summary

The different perspectives outlined here illustrate that, conceptually, literacy is multifaceted and thus requires different *levels* of analysis within a broad and flexible framework that incorporates complexities. These include, *inter alia*, historical relations, social practices and institutions, locality as well as individual and group subjectivities, and the tension that exists between agency and specific state-sanctioned political and hegemonic projects.

Luke (1996), for instance, arguing from a sociological perspective, critiques socially based models of literacy pedagogy including the Freirean approach discussed in the previous chapter, and the new 'genre-based' literacies within sociolinguistics (Veel & Coffin, 1996; van Leewen & Humphrey, 1996). He contends that these approaches 'stop short of coming to grips with their assumptions about the relationship between literacy and social power' (Luke, 1996: 309). These views, he suggests, define agency as an individual property which is 'neither collective or inter-subjective, nor necessarily connected with political ideology or cultural hegemony' (p. 311). Luke maintains that the history of literacy education is about power and knowledge:

> But it is about power not solely in terms of which texts and practices will 'count' and which groups will have or not have access to which texts and practices. It is also about who in the modern state will have access to a privileged position in specifying what will count as literacy ... Schooling and literacy are used to regulate and broker not just access to material wealth, but as well access to legally constituted 'rights', to cultural and subcultural histories and archives, to religious virtue and spiritual rewards, and to actual social networks, gendered desires and identities. (Luke, 1996: 310)

For Luke, a critical literacy approach extends beyond issues related to textual biases and representation, 'it is nothing less than a debate over the shape of a literate society, its normative relations to textual and discourse exchange, and the relative agency and power of the literate in its complex and diverse cultures and communities' (Luke, 1996 : 145). Luke's perspective is central to the view of literacy in the information age developed in Part 3 of the book.

Literacy as a Field of Inquiry: Levels, Contexts and Definitions

Since literacy spans such a broad terrain within various subject-disciplines, to address the complexities that surround literacy in the modern world necessitates an approach that incorporates many of the literacy meanings discussed earlier. In order to do so, I will explore the conceptualisation of literacy as a *regionalised field of inquiry*. A regional field of study according to Bernstein (1990: 156) represents a 'recontextualising of disciplines which operate both in the intellectual field of disciplines and in the field of practice'. Because literacy interpenetrates a wide range of subject-disciplines, we can argue that regions are the interface between subject-disciplines, and the literacy knowledges that are thus made available. These are illustrated in Figure 1.1.

The degree of overlap indicated in Figure 1 signifies the dialogical relationship between literacy knowledges and subject disciplines. This

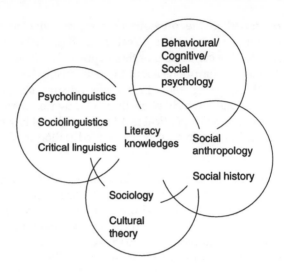

Figure 1.1 Literacy as a regionalised field of study

overlap, or interstices, represent the regionalised field of inquiry within which literacy will be conceptualised and discussed in the rest of the book.

The range of literacy meanings identified in the earlier critical paradigm highlight the fact that literacy constitutes, simultaneously, a *social practice*, an *ideological practice*, a *cultural practice* and an *educational practice*. Within the regionalised field identified here, discussion of these inter-related aspects would be able to draw on concepts and analytical categories across the disciplines. It would also be able to draw on analytic categories used in cross-disciplinary frameworks such as feminism and cultural studies. Crossing boundaries in this way provides opportunity to analyse the dynamic interplay that exists between specific literacy practices and the social, cultural, economic and political structures in which they are grounded, as is suggested by Luke (1996). Thus it would be possible to address educational meanings, whilst at the same time, take account of the fact that meaning production takes place organically within the complex power relations that traverse the social terrain. Moreover, it can take account also of agency, contestation and struggle which make possible the production of alternative meanings and practices as highlighted in the critical literacy framework.

The different interlocking aspects of literacy to be explored as a regionalised field of study in the rest of the book, are summarised in Table 1.2, and will be discussed in more detail below.

Table 1.2 Interlocking levels at which literacy needs to be theorised

Literacy as:	*Variables*
A social practice	Social life Institutions: state, industry, commerce, finance, media, education Social processes e.g. national language policy, educational policy, social policy (health, employment, economic) Social system: models of governance, social roles Structures e.g. social policy, language rights, ethnicity, gender, social position Religious-cultural practices
An ideological practice	Meanings produced in social discourse e.g. policy; media, political interest groups, industry, funding bodies Censorship Textual and contextual meanings Critical literacies/counter discourses
A cultural practice	Historical relationships Work-place literacy requirements Leisure/interest literacy requirements Literacy requirements to function in everyday life e.g. technologies, banking, health, social services, housing, civic engagement Range of cultural meanings produced and reproduced e.g. values, beliefs, expectations, aspirations Impact of religious-cultural beliefs on levels of access to literacy for particular groups e.g. women, religious minorities, ethnic groups
An educational practice	Models and forms of knowledge Technical literacy skills Technological skills and knowledges Theories of knowledge Pedagogical models Teaching methodologies Teaching and learning resources (including staffing; multimedia) Democratisation of sociopolitical structures and processes Literacy for democratic participation, e.g. decision-making, knowledge of rights and obligations, freedom of expression, freedom of access to information, knowledge of social system, citizenship, critical knowledges

Literacy as a social practice

Working towards concretising this framework and identifying analytic categories, I start with the argument that literacy defined as a *social practice* has to be contextualised within a general theory of society. As is argued earlier, its permeation into the social body requires that literacy as a social practice needs to be analysed in terms of its relationship with institutions, structures and processes and the social system in which they are grounded. The importance of this lies in the fact that these contexts constitute the key defining sites of what literacy is, who it is for and what purposes it should serve for the individual, specific groups of people and society as a whole. Scribner (1984: 8) concretises the intrinsic link between literacy and structures in the argument that:

> grasping what literacy 'is' inevitably involves social analysis: What activities are carried out with written symbols? What significance is attached to them, and what status is conferred on those who engage in them? Is literacy a social right or a private power? . . . Does the prevailing distribution of literacy conform to standards of social justice and human progress? What social and educational policies might promote such standards?

Such considerations should inform policy frameworks. Clearly then, the inter-relationship between literacy and knowledge needs to be concretised and theorised in relation to specific conditions that exist within particular societies — and the diverse uses of literacy within different societies. In positioning literacy within the context of societal relations, analysis would draw on sociological concepts and theories to explain the complex interactions in which literacy meanings are shaped — as well as what their concrete effects are on the lives of people. In terms of the latter, analyses of societal literacy levels should therefore also include a consideration of sociocultural factors such as ethnicity, languages, religious-cultural practices, gender and social position. Transferred to practice, this means that within culturally and linguistically plural societies issues of national language policy have to be considered in analysis of societal literacy levels.

It also means that literacy levels need to be discussed in relation to the role of women in society as is highlighted in the work of Stromquist (1990) and Rockhill (1987). These studies identify the fact that the social position of women and their differential levels of access to particular forms of literacy — or, literacy *per se* need to be addressed in relation to the social relations that inhere in particular religious-cultural practices within different societies. In relation to this, the emphasis in the UNESCO discourse currently on the need for higher literacy rates amongst women needs to be examined with regard to the particular value attached to the role of women in different societies.

Literacy defined in terms of 'individual empowerment' and 'social transformation' — and literacy defined as a 'fundamental human right' can only really be understood within the context of specific cultural formations and the diverse and complex power relations that traverse the social terrain. This incorporates political processes including models of governance and social policy (see Table 1.2). Ultimately, literacy policy and provision arise within the organisation of particular social systems, forms of governance as well as economic, social and political priorities identified within the context of the state. Related to this are issues that revolve around, for example:

- migration and the language rights of asylum seekers and refugees;
- routes of access to participation in the democratic process;
- fiscal policy as this affects approaches adopted to public expenditure — and thus funding for educational and/or language provision;
- social change related to technological developments.
- the linguistic and cultural rights of settled minority groups
- the role and influence of external funding bodies

Alongside these variables are issues that revolve around exclusion, subjugation and control exercised over particular forms of literacy — and the struggles and possibilities for transformation that these inequalities generate within the context of everyday life. Again, these multifaceted and inter-locking variables highlight the fact that because literacy is rooted in both the social and material world, discussions of societal literacy levels cannot be reduced to the level of discourse alone. To do so would be to present only a partial view of literacy as a dynamic social practice.

Literacy and technology issues

This is particularly important in the current period of technological change and rapid social transformation. Indeed, the organic links between microelectronics, and, especially, information technology and economic, social and political processes raise important questions regarding the conceptualisation of literacy as a social practice. The gains made in terms of time and space, facilitated by the new technologies, have resulted not only in the fact that the world is rapidly becoming smaller because of mass communication practices, but in the emergence of multifaceted networks of unequal social relations on a global scale. The new 'flexible accumulation' made possible by 'flexible' technologies enable not only speedier capital transfer to take place across the world but also contribute to new forms of control emerging within the restructured work-place. New realities are in the process of being constructed with the evolution of ever-newer, more adaptable and faster technologies. Thus, literacy defined as a social practice has also to address the effects of the uses of the new technologies on the social experience of people in their everyday social roles — as well as their quality of life as workers. This includes not only skills and knowledge requirements but also a consideration of the relationship between levels of technological literacy and broader social factors such as unemployment, intermittent or sporadic employment such as 'yearly work-time' and seasonal work — in addition to the variables of gender, race, their position as workers in the work-place as well as their everyday experiences as workers.

In definitional terms then, other than the necessary technical skills and knowledges required to function on an everyday basis, we need to move towards a re-conceptualisation of, *inter alia*, how we interpret the world, think on our lived realities and analyse the essence of power and control inherent in the technologies themselves — and the social processes through which they operate.

Literacy as an ideological practice

Literacy defined as an *ideological practice* needs to address the multiple meanings ascribed to literacy by different interest groups. First, this refers to not only the views of literacy legitimated in policy discourse, but also those articulated within other defining sites such as funding bodies, social institutions and political interest groups within society. For instance, UNESCO's current concerns with the breakdown of moral values in society and its growing emphasis on the role of education in inculcating 'those principles which are conducive to peace, human rights and democracy that finally must constitute the fabric of the "intellectual and moral solidarity of mankind"' (UNESCO, 1995b: 17) signify a clear move towards re-establishing a link between literacy and a moral economy. This, in turn, has to be seen in juxtaposition with the overall emphasis within the UNESCO framework, at least since the 1970s, on the principles of technological modernisation. It also includes a consideration of the mechanisms of control of information or censorship and the subjugation of local and critical literacies. Examples here can be taken from the particular forms of censorship that prevailed in pre-revolutionary Iran in the Shah's modernisation programme during the 1970s (see Street, 1984; Rassool, 1995). Within that context at the time, whilst the mass literacy programme launched by the Shah sought to increase literacy rates amongst the peasants, different forms of censorship affected those who could read and write. According to Kamrava (1992: 138–9) in Iran at that time '[p]eople were encouraged to read and write the alphabet, but reading and trying to understand books that were suspected of being threatening to the state was punishable by long sentences'. Oppositional literature, film, novels and essays were banned and the literati came under state surveillance by the notorious secret police, the SAVAK (Rassool, 1995).

Elsewhere, in Eastern Europe, Bulgaria pursued the same model of literacy that prevailed in the UNESCO framework; that is, literacy as a central part of societal modernisation, despite the fact that it was grounded in a different ideological framework. Yet algongside this process of rapid modernisation, the rights of ethnic Turkic and Roma people to become literate in their own languages were systematically repressed under the Zhivkov regime's policy of 'Bulgarisation' (Rassool & Honour, 1996). Again, what is highlighted here, first, is the overall ideological 'package' in which literacy is inscribed into state policy and practices — and the specific purposes that dominant forms of literacy served within these contexts within a specific time-frame — and as part of a specific hegemonic project of the state to assimilate minority cultural groups.

Second, the case of pre- and post-revolutionary Iran illustrates the point made earlier that literacy meanings are contingent; that they are subject to change within different sociohistorical frameworks — as well as in relation to the emergence of new technologies within the social terrain. Analysis thus has to draw on social history as well as the political economy of literacy programmes. Third, account has to be taken of the fact that literacy is also a signifier of cultural, social and individual aspirations — some of which may conflict with one another — as is the case for women in post-revolutionary Iran, and the empowering meanings inscribed into the revolutionary Nicaraguan literacy programme. The latter will be discussed in Chapter 4.

Literacy and technology issues

Fourth, the impact of the new technologies on the reconstruction of our social reality requires a re-conceptualisation of the literacy process. Apple (1987: 171), for example, argues that the new technologies are not only 'an assemblage of machines and their accompanying software', they also have potent symbolic power. Embedded within the communications industry, the new technologies make possible the construction of — and, relatedly, they have the capacity to sustain 'second order universes that increasingly are our experience of the cultural and social world' (Hall, 1989: 43). Applied to literacy this refers to the reality that we live today in a world dominated by the television advert defining our consumer needs, wants and desires; computer games in homes, shops, pubs and amusement arcades, video equipment in family homes having access to video libraries providing boundless popular entertainment. Alongside this is the power of communication contained in the almost unlimited textual interaction possibilities provided by the Internet as well as the multiple realities that inhere in CD ROM facilities. Computers form part of the taken-for-granted values, beliefs, material aspirations and expectations that we have of our everyday lives and thus they have been incorporated as hegemonic cultural capital. That is to say, technology has become an unquestioned, taken-for-granted 'must have' in order to function in everyday life.

In real terms then we have already moved beyond a one-dimensional view of text within our experience of everyday life. Indeed, because of the organic links between the new technology, the state and other power processes such as corporate business and the microelectronics industry, the concept of literacy today transcends written and other representational texts such as visual art, television, information technologies and photography to include also the social and political contexts in which communication practices are grounded. In other words, to be a literate citizen in the age of high technology means to be able read not only the word and image, but as is argued by Freire and Macedo (1987), also the world in its fullest sense.

Literacy as a cultural practice

As a *cultural practice* literacy has to be theorised in a conceptual-analytic framework that makes it possible to consider the subordinating meanings, values and beliefs that inhere not only in dominant discourse but also in traditional cultural practices. This refers to the maintenance of gender and political power elites legitimated in religious-cultural beliefs and practices, through which access to literacy can be controlled to exclude women and minority groups from acquiring particular forms of literacy. Dominant literacy practices also serve to subjugate local cultural literacies. The current rise of religious fundamentalism in countries such as Algeria, Egypt, Turkey and Afghanistan has implications for the range and types of literacy that would be made available to women within these societies.

In a more general sense literacy as a cultural practice also refers to the relative importance attached to particular types and forms of literacy within the culture. These comprise not only religious-cultural literacies, but also the range of social literacies required within everyday life including the work-place and leisure. Collectively, these influence the literacy knowledges that people would aspire to have in order to survive and become 'useful' citizens. Analyses should therefore also include the ways in which cultural meanings are produced and reproduced within and through literacy practices.

Literacy as an educational practice

As an *educational practice*, literacy has to be theorised in terms of definitions, models including pedagogy, assessment and measurement. Moreover, literacy as an educational practice cannot, reasonably, be conceptualised outside a theory of knowledge, or the function that it will serve in terms of the multifaceted purposes in people's everyday lives within society. As has already been suggested earlier, this extends beyond a direct link between literacy and the functional skills and knowledges required within the workplace to include also social and political purposes.

Scribner (1984: 8) emphasising the fact that literacy is a 'many-meaninged thing', tries to overcome this difficulty by identifying three metaphors, namely, 'literacy as adaptation, literacy as power, and literacy as a state of grace' around which to articulate the multiple and multifaceted meanings that surround literacy for the individual. *Literacy as adaptation*, involves the skills needed to function in a 'range of settings and customary activities' such as jobs, training and benefits, civic and political responsibilities. In this sense, she argues, literacy as adaptation is pragmatic and involves a range of competencies which should be broad enough to encompass new systems of literacy as is represented here in the new technologies. In this regard, account needs to be taken of the fact that literacy needs will not be the same for everyone; they may increase for some and reduce for others. *Literacy as power* is articulated around the 'relationship between literacy and community advancement' (Scribner, 1984: 11) and highlights the association between illiteracy and disempowerment grounded in the Freirean view of literacy. Scribner advocates mobilisation for literacy around local needs and small-scale activism. *Literacy as a state of grace* is defined in terms of the liberal tradition of intellectual, aesthetic and spiritual enhancement. Not all uses of literacy have a practical end. All these views of literacy, she argues, are inter-related and have validity for educational planning. Thus although there are obvious boundaries between these metaphors, they are not inflexible.

Another integrated view of what literacy is pertinent to the discussion here can be derived from the range of discourses described by the Russian literary theorist Mikhail Bakhtin. According to Bakhtin, discourse is not a fixed communication; it is intertextual (Todorov, 1984: x). That is to say, it exists in a dialogical relationship with previous discourses on the same subject; meanings are transferred from one discourse to another within a particular social context. Emphasising language and communication thus in relation to the social world, he argues that 'language is not an abstract system of normative forms but a concrete heterological opinion on the world' (quoted in Todorov, 1984: 56). In other words, it is constituted in a diversity of languages and a diversity of voices. Thus, both plurality and difference are intrinsic to discourse.

Bakhtin identifies a typology of socially located discourses essential to functioning in everyday life:

> (1) the communication of production [in the factory, shop etc.]; (2) the communication of business [in offices, in social organisation etc.]; familiar communication [encounters and conversations in the street, cafeteria, at home etc.]; [(4) artistic communication (in novels, paintings etc.]; and finally (5) ideological communication in the precise sense of the term: propaganda, school, science, philosophy, in all their varieties. (Bakhtin, quoted in Todorov, [1984: 57], information in brackets added)

To this we can add communication of the classroom defined in terms of learning processes. Literacy located within this framework of socially-based communication practices becomes linked with discursive sets of interaction in which a diversity of social and individual meanings are negotiated within the social terrain. What does this mean for education? I argue throughout the book that, first, in definitional terms, it would include a range of subject-registers in order to function within a variety of contexts — extending beyond those identified earlier in the OECD survey. Second, it also includes levels of access to adequate literacy provision which revolves around different forms of knowledge, cultural traditions, beliefs and values, resources, integrated teaching approaches as well as freedom of access to different forms of information. I return to these issues in more detail in Part 3 of the book.

Third, with regard to pedagogy, it includes a consideration of goal-directed learning and the specification of criterion-referenced learning outcomes. As is discussed later in Chapter 8, literacy for citizenship within a democratic framework is intrinsically bound up with access to different knowledges as well as with concepts of individual empowerment and social progress. Fourth, literacy defined in terms of its role in facilitating social transformation, needs to extend to the democratisation of sociopolitical structures and processes. This, implicitly, includes a contextualisation of literacy within models of governance, the nature of decision-making and the possibilities that they provide for bottom-up influences on policy frameworks. Collectively, these factors impact on the range and levels of literacies that can be made available to different groups of people within society — and, relatedly, influence the assessment and measurement of literacy levels in terms of the range of competencies required to function within society. Thus literacy as an educational practice is integrally linked with literacy defined as social and ideological practices.

Conclusion

Using these categories as guiding principles, literacy theorised within the regionalised field suggested here draws on all the major subject-disciplines without confining itself to the parameters of knowledge inscribed into them. Within this flexible and integrated framework, constituted in a dynamic interchange of concepts, criteria and registers, literacy can be analysed and theorised in relation to both individual and broader contextual issues. These refer to social and individual development in relation to complex political, cultural, educational and ideological processes and practices.

The broad categories and concepts identified in the integrated framework suggested here inform the discussion of literacy throughout the rest of the book. As such, it will draw on terms, concepts and categories within Sociology, Economics, Critical Linguistics, Political Economy, Cultural Studies, Critical Literary Theory, Sociolinguistics, Development Theory and Media Studies.

Part 2:
Literacy and Development Issues

Global Issues in Literacy Today

Statistical information on global literacy rates published within key defining sites such as UNESCO, the OECD and the World Bank reveal a picture of major improvements that have taken place over the past two decades. Much of this has been attributed to the success of, largely, externally funded mass literacy campaigns within a range of countries — and, particularly, 'developing' countries. The discourse on literacy within these contexts is generally presented in statistical terms, based on a clear distinction between those defined as 'literate' and those defined as 'illiterate'. This binary leaves huge gaps and silences on the often complex factors that contribute to, and sustain, high levels of illiteracy amongst specific groups of people, and also their levels of fluency in a variety of cultural literacies other than those defined within the dominant ideological framework.

In a recent UNESCO survey, for example, it is argued that the adult literacy rate in the world has 'increased from 69.5 percent in 1980 to an estimated 77.4 percent in 1995'. And, projections indicate that this could 'further improve to 80 percent by the year 2000'(UNESCO, 1995a: 1). It is suggested that, in numerical terms, this describes an increase in the number of literates world-wide 'to an estimated 3 billions in 1995' (UNESCO, 1995a). At the same time, it is argued that an increase in the world's population by 1035 millions during the period from 1980 to 1995 has contributed to an estimated net increase in the world's illiterate population of 8 millions (UNESCO, 1995a: 15). What do these statistics mean in real terms? How do they relate to the quality of life within particular societies? To what extent do they provide a true picture of literacy in the world today? What are the stories about literacy that they do not tell?

A more complex picture emerges when these claims are offset against a range of other determinants.

- _Despite levels of increase in literacy rates generally, women still represent almost two thirds of the world's illiterate population — the largest gender gap evident in SubSaharan Africa, the Arabs States and Southern Asia._ (UNESCO, 1995a)

It is estimated, for example, that the number of countries with female illiteracy rates of less than 50% to be within the region of 34 (UNESCO, 1995a). This identifies on average two out of three women who are illiterate in Africa, and one in two in Asia — with a literacy gap of 21 percentage points in favour of men (Stromquist, 1992: 55). Moreover, five low-income countries having female–male ratio of less than 50% at primary education level during the period 1986–88 were identified in the UN Human Development Report (1990). On a global level, the UNESCO World Education Report (1995b: 17) identifies women and girls as constituting the largest single category of persons denied 'full and equal opportunities for education for all'.

High levels of illiteracy amongst women in different societies can be ascribed to a variety of factors, including cultural values and belief systems, poverty and social disadvantage. In India, for example, high levels of illiteracy are prevalent among women of 'scheduled castes and scheduled tribes compared to women as a whole' — and more so in rural areas (Stromquist, 1990: 101). Women living in poverty, according to Stromquist, shoulder the burden of maintaining their families and households at a very basic level — a factor which often accounts for the high levels of drop-out from educational programmes amongst women and girls — despite high enrolment. Whilst, on the one hand, this reflects the effect of poverty on their lives, on the other hand, it can also be seen in terms of the cultural reinforcement of patriarchal relations. The ideology of patriarchy became ' codified in the laws of nation-states through regulations affecting institutions such as the family, work, land ownership, and voting rights' (Stromquist, 1992: 55). The sexual division of labour within many societies and cultures prevent women from fulfilling their roles as full citizens. In some societies, for example, in India and South America men often actively prevent women from attending literacy classes. In addition, Ryan (1992: 156) posits the view that 'despite notable gains, the persistent de facto discrimination of many education systems against women remain a blight on development today'. Within these contexts, the full weight of patriarchal hegemony comes to bear on women's social, economic, cultural and political marginalisation.

- *There are also wide variations in literacy levels between regions, subregions and countries.*

Based on past trends, the estimated number of illiterates have increased between 1980 to 1995 'by 70 millions in Southern Asia, 15 millions in SubSaharan Africa, and by 9 millions in the Arab States' (UNESCO, 1995a: 15). Countries such as Afghanistan, Niger and Ethiopia are reported as generally having low literacy rates within the population as a whole — as well as large differentials between male and female literacy rates. Furthermore, whilst according to recent information 'progress towards full literacy can be considered as self-sustainable in 36 countries' (UNESCO, 1995a: 1) in terms of the fact that they have reached the 70% literacy threshold, most of the world's illiterate population still reside in the 'developing' world.

The suggestion that although the *number* of literates might have increased globally, the *pattern of illiteracy* has remained the same, often serves as a universal explanation of social under-development. Such claims do not consider the complexity of social, economic, political and cultural relations within different societies — and, also, between regions. For example, contributing factors to disparities in levels of literacy between urban and rural areas are multifaceted and relate, at least in part, to differences between levels of poverty, the quality of educational provision, the availability of educational resources, lack of infrastructure as well as different national literacy priorities within these contexts.

Changing migration patterns within many 'developing' countries indicate a rapidly increasing urban population as people migrate to cities in search of jobs. It is estimated that urban populations in 'developing' countries will grow by at least 70% by the year 2000, in comparison with only 13% in the 'developed' world. The inability of cities to absorb this rapid increase in population levels, because of lack of adequate infrastructure, present further problems in providing appropriately for their educational needs.

- *Wide variations exist also within countries in relation to differences in literacy skills and the distribution of levels of proficiency.*

According to the International Adult Literacy Survey (IALS) conducted recently in eight industrialised countries by the Organisation for Economic Cooperation and Development (OECD), in some countries 'there is a wide range of difference between adults with low and high levels of literacy' (OECD, 1995 : 115). These differentials referred not only to marginalised groups but, according to the IALS, 'affect(ed) large proportions of the entire adult population'.

Despite its comprehensiveness, the International Adult Literacy Survey (IALS) survey nevertheless presents only a partial view of the literacy rates and related issues in metropolitan countries. This is the case if we take into account that the literacy differentials between immigrant groups and indigenous populations reported in the IALS (OECD, 1995: 71) result from the fact that the survey used as its basis for measurement, the dominant national language as the main literacy medium.

Literacy programmes available predominantly in the languages of the host country, in reality, exclude vast numbers of immigrants from participating in them. For example, many Bangladeshi women in Britain who were previously from peasant communities, because they tend to spend their lives mostly within their own communities, would be less motivated to attend adult literacy classes in English — which they might see as having little or no relevance to their everyday lives. Many of these women working in low-paid, low-skilled and un-unionised jobs in the informal sector such as clothes manufacturing, either in their homes or within their community, would have no or little need to be fully literate *per se* in order to earn a living, although they might wish to be literate in their own languages for their own cultural enrichment. This highlights the omission in most survey data of cultural literacies including reading for individual purposes such as leisure, and other ethno-cultural literacies and oral traditions that were often subjugated by different societies' experience of colonialism.

The complexity of the social practices and processes in which literacy is embedded highlights the fact that discussions of levels of societal literacy cannot take place realistically outside a consideration of broader social and political issues. This includes social policy and literacy provision, the impact of wider historical factors on shaping development priorities in different societies, the instability and corruption of some postcolonial regimes, and their collective impact on societal development.

In order to explore the range of meanings attached to literacy in relation to societal development, this section of the book focuses on the discourses that took shape within the policy frameworks of key defining sites such as national governments, UNESCO and the World Bank during the past three decades.

Chapter 2

Literacy and the Nation-state

The emergence of the modern secular state in Western Europe during the 19th century signified the end of absolutist monarchies grounded in the principle of divine sovereignty. The re-drawing of the territorial map of European states during that time resulted in the fact that 'the boundaries of state jurisdiction came to coincide more closely with that of peoples sharing the common characteristics of culture and historical identity that qualified them for nationhood' (Beetham, 1991: 209). Struggles for political power and control became articulated primarily around the concept of the 'people-nation' which cut across all social inequalities and exploitation to combine in a horizontally integrated comradeship (Anderson,1983). According to Anderson, the concept of the people-nation is defined first, in terms of its *territoriality* which refers to a given group of people residing within the boundaries of the nation-state. Second, it is defined in relation to its *sovereignty*, that is, existing independently and having its own exclusive rights within its domain; and the power to rule invested in the state. Beetham (1991: 209) argues that sovereignty also refers to the 'idea that the source of legitimacy for that jurisdiction derives from the people who constitute the nation' and that 'the nation forms the exclusive object of their political allegiance'. Third, the nation is imagined as a fraternal *community* (Anderson, 1983). This community is identified in terms of its own distinctive cultural identity, its own distinctive way of life and its own national language(s).

Language, Literacy and the Pluralist Nation-state

The 'pluralist' nation-state is defined as a poly-ethnic society dominated by one of the ethnic groups but which leaves broad areas of everyday life, for example, language and religion open (Bullivant, 1981). A central variable within the pluralist nation-state is the issue of language *choice*. The importance of language is its close relationship with fostering a national-identity. Within a pluralist society it provides the means by which a national consciousness is maintained by integrating diverse social groups within a heterogeneous society through its preferred official languages into a common value system; a common culture.

Language policy impacts on differential levels of literacy for particular groups in society, in the first instance, with regard to the choice of language(s) as medium/media of instruction at all levels of education. In the second instance, differential levels of communicative competence are also influenced through the preferred medium of official discourse in power institutions including, for example, local government, the mass media, business, commerce, and the law courts. As is discussed in the previous chapter, those not literate in the official language(s) can therefore be defined as illiterate although they may be able to read and write fluently in their own cultural languages or mother tongues, namely, the languages with which they have historically identified as a cohesive cultural group. Thus not all languages have parity in terms of their exchange value.

The relative value attached to particular languages in national policy derives from dominant ideas about what constitutes the 'nation' and, relatedly, the cultural, economic and linguistic factors that serve in the 'national interest' during different sociohistorical epochs. How the 'national interest' is defined varies between and within societies at particular stages in their development and, as will be seen later, also depends on specific political priorities defined by the state. These meanings are inscribed into their development objectives. In order to explore these issues, the next section considers the ways in which differentiated social meanings attached to literate 'functioning' within particular societies have a significant impact on how 'effective' different groups are expected, required, or allowed to become. This, in turn, would relate to the type of *political regime* in power within particular societies, the organisation of the social system, and the social roles adopted by people within these societies.

It is argued that language-state relations within autocratic, populist and techno-bureaucratic regimes often differ from those that exist in liberal pluralist democracies because they are pursuing different political aims. Moreover, different levels of importance attached to the role of civil society means that approaches to policy formulation would vary. This may have implications for minority language interests. Other influential variables include the stability of inter-ethnic group relations, the relative external and internal political stability of countries, as well as the politico-cultural ethos that prevails during specific sociohistorical epochs. Thus it can be argued that the literacy needs and expectations of people living within a society which is in the process of postcolonial nation-building, would be different from those living within colonial or a totalitarian context or the modern liberal democracy.

Changing literacy meanings in the liberal democracy

A key principle within the pluralist democracy is the need to preserve common institutions essential for the maintenance of the nation-state, for example, a common language, cultural values, legal system, political system and economic market system. Whilst government is seen as representing the interests of the 'people-nation', the system of government also constitutes the formal regulatory link between the state and civil society. Government intervenes strategically within the public domain at key moments to re-define 'national goals' (Jessop, 1990: 51), and to reshape or re-orientate the 'national-popular outlook' . This takes place either during moments of crisis for the state or in the interest of specific political projects pursued at the time or during periods of rapid social change.

For example, the drive for mass literacy in England and Wales during the period of the industrial revolution was, at least in part, a consequence of the invention of the printing press which had generated the need for mass readership (Williams, 1961). Thus it served in the interest of modernisation. Alongside this was also the need to stem the potential for social unrest within the rapidly expanding urban areas, by controlling working-class opinion through the popular press. The availability of family magazines allowed the respectable themes of moral and domestic development to become deeply entangled with the teaching of the social values of the emerging capitalist economic order (Williams, 1961). Literacy meanings at the time shifted from the erstwhile emphasis on the moral values of the Bible to serve more overtly in the interest of an emerging capitalist political economy. Significantly, with nationhood identified in terms of an English identity, literacy in Welsh as mother-tongue did not feature as an important variable in this process of development — and was not to be recognised educationally until 1907.

Major factors underscoring the need for government to redefine social goals at the time included:

(1) technological development and the resultant industrialisation;
(2) the changing mode of production altering ways of working — e.g. industrialisation and the transition from cottage industries to mass production in factories;
(3) changing patterns of consumption with the advent of mass production — and the development of wider markets within the colonies;
(4) the need to maintain social equilibrium threatened by high levels of poverty within urban areas due to rapid urbanisation, and rural–urban migration.

Within this context the drive for mass literacy served a dual purpose. On the one hand, increased literacy levels could contribute to a more skilled work force and also to facilitate consumption. On the other hand, it also provided a powerful means of securing social equilibrium and re-defining the social character in terms of the labour needs of a burgeoning capitalist system.

Literacy and colonial relations

Gray Cowan *et al.* (1965: 6–7), reviewing the framework of education in the pre–1950 colonialist period in Africa, provide an overview of the Education Policy in British Tropical Africa formulated in 1925, which outlined the direction of overall educational provision in Africa:

> [it] stressed that (1) the government reserved to itself the general direction and supervision of educational policy; (2) co-operation between government and other educational agencies should be promoted; (3) education should be adapted to the mentality, aptitudes, and traditions of the various peoples; (4) education should seek to strengthen what is good in the old beliefs; (5) the well-being of the country depended on the character of its people as much as on material prosperity; (6) voluntary agencies should be used in education; (7) grants-in-aid should be made, provided the schools conformed to the established standards; (8) the study of the educational use of the vernacular was of primary importance; (9) the 'native teaching staff' should be adequate; (10) a system of visiting teachers should be established to help in the training of teachers.

It also emphasised the importance of vocational and technical training, the education of 'women and girls' and regular monitoring of educational provision in the colonies. Education was organised to provide for both social cohesion and economic development. With regard to literacy it could be argued that despite the fact that British colonial policy encouraged the 'vernacular' as medium of instruction, that access to literacy would have been through English literary forms in Secondary and Higher Education. Thus a colonial cultural hegemony could be maintained although lip-service was paid to the right of indigenous peoples to retain their cultural heritage.

The subordinate positions occupied by the indigenous populations within the structure of the society would have meant that only a select few would have had access to the full range of educational opportunity. Ball (1983: 251) argues that we cannot assume a:

> straight-forward and unproblematic transfer of policy into practice. Figures from the 'Gold Coast Annual Education Report of 1934' analysed by Mumford and Jackson show the total numbers of children

attending school year-by-year for the previous 25 years (1911–1934). The trend of increase so shown reveals that it would have taken 600 years before the number attending school would have been as great as the child-population figures of the 1931 census. However, when these figures were amended to take account of the increase in population, the trend suggested it would take 3500 years before primary education would have been made available to 100% of the school age population.

Ball cites African resistance, restrictions imposed by examinations require-ments, the fact that English was taught only in the later years of schooling as inhibiting factors of expansion in colonial schooling. All education during the period would implicitly have been geared to producing an educational elite. Access to power within the state bureaucracy would have been controlled through literacy in the language of power which, during colonial times, was that of the colonising 'mother' country. Moreover, according to Ball (1983: 251):

> In 1939 there was still no secondary education for Africans anywhere in Central Africa. This position was carefully sustained in Central and East Africa by a rigid racial segregation of schooling for the European settlers, the Indians and the Africans . . . In 1934 Morris, Director of Education in Uganda, closed four of the eight junior secondary schools in the Protectorate because of what he saw as the consequences of the over-production of school graduates who would be the 'political emissaries of agitation and discontent' and have no outlet for their energies 'but political intrigue and the flouting of authority'.

The overriding factor in colonial education policy was to hegemonise relations of domination and subordination. As such, it underscored a model of social development that required a subservient, under-educated popu-lation which would provide a rich source of largely un-skilled and semi-skilled labour, with the exception of a core elite.

The imposition of the colonial mother tongue also influenced the educational possibilities for large groups of people. According to Ngugi (1993: 439) in Kenya during the 1950s:

> nobody could pass the [Kenya African Preliminary] exam who failed the English paper no matter how brilliantly he had done in the other subjects. I remember one boy in my class of 1954 who had distinctions in all subjects except English, which he had failed. He was made to fail the entire exam. He went on to become a turn boy in a bus company. I who had only passes but a credit in English got a place in the Alliance High School, one of the most elitist institutions for Africans in colonial

Kenya . . . English was the official vehicle and the magic formula to colonial elitedom.

He goes on to argue that the range of literature made available influenced the mental universes inhabited by the colonised by shaping people's perceptions of their world and their relation to it. Language as a primary mode of cultural transmission served an important means of shaping colonial cultural identities which, in turn, were offset against notions of ethnic 'Otherness' of indigenous peoples within the context of their own societies. Colonial education policies grounded in linguistic imperialism, and combined with differential levels of access to education, eventually contributed to uneven development within these societies.

Aspects of this have been continued during the postcolonial period. For example, Swahili as Kenya's official and national language, features mainly as a symbol of nationalism and unification within the political power structure of the country. Political discourse takes place in Swahili, whilst English has been retained as the language of economic and legal discourse. Social mobility still relies on fluency in English which is the language of social elite groups.

Similarly in Tanzania during the 1960s, although the country had adopted Swahili as its national and official language, it was the medium of instruction only until secondary school where it was replaced by English. This situation lasted until policy revision in the country's Third Five Year Plan in 1976. Since then Swahili has gradually been replacing English as medium of instruction throughout all phases in education (see also Chapter 4).

Literacy and postcolonial nation-building

During the postcolonialist period in the 1950s and 1960s, many societies engaged in nation-building focused on the socioeconomic value of education and defined their literacy needs in terms of unifying and extending the learning potential of their population to serve developing nations' economic and political needs or interests. However, the top-down policy approach adopted in many of these countries as well as residual power differences that had their origins in the colonial period, often resulted in continued political instability within some postcolonial societies.

Language and literacy provided primary arena in which these struggles were played out. Watson (1983) discusses this taking place in the education programmes fostered in post-independent Malaysia during the 1950s and early 1960s. The Razak Report (1956) he argues, provided the framework to an education policy oriented towards building a cohesive nation through centralised control over the curriculum and examination requirements. Successive governments have added to this the institution of a lingua franca

(Bahasa Malaysia) which has resulted in civil unrest particularly between the Malay and Chinese population groups in the country. Historically, the Chinese have been the more educated section of the population and have occupied powerful positions in commerce and industry. Urban Malays had been encouraged to join the civil service and those living in rural areas were predominantly farmers. The Indian section of the population are either plantation workers/owners or professionals.

The divide-and-rule policy of the colonialist period had resulted in deep ethnic cleavages within the society and it is the resentment that has grown between cultural groups, and the struggle for power among these, that contributed to social unrest in the immediate period that followed Malaysian independence. Ethnic group violence spread across the country in 1969. Watson (1983: 143) puts forward the view that:

> Since, in Malaysia, economic and social mobility are very dependent on the education system, and since the examination system is an effective instrument for regulating mobility through the system, any change in the language media, let alone a compulsory pass in Bahasa Malaysia, was bound to affect those not educated in Malay-medium schools.

Educationally, the institution of a lingua franca provided a barrier to literacy acquisition for the non-Malay population groups, a factor that profoundly shaped and influenced the social and cultural experiences of linguistic minority groups. Malay economic nationalism, articulated around the re-distribution of resources to the *Bumiputera* ('sons of the soil' or indigenous people), has continued since that time in order to facilitate the development of a Malay urban middle class (Khoo, 1999).

Postcolonial Malaysia typifies a model of authoritarian developmentalist growth in which the governing elite has a very strong ideological commitment to economic growth. Whilst this policy approach can stimulate rapid growth, it runs the risk of creating social instability because of the unequal distribution of services such as education and language rights amongst discrete minority ethnic groups. Social equilibrium has been maintained primarily as the result of the relative success of the restructuring of the economic base as part of the New Economic Policy (NEP) in the Second (1969–mid 1980s) and Third Phase (1984–1990s) of development. Khoo (1999) argues that luck with commodity prices, especially the discovery of off-shore oil during the 1970s, and relatively successful industrialisation have helped to pay for the expensive NEP.

The country, at least until the recent economic crisis, has been able to sustain high levels of economic growth throughout the 1980s and 1990s as a result of Mathathir Mohamed's liberalisation policies based on 'money politics'; the politics of the market. Through this, ethnic minority groups have been incorporated into the hegemonic vision of corporate nationalism, albeit economically at differential levels in comparison with the *Bumiputera*. In the late 1990s, the hegemony of a supra-class, supra-ethnic corporate nationalism is rapidly gaining ground in Mahathir Mohamed's project of re-orienteering national imaginings towards a 'Look East' perspective (Khoo 1999). This new corporate nationalism has been articulated in terms of the relative success of South East Asia's 'tiger' economies including Japan and South Korea during the 1980s. Ethnic particularities are rapidly giving way to a trans-ethnic capitalist entrepreneurism within a global market.

How this will work out within the current period of economic crisis remains to be seen. According to Khoo (1999), this vision of social corporatism may still be fractured by the growing nationalisms amongst indigenous groups such as the Dayak and Kadazan in East Malaysia, who have failed to benefit from the 'pro-*Bumiputera*' legislation. Language may yet re-emerge as an identity issue in Malaysia.

The role of literacy in legitimating the rise of the techno-bureaucratic nation-state in the USSR

Literacy levels for particular groups have, within some societies, also been carefully controlled through different forms of *censorship* validated by the official languages adopted. Censorship incorporated into national language practice played a key role in influencing societal literacy levels in the former USSR. Shorish (1984) argues that levels of literacy amongst the peasantry were carefully controlled in both pre- and post-revolutionary eras through the particular language policy pursued at the time. Under the Tsarist regime, successive russification policies had served to subjugate and colonise the different 'subnations' throughout the region by integrating them forcibly into a federal structure, with Russia as the dominant nation.

After the 1917 Revolution, the need to build a new Soviet nation had created an imperative to counter the traditional loyalties based on common language, culture and religion within the different regions. Both literacy and state censorship were to play key roles in this process. Within the framework of a mass literacy campaign, the 1919 Decree of Illiteracy required all citizens between 8 and 50 years to become literate. This programme built on a literacy initiative already started by peasants during the 1860s, and was integrated into the Red Army which coordinated literacy programmes through its *gramCheka* committees largely comprised by the secret police, the CHEKA (Eklof, 1987). Despite the regimented character of the literacy programmes, the principles of cultural pluralism were central to literacy development during this period. However, both pre- and post-revolutionary emphasis on cultural empowerment was to change when the political goals were re-defined in Stalin's cultural programme pursued during the 1930s.

The need to increase the low literacy levels that prevailed within Central Asia, which had a predominantly Turkic oral language base, contributed to the introduction of the Latin script for languages that were not alphabetised or that used Arabic script (Shorish, 1984). This formed part of Stalin's first Five Year Plan. However, this was to change again ten years later, when by the end of Stalin's Second Five Year plan in 1937, the Cyrillic script was introduced in Uzbekistan which had become the first Central Asian Soviet Socialist Republic. The transfer to the Cyrillic script affected literacy levels again in that those who had been made illiterate with the transfer to the Latin script now had to relinquish those skills they had acquired in order to function in the new milieu.

Stalin had argued publicly for the importance of regional autonomy and for the linguistic rights of minority groups to be sustained as a central element of their democratic rights. In reality, this was fractured by a national language planning approach that was integrally linked with the forging of a supra-class, de-ethnicised and secular Soviet 'nation' which, in turn, was to be incorporated into the Russian 'nation'. The adopted national language approach facilitated the building of a Soviet nation through the medium of the Russian language by socialising the discrete population groups into a common culture. The *Agency to Combat Illiteracy*, set up in 1930, served as a central means of facilitating Stalin's modernisation programme based on rapid industrialisation and the secularisation of the state.

Language has potent symbolic power, and the implications of Stalin's national language planning approach stretched beyond the links made between literacy and economic growth. An underlying function of this policy was to make censorship of the written word easier by making a limited range of literature available for popular consumption. Potential threats to the Soviet state could now be controlled in that would-be subversives were limited in terms of what they could read or write *officially*. Stalin's approach was primarily in response to the militant nationalisms that had emerged amongst rural population groups in the aftermath of the 1905 uprising. Stalin (1913: 2) commented:

The 'constitution regime' established at that time also acted in the same direction of awakening the nationalities. The spread of newspapers and of literature generally, a certain freedom of the press and cultural institutions, an increase in the number of national theatres, and so forth, all unquestionably helped to strengthen 'national sentiments' . . . The wave of nationalism swept onwards with increasing force, threatening to engulf the mass of the workers. And the more the movement of emancipation declined, the more plentifully nationalism pushed forth its blossoms.

Controlling the language of official publications thus served a powerful purpose in socialising the populace into Stalinist ideology. During the 1930s, unitarian class-based politics grounded in the ideology of 'homo soveticus' provided further legitimacy for the systematic marginalisation of ethno-cultural practices and religious institutions including mosques, synagogues and churches. Much of this took place through the Komsomol (Young Communist League) which comprised kultameitsy (cultural sol-diers) who were organised into kultbrigady (cultural brigades) (Eklof, 1987).

As is the case with present-day Malaysia discussed earlier, the USSR during Stalin's regime also represents an authoritarian developmentalist approach typified by an 'authoritarian political system committed ideologi-cally to economic development' (Ingham, 1995: 205). Whilst the country's economic and literacy goals were largely achieved during this period, this took place at the cost of freedom of information and speech. According to Eklof (1987) the stringent censorhip laws that prevailed in the USSR at the time prevented the populace from developing critical thinking skills and also from becoming discerning readers. He argues that they 'learned to decode but not to encode thoughts', and that 'people learned how to read and write but seldom to learn from reading' (Eklof, 1987: 144). These factors effectively inhibited the possibility of building a strong civil society.

Although bilingual policies did prevail within the different regions, Russian remained the official language of discourse within state institutions and thus became a primary means of access to political and economic power. Since the break-up of the Soviet Union in 1989, the struggle for the right to self-determination for social groups who previously had been relegated to 'subnations' has re-emerged. The various peoples of the Central Asian and Baltic regions started the process of reclaiming their languages, cultures and ethnic identities.

The role of literacy in legitimating a totalitarian regime

Pursuing a policy of cultural pluralism to legitimate its political aims of separatism, South Africa during the Apartheid years adopted a national language policy which, since 1948, aimed at consolidating white rule. Afrikaans and English became the official and national languages, with more emphasis placed on Afrikaans as the national language. Differential levels of access to literacy were provided for different ethnic groups banished to 'Coloured townships' and 'Bantu homelands' within the boundaries of greater South Africa. African children schooled in the under-resourced and under-funded 'Bantu' Education system were provided with a minimal level of functional literacy predominantly in Afrikaans and, to a lesser extent, English and, in Apartheid parlance, also an 'ethnic' language. Both Afrikaans and English were barriers to literacy acquisition as they were not the first languages of most of South Africa's Black population groups. As was the case in colonial Kenya discussed earlier, all major examinations could be passed only on the basis of a pass in both official languages.

In a situation where most pupils were forced to leave school before the age of 15 to earn a living as quickly as possible because of family poverty, many left as illiterates. Useful knowledge and basic education for these pupils were limited to those skills that would make them productive only as manual labourers within the Apartheid system. Unequal access to knowledge and literacy for the different population groups had been inscribed in the Bantu Education Act of 1953, the Extension of University Education Act (1959) which segregated higher education by setting up black universities also referred to as 'tribal colleges', the Coloured Person's Education Act (1963) and the Indian Education Act (1965). These introduced the framework of Apartheid education which was based on the principles of Christian National Education (CNE). CNE which was grounded in the hegemony of *eiesoortigheid* (ethnic purity) and white supremacism, became consolidated in the National Education Act (1967) that applied to the white population group.

The inferior social, cultural, political and economic position of the (heterogeneous) black population group was a key principle of CNE ideology. It stated:

Native [black] education should be based on the principles of trusteeship, non-equality; its aim should be to inculcate the white man's view of life, especially that of the Boer nation, which is the senior trustee. (CNE, 1948: 23; information in brackets added)

Later in 1953, Dr Hendrik Verwoerd, then Minister of Native Affairs (quoted in Sached, 1986:12) augmented this in his declaration:

The native must not be subject to a school system which draws him away from his community, and misleads him by showing him the green pastures of European society in which he is not allowed to graze.

Two years later he underscored this in his statement that 'there is no place for the Bantu in the European community above the level of certain forms of labour' (Verwoerd 1955, quoted in Sached 1986: 12.). Education under the Bantu Affairs Department (BAD) was removed from the control of the various provincial councils which presided over the syllabus content for the white population group.

On the second tier of education provision were the population groups defined as 'Coloureds' and 'Asians' schooled under the Coloured Affairs Department (CAD) and Indian Affairs Department to occupy only certain unskilled, semi-skilled and lower professional positions within the service industry. These differential levels of access to knowledge would, it was assumed, produce a stratified consciousness in which the 'master–servant' relationship would be reinforced.

Teachers who, during the late 1950s, aimed at subverting the dominant definition of 'useful knowledge' by inducting pupils into a critical social literacy were persecuted by the Security Police, imprisoned or placed under 'house arrest'. This culminated in the banning of all major educational and political organisations after the Sharpeville uprising in 1960. Stringent censorship laws meant also that a limited range of literature was available in the country and thus, theoretically, the potential for counter-hegemonic or critical knowledges could be curtailed.

Shakespeare's *Othello* and Alan Paton's *Cry the Beloved Country* did not form part of the set textbooks of the Matriculation Examination as they were seen as constituting a threat against the 'national interest'. The struggle against Apartheid education continued underground and found expression in the student uprising in 1976 when black children across the country revolted against Afrikaans as the medium of instruction and, *ipso facto*, 'Bantu' and 'Coloured' education circumscribed by CNE educational policy.

Post-Apartheid South Africa has been involved in the process of redefining its language policy in favour of the many sublimated cultural literacies of its diverse population groups. The country has opted for 11 official languages to suit the linguistic needs of the various regions. Language rights within this new context are viewed as being part of re-dressing the human rights of its minority groups and are regarded as central to the overall development of society as a whole. How this situation will develop in terms of the demographic changes that will inevitably take place as people migrate because of the new freedom of movement within the country remains to be seen. Educational policy is similarly being re-defined in the interest of all its peoples, accompanied by the re-distribution of resources to cater more equitably for the literacy needs of all the population groups.

Post-Apartheid South Africa has defined language as a basic human right. The new constitution states that 'every person shall have the right to use the language of his or her choice', that ' no person shall be unfairly discriminated against, directly indirectly, on the grounds of language', and that 'each person has the right to instruction in the language of his or her choice where this is reasonably practicable'. Collectively these principles underscore equity, social justice and the power to self-define and, in terms of this, the country has adopted 11 official languages as a means of cultural reparation and individual and social empowerment. Emphasis has been placed on re-instating previously subjugated languages and thus powers have been extended to school governing bodies to 'determine the language policy of the school', subject to the Constitution, the South African Schools Act (1996) and provincial law. Sign Language has been incorporated as an official language ' for the purposes of learning at a public school'.

Following the Constitution, a Language Plan Task Group (LANTAG) was established by the Minister of Arts, Culture, Science and Technology with the brief of helping to devise a National Language Plan for South Africa. The proposed plan is supported by the following principles:

(1) All South Africans should have access to all spheres of South African society by developing and maintaining a level of spoken and written language which is appropriate for a range of contexts in the official language(s) of their choice.
(2) All South Africans should have access to the learning of languages other than their mother tongue.
(3) The African languages, which have been disadvantaged by the linguicist policies of the past, should be developed and maintained.
(4) Equitable and widespread language services should be established. (LANTAG, 1996: 7)

The National Language Plan represents direct state intervention via national language planning, to alter the language culture in the country. That is, to re-instate previously subjugated languages, to support multilingualism as an intrinsic part of the culture as part of the process of overcoming the linguicism that framed national language policy during both periods of colonialism in the country. The report *Towards a National Language Plan for South Africa* published by LANTAG (1996) identifies both short- and long-term measures. Short-term measures include:

(1) initiating language awareness campaigns to sensitise people to the importance of language in society and to persuade them to the view that equity is an essential component of democracy in a multilingual society;
(2) developing a Language Code of Conduct for the Public Service to end the abuse of power through language practices;
(3) enjoining the political, economic and cultural leadership to use the

African and other marginalised languages on important and prestig-
ious occasions;

(4) putting pressure (legislative and otherwise) on the sate and privately
owned media to give equitable time and space to all official languages
and to use Sign Language and other languages where appropriate;

(5) using incentives to encourage employers and employees in both the
private and public sectors to learn additional languages, especially
those which would help to improve efficiency and productivity in the
work-place;

(6) regulating the use official languages in the Public Services;

(7) expanding state and state-supported provision for adult basic education and training.

Long-term measures include, *inter alia,*

(1) establishing appropriate and accurate demographic statistics, language
maps and language surveys for South Africa;

(2) consulting with communities to work out strategies for improving the
status of marginalised languages;

(3) establishing a solid nation-wide infrastructure of language services
involving adequate numbers of well-trained translators, interpreters,
terminologists, terminographers, specialist dictionaries, glossaries,
telephonic and other electronic facilities for verbal communication and
a language industry orientesd to trade and other interactions with the
African continent;

(4) eradicating illiteracy by giving support to literacy campaigns and
ongoing basic education projects;

(5) using extra-linguistic strategies and policies to enhance the status of the
African languages.

The LANTAG report argues further that multilingualism is more often the
norm in societies than monolingualism which is a powerful social construct
in the nation-states of the West. It is suggested that as a result of the flexiblity
of the post-Fordist workplace and international market 'monolingual
work-places and trading environments are fast becoming anachronisms'
(LANTAG, 1996: 96).

What this unity-in-diversity approach to national language policy holds
in store for the development of a cohesive South African nation as well as
the nature of societal development, will depend largely on equity in relation
to the distribution of political and economic power to the different social
groups in that country. It would also depend on the strength of support
amongst the diverse social groups for the development of a plural society.

Key issues that emerge in the discussion so far, revolve around the central role that language policy and, relatedly, literacy practices have historically played in managing the process of social change. This discussion is continued later with special regard to the identification and management of literacy priorities within the liberal democracy during a period of rapid social transition.

Conclusion

This chapter examined literacy as a *social practice* with regard to its interactive relationship with social institutions, structures and processes. It explored the impact that the ethos and organisation of particular social systems have on the structuring of language relations within the pluralist nation-state. The importance of this lies in the fact that the principles, political values and systems that govern society, create or inhibit the levels and forms of literacy knowledge made available within society. It highlighted the fact that political interests play a key role in influencing definitions of legitimate 'high-status' and 'useful' knowledges within the culture. In terms of this, decisions about levels of access to different forms and types of literacy depend on the particular regime in power and what its specific ideological and political aims are in relation to different population groups within society.

Implicit in this are also specific ideas about citizenship and, *de facto*, the role of citizens within society. This refers, on the one hand, to national aspirations and expectations about individuals' levels of personal 'efficacy' in relation to their usefulness and value as workers and consumers to the overall economic development of society. On the other hand, with regard to citizenship it also refers to their social roles and positions in relation to national decision-making processes including opportunities (or lack of them) for co-determination and, therefore, their role in governance.

In the case of Apartheid South Africa, vast sections of the population were excluded from this process, first, because Apartheid social policy ensured that they remained at the margins of society. Second, the particular language policy pursued by the Apartheid State framed an education system grounded in the overt subjugation of its black population groups. Black people did not form part of the citizenry; and because they had very limited access to education the majority were, largely, illiterate. This strategy also served an important economic purpose. South Africa during the period of Apartheid managed to develop a strong economic base made possible largely by the availability of low-waged, illiterate and politically disempowered manual labour in the mining, services and agricultural industries. High levels of *illiteracy* amongst black population groups were therefore a necessary prerequisite for an intentional policy of uneven social development which provided the economic and political basis of Apartheid policy and practice. Economic development could take place only on the basis of social inequality for a large proportion of that society, whilst at the same time retaining white supremacy.

The example of social change in England and Wales during the 19th century illustrates the ways in which government policy re-define social goals at key moments in a country's development. This highlighted the fact that levels of access to different forms of knowledge and types of literacy skills can alter with the types of skills and training required by industry, the defined needs of the national economy at a given time as well as the social cohesiveness needed to sustain the nation during periods of crisis or transition.

The examples of postcolonial Malaysia and Apartheid South Africa, which here represent autocratic regimes, showed how government often also functions overtly to serve the specific ideological and political interests of powerful elite groups within society. The discussion on post-revolutionary USSR, illustrated the contingency of literacy meanings; that they are always subject to change in terms of what constitutes the 'national interest' at particular times. Whereas literacy meanings were culturally empowering to all population groups during the period before and immediately after the revolution, the emphasis on language medium and forms of literacy altered within the framework of Stalin's economic project of modernisation, and his cultural project of creating the ideal soviet nation during the 1930s.

Collectively, these factors impact on the range and levels of literacy made available to different groups within society as well as their relative access to participation in societal decision-making. They also highlight the fact that the situation regarding societal literacy is not the same in every country. It tends to vary according to:

(1) the type of regime in power — and its historical antecedents;
(2) models of governance;
(3) social ethos and organisation of society;
(4) dominant ideologies and political interests.

These factors underline the argument that although there are over-riding principles, we cannot have a universalised discourse on societal literacy levels. Analyses need to take account of specific conditions that prevail within different societies.

Models of government and governance in relation to policy and provision for societal literacy within different sociohistorical contexts previously discussed, are summarised in Table 2.1.

What also became evident is the complexity of linguistic needs within

Table 2.1 Models of governance and language relations within the pluralist nation-state

Model of government	Patterns of power	Concept of governance	Patterns of interest	Language relations
Colonial rule, e.g. British, French, Belgium throughout Africa	External 'mother country'; colonial government comprising representatives of mother country	Indirect governance; limited popular involvement in decision-making	Circumscribed by colonising state	Externally imposed 'mother tongues' to socialise colonised into language, culture and belief system of 'mother country'; subjugation of local literacies and linguistic-cultural traditions
Postcolonial, e.g. countries throughout Africa and South East Asia since de-colonisation started in the 1960s	National development priorities; party political interests — varies with type of regime	Vary from autocratic; populist; to democratic decision-making	Nation building; sometimes emergence of nationalist agenda	Re-defining status of national languages; re-assertion of mother tongue/s — sometimes representative only of dominant cultural groups — literacy as essential aspect of societal modernisation
Totalitarian/ autocratic regime, e.g. Apartheid South Africa	Defined within context of centralised state	Power to govern is invested in strong state — often exercised through dominant ethnic/social/ cultural group eg. white 'Afrikaners' in Apartheid South Africa	'Needs' of the state; needs of dominant power group often articulated around ethnic nationalism e.g. 'Afrikaner' creed: '*Een Volk, Een Taal, Een Land*' = ethnic nationalism	Imposition of language of ruling group; limited range of provision for linguistic/cultural minorities; subjugation of local literacies; literacy as key cultural variable to sustain hegemony of ruling group
Liberal democracy, e.g. Western Europe, USA, Australia	'National interest'; business; political parties; political, cultural, economic power interest groups	Representative government; structures exist within society to facilitate democratic decision-making, interactionist; need to maintain consensus — and social cohesion;	National interest, economic needs; business interest groups linguistic and cultural minority interest groups; political projects amongst different interest groups within the context of the state	Dominant mother tongue as official language; cultural and linguistic pluralism
Neo-liberal Democracy, e.g. UK during period of Thatcherism 1980s; US during period of Reaganism 1980s	Centrality of the market	Minimal government intervention; free-market democracy; transnational governance through funding	Primacy given to economic and business interests; 'needs' of the market	Importance of literacy in 'world languages' to facilitate participation in global market; practical knowledges and flexible skills, computer literacy

the majority of the nation-states. This, in turn, raises questions about the implications of national language policies on the literacy entitlements of different linguistic minority groups with regard not only to improving personal efficacy, but also in terms of maximising their cultural capital. Balancing human resource development needs that are defined in terms of maximising productivity to sustain economic growth, against basic human needs that include factors of language and culture remains a problematic area. Overall, the examples highlighted throughout this chapter have illustrated that national language policy structured into educational policy frameworks forms an integral part of society's implicit or explicit development goals. This, in turn, impacts on the distribution of particular types and forms of literacy in society. These issues will be discussed further in the next two chapters.

Chapter 3

Literacy and Social Development

The nation-state has, at least since the 1950s, provided the focus for development policies geared to foster national independence and self-reliance through a process of sustained economic growth. Literacy has featured centrally in this discourse on societal development, especially within the context of national modernisation programmes adopted since the 1960s. Whatever the type of regime, provision for and funding of national literacy programmes are grounded in policies influenced by particular understandings of societal 'development' and, *de facto*, 'under-development' as well as the factors that contribute to these.

As is the case with definitions of literacy discussed in Chapter 1, views on what development is differ within the social sciences. And, as such, it remains a contested concept. In order to clarify the position of literacy within societal development policies, the next section summarises some of the major theories that have framed discussions of national 'development'. These will then be integrated into the discussion of the influences of different models of development on views about the relative value of literacy to social development.

Theories of Development

The concept of development used in *economics* has traditionally been explained in terms of the ability of countries to '*generate and sustain* an annual increase in its gross national product at rates of about 5 to 7% or more' (Todaro, 1989 : 86, original emphasis). Other, non-economic indicators of social development include gains in literacy, schooling, health conditions and services, and provision of housing, character of basic social organisation, extent of mass communication, degree of national integration and sense of national unity, level of effectiveness of financial institutions and — political stability (Todaro, 1989; Adelman & Morris, 1967). These social indicators occupy a secondary position to those related directly to economic growth since it is argued that the gains made would benefit society as a whole.

77

Providing an *historical,* that is, a perspective over time of societal development, Rostow's (1960) *stages of economic growth* became the most influential in development theory during the 1960s and 1970s. The stages of development included:

(1) the traditional society (predominantly agrarian);
(2) the pre-take-off society (increased levels of agricultural productivity, development of effective infrastructure: change in people's mentality; emergence of entrepreneural class);
(3) take-off into self-sustaining growth (share of net investment and saving in national income rises from 5–10%; industrialisation; use of modern technology);
(4) the drive to maturity; and
(5) the age of high mass consumption.

Mass communications came to be seen as playing an instrumental role in economic and social development within this framework. Television, in particular, was seen as offering the potential to 'inform, persuade and educate and thereby facilitate development' (Dordick & Wang, 1993: 20). The mass media came to be seen as providing the mechanism to achieve Rostow's 'take-off' stage of development. Underlying this was the view that 'urbanisation increases literacy, literacy increases mass media consumption, and mass media consumption increases electoral participation — all of which are necessary for development to occur' (Dordick & Wang, 1993: 21). Another view was Windham's (1970) argument that 'communication causes urbanisation, education, and development; urbanisation causes education; and education causes communications and development' (quoted in Dordick & Wang: 21). Developing countries were to be encouraged to invest in communications infrastructure and extend mass media with the aim of altering people's expectations and to re-orientate them towards entrepreneurism, which would benefit economic development. As can be seen later, these views essentially subscribed to a technical, rational view of development in which technology was to provide a 'quick-fix' to complex societal problems.

Within a *philosophical* framework, development has been regarded as, 'an *attribute of history,* as a specific *historical transitional process* and as a certain *development policy'* (Hettne, 1995: 50, original emphasis). In his critique of traditional views of development, Hettne outlines the principles that underscored the *modernisation* paradigm which dominated development theory during the 1960s and 1970s:

• Development is a spontaneous, irreversible process inherent in every single society.

- Development implies structural differentiation and functional specialisation.
- The process of development can be divided into distinct stages showing the level of development achieved by each society.
- Development can be stimulated by external competition or military threat and by internal measures that support modern sectors and modernise traditional ones.

Key elements in this paradigm are the range of factors that stimulate social change, organisational complexity as a fundamental goal of development and, significantly, the notion of progression derived from Rostow (1960).

A more *critical theory* of development emerged during the 1970s when, despite the fact that some developing countries did achieve high rates of growth which, theoretically, placed them within Rostow's 'pre-take-off stage', they were still experiencing high levels of unemployment, growing poverty and social inequality. Academic discourse structured around under-development provided a critique of the linearity and technicism of modernisation. Summarising this debate at the time, Owens (1987) argued that:

> development has been treated by economists as if it were nothing more than an exercise in applied economics, unrelated to political ideas, forms of government and the role of people in society. It is high time we combine political and economic theory to consider not just ways in which societies can become more productive but the quality of the societies which are supposed to become more productive — the development of people rather than the development of things. (Quoted in Todaro, 1989: 88)

The re-defined view of development that emerged within this debate stressed the need to reduce levels of 'poverty, inequality and unemployment within the context of a growing economy' (Todaro, 1989: 87). In terms of this, Todaro (1989: 88) argued that development is to be:

> conceived of as a multidimensional process involving major changes in social structures, popular attitudes, and national institutions, as well as the acceleration of economic growth, the reduction of inequality, and the eradication of absolute poverty.

Todaro identified three core values of development, namely, lifesustenance (the ability to provide basic needs); self-esteem (to be a person); and freedom from servitude (to be able to choose). These factors referred to the need to lessen absolute poverty, and inequality in income distribution. It advocated improvements in levels of employment, the nature and quality of basic services such as health, education and other social and cultural services. It also included overall improvement in a nation's collective esteem — in relation to itself as well as with other nations; freedom from external dependence and 'internal servitude to other people and institutions' (Todaro, 1989: 91). Emphasis shifted to concerns about countries' ability to provide for 'basic needs' and facilitating a nation's 'self-help' capabilities by planning their own routes to development and choosing appropriate technologies.

Whilst modernisation theory including Rostow's model is criticised in terms of the fact that it advanced a neutral, value-free model of development, the views expressed within the critical framework can be questioned on the basis of their assumptions about the relative power that developing countries have to define their own development goals. This is especially important if we take account of the power exercised by international agencies such as the World Bank and the International Monetary Fund (IMF) over the particular economic policies adopted in aid-receiving countries. This issue will be discussed again later in the chapter.

The ways in which different theories of development have framed models of development, and their influence on shaping societal literacy meanings are explored in the next section.

Literacy and Models of Development

Modernisation

The concept of societal modernisation, *historically*, derives its meaning from the process of social, economic, political and cultural change that swept across the Western world during the 18th and 19th century (Ingham, 1995). As a *social scientific construct*, modernisation is a multifaceted concept and refers to various aspects of societal development. Ingham (1995: 40) explains:

> In economic terms, it implies industrialisation and urbanisation and the technological transformation of agriculture. Socially, it involves the weakening of traditional ties, and the rise of achievement as the basis for social advancement. Its political dimension is in the rationalisation of authority and the growth of bureaucracy. Culturally, modernisation is represented by increased secularisation of society arising from the growth of scientific knowledge.

The concept of modernisation revolves also around the need for geo-political re-organisation (rural–urban), technological re-structuring, building an effective infrastructure and the re-constitution of cultural relations to suit the diverse needs of a more complex scientific society. Key principles in the argument for modernisation included the need to develop:

(1) rationality as a basis for logically informed economic planning to replace traditional forms of thinking and organisation.
(2) 'improved institutions and attitudes to increase labour efficiency, promote effective competition, social and economic mobility, individual enterprise; permit greater equality of opportunities; make possible higher productivity rates; raise levels of living; and promote development' (Todaro, 1989: 123).

The significance of literacy as providing a means of access to both knowledge and skills is implicated in both these principles.

Increased literacy levels as an essential variable in facilitating popular participation in societal development have, at least since the 1960s, featured centrally in theories on societal modernisation. These meanings were underscored in the claims made by influential writers such as Goody and Watt (1968) and Oxenham (1980) about the intrinsic value of literacy for both individual and societal development. As is discussed in Chapter 1, literacy was regarded as the technology of the intellect; that it strengthens the power of thought and contributes to the growth and development of rational, human reasoning (Goody & Watt, 1968). And it was seen to play a role in the development of 'empathy', 'flexibility', 'adaptability' and 'willingness to accept change' (Oxenham, 1980:15) which, in turn, would contribute to the development of a modernised, technologically advanced society.

An overt link between literacy and development was provided by Anderson's (1966) claim that a society requires a 40% literacy rate to enable it to enter Rostow's 'take-off' stage. Collectively, these meanings provided educational and economic legitimacy to the incorporation of literacy as a key variable in the project of societal modernisation (see also Chapter 4). Anderson's claim had a major impact. Indeed, according to Street (1984: 184):

Anderson's conception of a development threshold at a 40% literacy rate, . . . affected perceptions of what investment in literacy might lead to, and it in turn was 'explained' by various theories, . . . regarding the significance of literacy for logic, problem-solving abilities and other 'cognitive' skills.

As a result, national expenditure and external funding for literacy became increasingly targeted to people directly to maximise their productivity levels in order to facilitate economic growth.

The economic meanings attached to literacy were subsequently inscribed into the framework of the UNESCO Experimental World Literacy Programme (EWLP). Consequently, the concept of 'functional literacy' became an important component of development programmes throughout the developing world. The distinction between 'traditional' literacy and 'functional literacy' was stressed in the argument that 'whereas traditional literacy can be offered in isolation, functional literacy must be a part of a broader development effort; provided in a vacuum it only disappoints expectations' (UNESCO, 1972: 42). Literacy geared to specific learning needs within the work-place became seen as an essential means of maximising 'human capital' in the development process. According to Jones (1990: 55):

> functional literacy referred to an approach to literacy in which mass attacks on illiteracy were rejected, traditional patterns of motivation, infrastructure, teaching methods, and reading materials were set aside, and key (largely economic) sectors, where literacy hindered develop-ment, were identified to determine who would receive instruction.

Particular groups targeted for inclusion in functional literacy programmes included 'those groups whose illiteracy presents the most immediate block to progress and who stand the most chance of using and thus retaining literacy skills once they were acquired' (UNESCO, 1972: 42).

The fact that UN funding became integrally tied to functional or 'work-oriented' literacy programmes (Jones, 1988) resulted in pilot projects being set up in countries such as 'Algeria, Ecuador, Ethiopia, Iran, Madagascar, Mali, the Sudan and Tanzania' (UNESCO, 1972: 44) as part of the EWLP. Functional literacy was integrated also into aspects of agricul-tural programmes in Afghanistan and India. A survey conducted by UNESCO (1969–71) reflects the extent to which countries had adopted this approach. Comments from Peru stated that 'at present, isolated literacy programmes are no more conceivable than development programmes without literacy. In their development plans sectors such as agriculture, mining, fisheries, industry, trade etc., give priority to literacy activities' (UNESCO, 1972: 51). Mali similarly stated that 'as of 1 January 1971, the literacy policy of the Government has been exclusively oriented towards functional and selective literacy linked to the priorities of the country's economic development' (UNESCO, 1972: 51).

Because of the work-oriented focus of functional literacy, the teaching resource base altered. It extended from a previous dependence on traditional educational providers to one that incorporated a wider pool of expertise, such as agricultural and technical experts (UNESCO, 1972). UNESCO experts were subsequently included in the Technical Assistance

Programme and were sent to a variety of countries to assist them in the design of functional literacy programmes (UNESCO, 1972).

Yet, despite this massive input of resources into national literacy programmes, variations in literacy levels and levels of proficiency emerged between regions, subregions and between countries. Jones (1988: 149) highlights this in his argument that 'the programs for cotton growers in Syria, Tanzania and Mali, for example, were quite dissimilar, not just because of the linguistic differences between the regions, but because of obvious social, vocational and psychological variance as well'.

Very little significant change took place in the quality of life of people generally, despite the fact that there were relative levels of increase in the Gross National Product (GNP) of some countries. The principles of equal opportunities, raising standards of living and facilitating social and economic mobility which were seen as being central to the modernisation project were therefore not achieved fully. In other words, functional literacy as a 'quick-fix' strategy for societal development had failed.

Focusing on literacy in relation to the work-place *per se*, outside a consideration of cultural, sociohistorical and political relations within different societies, was highly problematic. At the time, many developing countries had just emerged from sustained periods of colonisation, and had more complex social needs and political instability than the developed world. As was discussed in Chapter 2, in many colonised societies, particularly throughout Sub-Saharan Africa, colonial education policy had ensured minimal levels of literacy and, as a result, a vast pool of un-skilled labour. In addition, the tendency during the postcolonial period to encourage literacy in defined 'national languages' as part of the process of nation-building, contributed further to the marginalisation of local languages and, therefore, minority cultures. Many developing countries were at base multilingual, and it is now widely accepted in linguistics research and in educational discourse that people acquire literacy more easily in their first language (Skutnabb-Kangas, 1990). In not fostering local literacies, development within the modernisation paradigm, paradoxically, did not maximise societal development.

Furthermore, social and economic development are also dependent on the type of regime, and relatedly, forms of governance, as well as the relative power of interests groups. Power struggles and other conflicts played out around sovereignty, territoriality, ethnicity and language during the period of postcolonial nation-building resulted in social instability in many developing countries. This factor impacted on the extent of social development that could take place within these societies.

In turn, as can be seen in Chapter 4, lack of social and political stability during this period also had an influence on the possibility to maintain continuity and progression in literacy programmes.

Whilst national drives for increased levels of literacy can provide an important hegemonic factor in managing the process of societal change, as was the case in England during the industrial revolution (see Chapter 2), increased literacy levels on their own are not necessarily significant with regard to their direct value to economic growth. As was discussed in Chapter 1, as a social practice, literacy combines with a range of social and political variables to influence societal development.

Summary

The modernisation paradigm assumed a bi-polar perspective of development grounded in the notion of traditional versus modern capitalist society, in which the latter represented the preferred aspiration of all societies. And, relatedly, the principles of modernisation inscribed into Rostow's stages suggested a linear and rational process of getting there. There were also strong, implicit, elements of 'moral' deficit in the association of illiteracy with under-development within these societies. The fact that the cultural, political and economic traditions through which many of these societies had sustained themselves historically had been systematically eroded during centuries of colonial rule, raises difficulties with regard to how 'traditional' societies would be defined in the modern world.

Having a different sociohistorical base to that which shaped the project of modernity in Western Europe during the 19th century meant that different conditions prevailed within the developing world. Their development trajectory would therefore be quite different to that which typified development throughout Western Europe since the industrial revolution.

Western European modernisation during and after the industrial revolution rather than constituting development from within (endogenous), in reality, could take place only because of profits generated within and extracted from the colonies — as well as the rapidly expanding markets that colonialism offered. Smith (1995: 255) highlights this in his argument that:

> the emergence of the great colonial empires was accompanied by several significant trends in domestic statehood: the growth of bureaucracy and military organisation, the expansion of government budgets, the development of corporate commercial organisation and the consolidation of the technological and scientific base for state activity.

Within this time-frame then, Western Europe benefited from a transnational capital flow that enabled the infrastructural base of the nation-state to be secured.

These factors suggest that increased literacy levels, in these instances, were the *outcomes* of the possibility for mass schooling provided by a strong economy. Indeed, technological development and social change had provided the *impetus* for mass schooling. Similar conditions do not exist for the now 'developing' world — which has been, at least since the 1960s, engaged in a process of re-defining itself *against* their history of exploitation.

Lacking a consideration of broader factors such as historical relations, societal ethos and cultural aspirations, the modernisation model essentially imposed a Western model of development on these countries. In doing so, it neglected consideration of the fact that many developing countries have a legacy of uneven development grounded in the unequal relations of colonialism which, as could be seen in the examples of Kenya and Tanzania discussed in Chapter 2, also included linguistic inequalities. This meant that during the process of change towards a re-defined nation, they would have had a set of development priorities that reached beyond the economy.

Also significant is the fact that many postcolonial societies were dogged by long periods of social instability as the result of struggles for power amongst elite groups. This had a major impact on the levels of development that could take place within these societies. Both baseline and subsequent levels of development could therefore be measured meaningfully only in relation to the specific sociohistorical relations that had shaped conditions within each society.

The new international economic order (NIEO)

By the time that UNESCO's Experimental World Literacy Programme concluded in 1974, the world was in the midst of a deep recession sparked, in part, by the OPEC oil crisis of 1973. It was within this context that a critique of Western development theory emerged within the postcolonial world and re-focused attention on the issue *of under-development* within developing countries; and *unequal development* between the industrialised world and the under-developed world. Social and economic inequalities were ascribed to historical relations of dependence and domination structured between the colonised and colonising world. These relations, it was argued, were now perpetuated in the unequal economic relations that existed between countries at the centre (developed) countries and those existing at the periphery (under-developed countries). Under-development became defined as constituting *dependent capitalism*.

Measurement of social development in terms of net increases in the GNP which, as is argued earlier, provided the basis of the modernisation model, came under fierce criticism. Under-development was seen as a direct result of international power imbalances, and arguments were made for the need to move towards a new international economic order (NIEO) in which these inequalities could be addressed through economic, political and institutional reforms. The UN General Assembly adopted a resolution in 1974 to consider a new international economic order 'based on equity, sovereign equality, interdependence, common interest and co-operation among all States . . . which shall correct inequalities and redress existing injustices' (quoted in Jones, 1988: 217).

Within an increasingly politicised discourse, literacy definitions within the UNESCO framework changed at the Persepolis Symposium in Iran (1975). Literacy was defined as being more than reading and writing. It was 'a contribution to the liberation of man and to his full development; literacy is not an end in itself — it is a fundamental human right' (quoted in Tanguaine, 1990: 20). This shift in definition from purely economic concerns to those focused on human rights can be attributed, to a large extent, to criticism from the postcolonial developing world and, particularly, the impact of the Freirean model of literacy on discourses of adult literacy.

This politicised debate around literacy and development was to dominate UNESCO for the next 14 years during the period when Amadou-Mahtar M'Bow served as the Director-General (1974–87) (Jones, 1988). Within the critical discourse that prevailed, the meanings attached to literacy by developing countries became part of a different political project of national empowerment to the one underscored in UNESCO's modernisation programme. Literacy now became tied to another discourse focused on seeking means to re-adjust the unequal power relations between the 'developed' and 'developing' world. The debate taking place within UNESCO foregrounded the primacy of 'endogenous development' (Jones, 1990: 220) and centred on economic and political redress in relation to historical forms of control and exploitation. This view, which derived from the Freirean approach to literacy, reflected the concerns expressed also within dependency theory at the time. As can be seen in Owens' (1987) argument above, the critique extended beyond concerns with literacy levels to include concerns about external control over information as well as mass communication practices. This broader perspective of literacy sought to empower developing countries by helping them 'to build their own media infrastuctures through the provision of equipment, the planning of systems of communication and the training of journalists and technicians' (Jones, 1990: 224).

Advocacy of the need for developing countries to build their own infrastructure to support mass communication processes would, it was argued, enable them to extend their literacy, technological and human resource base. This could, potentially, improve decision-making processes on the basis of enlarged information and knowledge and, in the process, facilitate a more informed participation in the democratic process. Another factor underlying this drive for control over information was the hope to free the 'developing' world from dependence on transnational communications services based in the 'developed' world.

The counter-hegemonic discourse that ensued against what was perceived as the expansion of Western imperialism during this period resulted in UNESCO becoming an arena of struggle for control over literacy meanings as well as for control of the political agenda. The response from key actors such as the United Kingdom, Singapore and the United States to developments during this period was to withdraw their funding contributions during the early 1980s.

Critique

Whilst the new 'empowering' statements in the critical discourse generated within the framework of UNESCO during the M'Bow period were clearly significant in terms of their rhetorical value, in practical terms, their meanings were much more problematic. Although the ideological framework was clearly defined, the NIEO programme lacked clarity with regard to definitions, pedagogy, literacy models and criteria for the measurement of both individual and societal literacy levels. Indeed, subsumed within a counter-ideological discourse on development issues, literacy became divorced from its educational base (Jones, 1990). Moreover, concentrating predominantly on exogenous factors that impeded development within postcolonial societies, in effect, meant that internal national issues related to autocratic regimes, government corruption, state censorship and their impact on linguistic, political and cultural rights of minority groups were, largely, left unaddressed. These issues were to emerge in the social unrest, articulated mainly around ethnicity and language, that have taken place in many developing countries since the late–1980s.

Neo-classical model

Since 1989 UNESCO has been in the process of yet again re-defining its views of literacy in line with the concept of 'functional illiteracy' which, in addition to a lack of ability in reading, writing and arithmetic, also includes practical skills as well as technological and technical illiteracy (Tanguaine, 1990). Much of this has been articulated again within a discourse on 'empowerment'. However, this notion of empowerment has a different ideological basis to that which supported the Freirean approach to literacy. Within the redefined discourse framework the notion of 'empowerment' centres on the need to adapt to changing skills needs in the labour market, and changes within the labour process. Emphasis has shifted to concerns about the mismatch between existing skills supply and new skills demands requiring different competencies (OECD, 1995). Lack of adequate levels of literacy is seen as a barrier to productivity and innovation and it is argued that:

> governments can no longer rely on a policy of gradually expanding school enrolments and improving the quality of education over time to meet the demands for new and high-level competencies generated by the economy. (OECD, 1995: 22)

In addition to the new skills demands evolving within the new technological production process, this change in literacy definitions and priorities also accompanies an ideological shift towards the principles of neo-liberalism within the developed world since the late 1970s.

Foregrounding the market as primary regulatory mechanism, neo-liberalism advocates freeing capital by reducing the role of the state in the management of the economy. This, it is suggested, would be accomplished by exercising cuts in public expenditure which would, in turn, boost the private sector. It is argued that:

> by permitting free-markets to flourish, privatising state-owned enterprises, promoting free trade and export expansion, welcoming foreign investors, and eliminating the plethora of governmental regulations and price distortions in factor, product, and financial markets, both economic efficiency and economic growth will be stimulated. (Todaro, 1989: 83)

Emphasis has shifted towards human resource development (HRD) which centres on targeting expenditure to people directly in order 'raise the actual and potential productivity of the population, identified as 'quality' ' (Gould, 1993: 149).

Lawrence (1992: 50) defines the concept of HRD as:

> sustaining equitable opportunities for continued acquisition and application of skills, knowledge, and competencies that promote individual self-sufficiency and are mutually beneficial to individuals, the community, and the larger environment of which they are a part.

He goes on to argue that successful implementation would depend on a re-conceptualised view of learning and the educational process, which should be regarded as a life-long experience. Education and training, he claims, should also be 'winched closer to actual settings in which competencies are applied', not as a process of ' 'vocationalising' education but rather to teach people flexible skills which they would be able to transfer to different contexts, and thus help to shape their own and others' futures' (1992: 52). Although an attempt has been made to acknowledge some of the complex needs that exist in the developing world, the meanings attached to HRD within this re-formulated framework essentially support the principles of work-place flexibility. The implications of these new and evolving skills requirements in relation to literacy and development will be addressed in more detail in Chapter 5.

Literacy as a central variable in human resource development became incorporated into World Bank discourse in 1980, following arguments made by the agricultural economist, Theodore Schultz. In his Nobel Prize address in 1979 Schultz argued that:

> investment in population quality and in knowledge in large part determines the future of mankind ... the decisive factors of production in improving the welfare of poor people are not space, energy, cropland; the decisive factors are the improvement in population quality and advances in knowledge. (Quoted in Gould, 1993: 148)

These meanings derive from the view that new and evolving technological production processes have created the need for *flexible workers* who possess *transferable skills and knowledge*, and who can engage in *constant innovation* within the production process in order to cater for *evolving market needs*.

Some of these meanings have been taken up in the OECD literacy discourse which underlines the significance of increased literacy levels — and different range of literacies, skills and knowledges. It is argued:

> As firms and labour markets change, some jobs become obsolete and new ones are created. The new jobs require literate workers. In a flexible economy that is well positioned to take advantage of change, people will need to change skills and qualifications — perhaps many times. (OECD, 1995: 22)

Moving away from the bi-polar perspective of literacy, that is, that people are either literate or illiterate, the OECD places emphasis on the growing need in the work-place for skills-updating, and the need for learners to *want* to learn. The influence of literacy on creating workers who are flexible and efficient in their learning is seen as an important variable in the new *learning society*. Literacy is seen as formative in terms of facilitating work-place learning (OECD, 1995); it is a key element in HRD.

Decentralised planning and management of literacy programmes

Within the framework of neo-liberalism societal underdevelopment is ascribed to lack of efficiency, centralised planning, corruption and lack of economic incentives, rather than the relations of domination and subordination as is suggested by dependency theorists. Significant shifts started to take place during the 1980s to decrease the role of government in the public sphere. The need for internal administrative reforms focusing on management capacity, cost-effectiveness and quality control in aid-receiving countries became highlighted. De-regulation of the market and self-regulation of services within the public sphere, it was suggested, provided increased opportunities for stimulating competition amongst providers — and also 'in particular private, non-profit providers often organised by NGOs' (World Bank, 1996: 129). Within the World Bank's policy guidelines NGOs (Non-government organisations) are defined as 'entirely or largely independent of government, and characterised mainly by humanitarian or cooperative rather than commercial objectives' (Korten, 1991: 18). The important role of NGOs in education for development programmes was acknowledged at the UNESCO World Conference on Education for All (1990).

NGOs have, at least since the 1960s, featured centrally in development programmes grounded in social action. During the 1970s, the period when dependency theory prevailed as counter-hegemonic discourse, NGOs became rooted in community self-help and placed emphasis on the need for development to engender self-reliance, responsibility, human dignity and freedom from oppression (Korten, 1991). Some of these influences derived from the liberation theology embedded in the encyclical letters of Popes John XXIII and Paul VI, who held the view that human beings should be both the agents and goals of development. In many instances this approach combined with the revolutionary ethos that prevailed in many developing countries at the time, especially throughout South America. Clark (1991: 36) maintains that, during the 1970s,

> development was increasingly viewed as a *process* of liberating the poor, both from their physical oppressors and from their own resignation to poverty . . . Brazilian NGOs (particularly inspired by the ideas of Paulo Freire) pioneered the approach of 'conscientisation' — a combination of political education, social organisation and grassroots development . . . The resulting grassroots organisations were rapidly shifting, often informally constituted, and sometimes unrecognised by their governments. (original emphasis)

Alternative structures and processes of governance to those that inhere in state structures emerged to cater for areas such as non-formal education and adult literacy programmes. Locally funded and organised, these NGOs supported an endogenous model of development that had the aim of transforming societies from within.

The incorporation of many NGOs into the discourse and policy framework of international bodies such as the World Bank and the International Monetary Bank (IMF) has far-reaching implications not only for the types of literacy programmes, but also the types and levels of social development that can take place in aid-receiving countries. These issues are addressed in the typology of NGOs involved with literacy programmes which follows.

Governance Beyond the Nation-state: The Role of Non-government Agencies in Literacy and Development

It is estimated that NGOs currently provide 10% of donor aid to the South (Allsop & Brock, 1993). Different types of NGOs with different scope, range of foci and approaches to provision exist. The first category of NGOs can be said to include church groups, national and international charities, missionaries, minority religious-community groups and grassroots political organisations. Some classifications do not include the last as NGOs and refer to them as GROs. In many instances, these NGOs often serve to fill the gaps left by government laws and policy in the provision of education for specific groups of people and, therefore, literacy (Zabala, 1992). Operating generally outside government structures provides them with relative autonomy in the nature and types of literacy programmes made available to particular constituencies. This, combined with the fact that they tend to operate on a small scale basis, contribute to their being more flexible and able to establish effective local networks than the more bureaucratised government structures.

At the same time, however, smaller NGOs are limited in scope and because their work is often transitory, some find it hard to maintain coherence and to sustain a lasting impact (Edwards & Hulme, 1992). Smaller NGOs also have problems with regard to the range of technical expertise that they can offer. In order to maintain ongoing literacy development, some have linked with government programmes, as was the case with the National Rural Workers Congress (CNTC) in Honduras (Archer & Costello, 1990).

As can be seen in Clark's (1991) discussion above, some of the literacy knowledges within these types of NGO programmes are often counter-hegemonic in their practices or overtly critical of government policy. Many of these literacy programmes also centre on 'giving voice' to disempowered groups within society such as women, ethnic minority groups and rural communities. However, a fundamental contradiction of this form of this approach has been that, although participants often do become highly politicised, because literacy measurement is arbitrary, many participants may still remain functionally illiterate in vast areas of everyday life.

The second category includes those NGOs that are created by, or have close links with governments — and, therefore, can have a different political agenda to the other NGOs discussed here. Often these, government-funded national NGOs (NANGOs) (Zabala, 1992) are highly bureaucratised and exist to implement specific policy reforms beyond the formal educational system. Essentially, they provide additional services to those operating within mainstream education. An example of this form of NGO is the Adult and Basic Skills Unit (ALBSU) in England and Wales which has traditionally operated through a pump-priming government-funding approach. The role of ALBSU will be discussed in further detail in Chapter 4.

The third category includes NGOs that are funded through international charities such as the World Council of Churches and Christian Aid. Zabala (1992) argues that many externally funded organisations tend to make use of outside consultants in literacy projects and are imposed on local NGOs through donor agreements. The views of these consultants regarding literacy priorities often conflict with those defined locally.

Other forms of intervention include literacy programmes provided for by official para-national funding agencies such as, UNESCO, and donor-aid from national governments such as Sweden and Germany, United States, the Overseas Development Agency (ODA) who fund specific NGOs. Organisations such as the World Bank and IMF, because of their funding processes, have formal links with government programmes — and, as such, have a more influential relationship with the process of national governance than NGOs. Whilst countries can benefit financially from donor-aid, it can be a double-edged sword. This has been the case, for example, with NGOs funded by the United States which, it argued, has been able 'through its aid ministry, USAID, to influence greatly the shape of the NGO community and mould NGO objectives to fit its own foreign policy and aid objectives' (Clark, 1991: 49). The literacy meanings that emerge within these contexts are often at variance with those defined by the countries involved themselves, especially as they relate to the different linguistic needs and entitlements of minority groups.

Moreover, NGOs themselves are positioned within particular ideological frameworks and therefore operate within a context defined by particular sets of values about, for example, people, education, health and the environment. As was suggested earlier, sometimes this is imposed on them through their funders. Many of these organisations implicitly articulate and underwrite particular views of social development, and at the level of educational practice, support specific pedagogic models. As such they can be seen as constituting external forms of governance.

Models of governance

Whereas governance operating within state structures exercise overt control over political aspects of literacy provision such as national language policy within the broader framework of social policy, NGOs tend to have a narrower remit — and therefore have limited levels of influence. The different areas of governance within the framework of government and non-government structures are summarised in Table 3.1.

Table 3.1 Governance in formal and non-government structures

Government structures	*Non-government structures*
National language policy	Local or regional levels of literacy need
Media of instruction	(community groups; charities;
National levels of literacy need	grassroots political groups etc.)
Form and content of educational/	Regional levels of literacy needs
literacy programmes	Form and content of
Range of literacy technologies made	educational/literacy programmes
available in educational programmes	Media of instruction
Public expenditure in educational and	Teaching methods
adult literacy programmes — social	Range of literacy technologies made
policy	available in educational programmes
Who exercises overall budget control	Expenditure in specific educational
in national or regional education	and adult literacy programmes
programmes	Who exercises budget control in
Access to information	individual programmes
Funding of teaching and learning	Provision of teaching and learning
resources	resources
Rural and urban emphases	Rural and urban emphases
National monitoring standards	Measurement criteria within particular
Standardised measurement criteria	programmes
	Monitoring of specific literacy
	programmes
	Popular participation in
	decision-making

Table 3.1 shows that governance within non-government structures tend to centre on actors, advocacy and practical influences within the policy-making arena. That is to say, NGOs foreground agency and seek to involve key participants in decision-making at different levels. This has contributed to greater efficiency, local resource allocation and capacity-building (Stiefel & Wolfe, 1994). The increasing recognition of the important role of NGOs in development programmes stem from the fact that they:

facilitate access to technical knowledge and information and to funds and material support; they help establish horizontal lines of communication between different movements and organisations that allow for the exchange of experiences and the co-ordination of supra-local action; and they establish contacts between grassroots action and sympathetic and influential individuals, groups and institutions at national level. (Stiefel & Wolfe, 1994: 207)

In other words, they manage to establish broad networks through which they can operate more effectively.

The ineffectiveness of the state in some developing countries to provide adequately for diverse social needs, and concerns about 'ingovernability' within different societies have provided the bases for arguments in support of alternative institutional structures such as NGOs to foster participatory development. The World Bank has been involving NGOs since 1989 in its development projects as a means of ensuring the 'efficiency and sustainability of its operations' (Stiefel & Wolfe, 1994: 206) by increasing public accountability and transparency of decision-making processes.

It is argued further that the general encouragement given to NGOs to adopt 'a wider role in implementing education projects and programmes, raises the wider question of the role of governments in the provision of education in the South' (Allsop & Brock, 1993 : 8). Such views support a decreased role for government in education which it is argued, should focus specifically on the overall monitoring of education, whilst the 'running' of schools are to be left in the hands of NGOs. This view is supported further by arguments that decentralised planning of programmes 'will result in improved service delivery by enabling local authorities to perform tasks they are better equipped to manage'; that decentralisation will improve economies of scale 'and will lead to more appropriate responsiveness to the particular needs and situations of different regions and groups', and also, facilitate equity in decision-making (Govinda, 1997: 5.33).

Strong arguments can clearly be made for the success of NGOs in facilitating micro-development, based on their potential to cater for individual development needs because of their close links with and knowledge of localities. Nevertheless, there still remains considerable doubt about their effectiveness in relation to maintaining nationally coherent development programmes that can cater for the complex literacy needs within different societies. The wide range of financing sources raise fundamental questions about the future role and long-term obligations of governments in the provision of education for all. Control exerted by para-national organisations can be seen as implicitly undermining the management role of government and, potentially, subjecting the state to ideological and economic control of para-national structures.

The latter also have the power to define development needs in terms of the exigencies of ever-evolving global market needs, which may not coincide with what is necessarily good for the development of the country itself ecologically, socially and culturally. External funders are not necessarily altruistically motivated. As could be seen in the example of USAID, funding from external governments can, potentially, be politically or economically driven. It is argued, for example, that much of the international aid package is ultimately spent on securing export contracts with developing countries — with the bulk of the aid money spent within the domestic market (Hancock, 1989). Moreover, macro decision-making such as priority-setting, consultancy, project approval and evaluation still largely take place within the context of donor countries. If this is the case then it means that most of the major decision-making would not involve the people who will be affected in real terms.

Already, according to Gould (1991: 49), 'it is feared that NGOs are starting to plan projects based on the interests of the funders'. In terms of this, they risk becoming incorporated into the specific ideological, economic or political project of their funders which makes it more difficult for them to be critical of both their funders and governments. Their incorporation into larger, external structures could also, potentially, limit their traditional advocacy role. Thus, rather than facilitating the democratic process, politically progressive NGOs could potentially end up working against the very principles that generated their existence in the first place.

The increasingly popular notion that NGOs are inherently 'good' for societal development also needs to be questioned on the basis of their accountability, ideological biases and their interest in achieving sustainable and equitable national outcomes. Again, this factor is significant particularly within a competitive global market. Absolving governments in the South from responsibility for educational provision could ultimately serve to reinforce their dependency on external donor-aid. Rather than become self-sustaining developing countries could, rather paradoxically, be colluding in the perpetuation of the North/South economic and social divide. Indeed, it could be argued that making education and, *de facto*, adult literacy the primary remit of NGOs would constitute a powerful means of de-regulation which would leave education within these societies to function according to the economic, ideological and political exigencies of donor countries. On a more practical level, it would also raise questions about media of instruction, official languages and, relatedly, the ability or willingness to secure equitable provision for linguistic human rights. Attempts at linguicism, that is, the imposition of common languages with 'economic currency', but without a natural social base, would need to be part of the process of monitoring literacy provision. The general lack of awareness of the complexities of language issues in the discourse of major NGO funders such as the World Bank is discussed by Skutnabb-Kangas and Phillipson (1995). Similarly, postmodern arguments focused on multilingualism and cultural hybridity exist in tension with the realities of ethnic violence within many of these societies.

The appeal of NGOs to external funding agents such as the World Bank could also be seen as a means of underwriting a form of quasi-privatisation of whole systems of education within the developing world. Indeed, NGOs appear to have all the requisites of neo-liberal market theory in that they are flexible, adaptable, innovative and provide a cost-effective service delivery. Their replacement of government within key areas such as education would, in effect, fulfil the neo-liberal requirement of decreasing the role of the state in the public sphere. The concept of 'good governance' celebrated in NGOs can only be effective to society as a whole if it forms an integral part of the reforming state. Governance grounded in a model of self-management and self-reliance but which, to a large extent, is imposed through donor-aid agreements will be able to be sustained only as long as it does not challenge the hegemony of external or internal political forces (Hettne, 1995).

Implications for Literacy for Sustainable Development

In an overall sense, the issues raised throughout this chapter have highlighted the important fact that the concept of development needs to extend beyond technicist perspectives to include also the basic human needs and the social roles of people. Indeed, there is growing acceptance within UN development discourse about the limited value of a modernisation approach. Thus it is argued that:

> the automatic equation of a single technical measure of 'development', usually GNP, with the society's overall progress and well-being is pervasive. It is part of a 20th century mind set that means are more important than ends, levels of activity more important than the purposes served. (UNESCO, 1997c: 11)

Emphasising the importance of education in the process of sustainable development UNESCO foregrounds the need for 'a critical reflection on the world, especially its failings and injustices, and by promoting greater awareness, exploring new visions and concepts . . . disseminating knowledge and skills' to effect changes in behaviours, values and life-styles (UNESCO, 1997c: 16). The need for effective communication in terms of disseminating scientific knowledge and information are also highlighted as a basis for having an informed public.

The need to understand these knowledges and information clearly identify the imperative for more than 'basic' literacy and basic education. If, as is argued in the Introduction to the book, the concept of sustainable development highlights the responsibility that we all share in shaping the world of the future, then it follows that people must be provided with the skills, knowledges and expertise to shape their own development priorities. Literacy defined within the framework of sustainable development would therefore include a broad and critical knowledge base, and an understanding of how societies function, and the complex ways in which they are linked with global processes. As such, the economic and political context should be created in which literacy provision can be organised in a coherent and equitable way for all citizens within different societies as part of the process of political enfranchisement. This can take place only if knowledge-based literacies are accorded their proper status in the discourse on the democratisation of the political process. Unless this takes place, the social and cultural basis of development runs the risk of being undermined which, in turn, would impact on the quality of civil society that provides the basis of the democratic process.

Civil society here refers to the informal organisation of social life which operates beyond the direct control of the state, and which serves as an arena in which people can 'exercise pressure and restraint on the state and thereby strengthen the assumptions and practices of democratic self-management' (Leftwich, 1995: 435). The importance of cultivating a literate, knowledgeable and active civil society to regulate internal inequalities, their ability to interpret and analyse inequalities that are externally imposed and, moreover, having adequate levels of communicative competence to build links with international pressure groups, and their ability to interact effectively within the re-defined textual environment provided by information technology, can therefore not be over-emphasised.

Literacy linked with social knowledges plays an important role in influencing the ways in which people would be able to name the multiple conceptual worlds in which they increasingly live. As such, literacy can no longer be divorced from its knowledge base, as a mode of discourse and its links with social structures. I return to the issue of changing definitions of literacy within the context of the 'information' society in Part 3.

Chapter 4

The Role of Mass Literacy Campaigns in Social Development: Some Lessons to be Learned from the Past

As could be seen in Chapter 3, mass literacy campaigns came to play an important role in the modernisation development paradigm during the 1970s. Within that framework, they were seen as providing an accelerated means of providing workers with the functional literacy skills that would make them more willing to learn, and to become more productive. Literate workers, it was argued, are more adaptable to change. Again, as is discussed in Chapter 3, during the 1960s, a 40% literacy rate became regarded as a necessary pre-requisite for societies to enter Rostow's 'take-off' stage of development (Anderson, 1966).

Bhola (1984: 35) defines mass literacy campaigns as 'a mass approach that seeks to make all adult men and women in a nation literate within a particular time-frame. Literacy is seen as a means to a comprehensive set of ends — economic, social-cultural, *and political*' (original emphasis). Bhola goes on to make distinctions between mass literacy campaigns which, he argues, 'suggest urgency and combativeness; it is in the nature of an expectation; it is something of a crusade' — and literacy programmes, 'which even though planned systematically to meet certain objectives, may lack both urgency and passionate fervour' (Bhola, 1984: 176). This view suggests that literacy campaigns are extraordinary events within the political life of the particular society and are largely oriented towards the fulfillment of the aims of specific hegemonic, economic or political projects. Literacy campaigns, in other words, represent overt intentionality and, involving mainly the adult section of the population, tend to take place outside the general framework of mainstream educational provision.

Theorising Mass Literacy Campaigns

Mass literacy campaigns have served, historically, as a powerful means of mobilising popular interest and support for increasing societal literacy levels. Bhola (1984 :35), for example, regards mass literacy campaigns as having constituted a 'moral equivalent of the "Long March" ' in mobilising postcolonial peoples towards nationhood. And, indeed, a campaign does suggest a military offensive; a number of operations aimed at a single objective which, within this context, refers to 'eradicating literacy. According to Arnove and Graff (1987: 2), mass campaigns have 'historically and comparatively, formed part of larger transformations in society' and tend to emerge during periods of social and economic transition.

Since the onset of modernity during the late 19th century, these transitions were exemplified, for example, in the emergence of market economies in Europe (Arnove & Graff, 1987). Modernity here refers to the sweeping social, economic and political changes brought about by industrialism at the time, the rise of the nation-state, the formation of distinct social classes, an advanced sexual and social division of labour and the transition from religious to secular culture (Hall *et al.*, 1992).

The role of language and literacy in the social construction of reality

The reasons for literacy assuming such a high level of importance at key historical moments are complex and need to be examined in terms of the ideological, political and economic value attached to it in social discourse. Language provides the primary means through which we interpret and construct the world in which we live. Together, language and literacy provide powerful means, ideologically, through which cultural hegemony can be re-organised in order to secure the social relations of the emerging sociocultural and political milieu. This refers to the fact that, as the economic, political and cultural bases of society change, people's re-defined roles and positions within the changing landscape need to be accommodated in social consciousness. Within these circumstances, 'the emphasis shifts onto literacy, not as an end in itself, but as a means to other goals — to the ends of national development and to a social order that elites, both national and international, define' (Arnove & Graff, 1987: 2).

At the same time, as is discussed later, literacy campaigns geared towards effecting liberatory change from social and political oppression also provide key means by which alternative realities can be structured in social discourse and, through this, allow collective subjectivities to become re-oriented towards creative possibilities to effect societal change. It is largely because of the importance of its *symbolic power* that literacy features as a central variable in the mobilisation of populations to effect social change or, alternatively, in the management of social change, economic crisis or crises of hegemony. In each of these circumstances, literacy becomes both signifier and signified in the discourse about what society is not, as well as what it should be, or should aspire to become morally, socially and economically. On the one hand, it serves to re-define social development goals and, on the other hand, to re-orientate individual and social awarenesses in terms of the goals identified for social and individual development. At such moments, literacy becomes signified as the primary means by which this multilevelled process of change can be secured. The relative emphases placed on particular forms of knowledges within the culture, and who should have access to these, will depend on the particular ideological milieu and the specific political and economic aims that underscore societal development. Mass literacy campaigns, forming part of this process, can be seen as serving particular political, economic and cultural ends.

Mass literacy campaigns as power/knowledge discourses

What I am arguing then is that mass literacy campaigns do not emerge within a social, political and ideological vacuum; they find their rationale in changes already taking place within society. And the discourse in which they are legitimated key into 'real' events which then are re-defined, and inserted into a different discourse focused on eradicating *illiteracy* as an urgent national or international priority. Hence, mass literacy campaigns implicitly help to set policy priorities as well as the parameters and terms of reference of the debate about literacy.

Ultimately, they are also embedded in particular models of social development. In the process of defining their development goals, mass literacy campaigns, as Ball (1990) argues regarding educational policy generally, make projections 'about the way things could be or should be — which rests upon, derive from, statements about the world — about the way things are' (Ball, 1990: 22). To achieve maximum effect, they tend to be constructed around 'moral panics' about, *inter alia*, 'poverty levels', 'falling standards in education', 'criminality and lawlessness' or 'freedom and democracy'. Or alternatively, literacy is articulated in terms of a bi-polar 'backwardness' versus 'civilised society', and thus it helps to legitimate powerful meanings revolving around illiteracy and moral deficit. Drawing on the knowledge of development experts or inspirational political leaders, they 'speak with authority, they legitimate and initiate practices in the world, they privilege certain visions and interests' (Ball, 1990: 22). Depending on 'expert' information, they select particular forms of literacy as a legitimate target for social action, define what literacy is or should be, what its value is for the individual and for society, and that everyone who does not have it, should have it.

Mass literacy campaigns can then be seen as constituting what Pecheux (1982) calls 'discursive processes' operating within the social terrain. Discursive processes refer to institutional practices, ideological positions, power relations and social position which influence how words change their meanings within and between discourses. In claiming 'to bring about idealised solutions to diagnosed problems' (Ball, 1990: 22), they serve to construct particular views of reality, legitimate particular understandings of societal needs and, in the process, serve to regulate cultural knowledges.

Mass campaigns articulated from within key institutional, community or political contexts operate from relatively privileged positions to define societal needs and wants. These power positions influence who is allowed to speak, who has the authority to define, as well as the legitimacy and statuses attached to the 'truths' produced in discourse (Pecheux, 1982). Constituted thus in power relations, mass literacy campaigns 'construct certain possibilities for thought; they order and combine words in particular ways to exclude or displace other combinations' (Ball, 1990:18). For example, discourses structured around literacy and economic growth would place emphasis on functional skills and knowledges, the affective attributes such as 'flexibility' and 'efficiency', and their association with personal efficacy and the 'employability' of workers. In circumscribing the knowledge framework, they often displace local literacies and other forms of cultural knowledge valued by individuals or minority groups as important elements in maintaining cultural or self-identity. As such, they can be viewed as constituting 'power/knowledge' (Foucault, 1980) discourses that make available 'truth' as perceived by those who possess power and control.

Historically, the multilevelled discourses constructed around literacy and social development in these campaigns, have provided the arena *par excellence* in which preferred cultural knowledges could be defined through particular emphases given to specific skills and forms of knowledge, and the exclusion of other, often competing, meanings in social discourse. Thus they have served to identify 'useful' knowledges within the culture. 'Useful knowledges' refer to the particular knowledge areas defined in terms of 'what we need to know' to be able to function within society at particular moments of its development. Mass literacy drives within the nation-state can therefore be viewed as constituting forms of strategic state intervention to re-define the 'social character' in terms of the specific development goals identified for society as a whole at a particular moment in its development. Williams (1961: 146) defines the 'social character' as constituting much more than new behavioural norms and attitudes, to include also 'a particular system of values, in the field of group loyalty, authority, justice, and living purposes'. In relation to this, ' the prevailing ideology will reflect a particular political culture which, in turn, will determine the organisational, mobilisational and technological choices that can be made in the planning and implementation of a mass literacy campaign within a particular society' (Bhola, 1984: 177).

Depending on the ideological framework in which societal needs are defined, it can serve either to maintain the received order or to effect fundamental changes within society. The next section explores the ways in which these discourse meanings have been shaped within different ideological milieux.

International literacy campaigns

Since its inception, the discourse on literacy within UNESCO has been grounded in the principles of promoting 'international understanding, a commitment to mass education, and through it the promotion of peace, human rights and progress' (Jones, 1988: 125). The 1960s, which had been identified as the 'First Development Decade', was to provide a testing point for these principles. The 1960s represented a period of significant social and political change in the developing world as many countries were emerging from centuries of colonialism into self-government. The significance of having a 'development decade' was to address issues of disease, hunger, ignorance and poverty (Jones, 1988).

Following proposals for a global literacy campaign from the Ukraine in 1961, the UN General Assembly invited UNESCO to explore the possibilities for the mass eradication of illiteracy. The UNESCO report *World Campaign for Universal Literacy*, which incorporated a global survey of illiteracy and recommendations for the design and implementation of a global campaign, was presented to the General Assembly in 1963. It was proposed that the campaign should be aimed at two thirds of the world's adult illiterates for a period of ten years (Jones, 1988).Within the subsequent debate about the relationship between literacy campaigns and economic development, the theme of cost effectiveness became a justification for its inclusion in a development plan. The US representative argued that:

> the struggle against illiteracy, particularly amongst adults, must not be pursued at the expense of other aspects of a country's development plans, particularly in the educational field . . . [that] an all-out crash program could be inconsistent with the achievement of balanced educational development. (Quoted in Jones, 1988: 136)

In line with this, the US later expressed its opposition to UNESCO's 'plunging into the limitless quicksands of the attack on illiteracy'.

A written critique of the UNESCO proposals for a global literacy campaign was to become highly influential in defining the framework in which UNESCO was to operate with regard to adult illiteracy in the future. The article, written by Adam Curle at the Harvard Graduate School of Education, argued against the idea of having a campaign for universal literacy and suggested instead a selective literacy approach which targeted the work-place (Jones, 1988). This approach, he argued, would result in education yielding better economic returns.

The Experimental World Literacy Programme revisited
It was within this context that the idea of functional literacy was given voice and later provided the basis of the Experimental World Literacy Programme (EWLP). Although the EWLP did not constitute a campaign according to Bhola's criteria, its high-profile launch and subsequent high-media profile ensured topicality. Several strategies were used to raise awareness, and to mobilise countries to participate in what became seen as a crusade against illiteracy. In preparation for the launch of the EWLP a World Congress of Ministers of Education on the Eradication of Illiteracy was convened in Tehran in 1965 which provided political support and technical content to the EWLP (Gillette, 1987: 200).

In a background paper for the World Congress the UNESCO Secretariat had expressed the view that ' literacy, the bridge between passivity and real participation, is a pre-requisite of democracy' and that we all should have 'a clear awareness of the relationship of education to one's work and one's civic, political and social role in life'. These meanings were picked up in the 1965 Tehran Congress which defined functional literacy in the following way:

> Rather than an end in itself, literacy should be regarded as a way of preparing man for a social, civic and economic role . . . reading and writing should lead not only to elementary general knowledge but to training for work, increased productivity, a greater participation in civil life and a better understanding of the surrounding world and should . . . open the way to basic human culture. (Quoted in Gillette, 1987: 203)

UNESCO launched the EWLP in 1967. It was to last for five years, within 11 targeted countries. The campaign was characterised by three key elements, namely, intensity, selectivity and experimentation which together constituted an overall strategy to the campaign (UNESCO, 1976). The underlying objective of the EWLP was 'to test and demonstrate the economic and social returns of literacy' on which to base further considerations for 'launching a campaign for the eradication of illiteracy throughout the world' (Jones, 1988: 161).

In the publicity generated around the EWLP, literacy caught the hearts and minds of world leaders on a global basis. 1970 was declared 'International Education Year' — and 'International Literacy Day' held on 8 September, coincided with the publication of *Literacy and Development*, by H.M. Phillips. According to Jones (1988: 147) Phillips argued that:

> much evidence existed that literate workers — both urban and rural — were more productive. For factory workers, he presented a rather wide-ranging list of areas in which literates are seen to excel. This included dexterity, speed of output, learning aptitude, conscientiousness, thrift, better health, punctuality, safety, and team spirit.

This provided further legitimacy to the strategy of functional literacy adopted in the EWLP and consolidated the link already made between literacy and societal development. The emphasis on literacy was maintained further in 1972 being declared 'International Book Year'. Summarising the first stage of the EWLP, the UNESCO (1969–71) Report described the benefits of literacy to the individual and society as follows.

> For the individual, it should improve productivity, thus increase wages ... and raising the standards of living. For the industrial enterprise, increased productivity for workers should reduce costs and raise profits; in some situations, local workers may by able to replace more expensive foreign skilled labour . . . For the nation, gross national product (GNP) should rise, tax revenue should increase, and dependence on imports — both of goods and manpower should fall. Where widespread unemployment is coupled with a shortage of appropriately trained skilled labour, work-oriented literacy should help alleviate unemployment. (UNESCO, 1972: 29–30)

In other words, literacy became the primary means through which a nation could achieve a liberation that was truly comprehensive in its scope. It became a technical 'panacea' to the developing world's diverse problems and, as such, justified capital investment. Gillette (1987: 197) argues that the 'EWLP was an unprecedented, and remains in educational history an unequaled, multilateral literacy venture in terms of international resources mobilised, political and technical interest aroused, and controversy unleashed'. The shortcomings of the EWLP generally in terms of the ideological interests that underscored it have already been discussed in Chapter 3.

Centralised mass literacy campaigns in the nation-state

Centralised national literacy campaigns generally constitute top-down policy approaches and, in most cases, represent strategic forms of state intervention to pursue specific hegemonic, economic or political projects that are deemed to serve the 'national interest'. They play an instrumental role in the social construction of reality at particular moments in order to accommodate real, or the perceived changing needs of society. Their primary function is to secure either a moral or political consensus, and since the 19th century, have played a significant role in nation-state building (Arnove & Graff, 1987).

Mass literacy campaigns and nation-building

Mass literacy campaigns that emerge within societies engaged in nation-building find their rationale in the *central role that literacy plays in building a cohesive nation*. As is argued in Chapter 2, within the liberal pluralist nation-state, the acquisition of literacy through the medium of official or national languages is seen as providing an important means of integrating diverse elements into a common culture. However, whether a common language necessarily integrates people into a common national culture is a debatable point. Common languages, according to Hobsbawm (1990), are constructed; they do not evolve naturally within society. He goes on to argue that historically 'the official or culture-language of rulers and elite usually came to be the actual language of modern states *via* public education and other administrative mechanisms' (Hobsbawm, 1990: 62). Incorporated thus into societal structures they serve to acquire status and currency over and above other minority languages. This has been the case in the language policies and, *de facto*, the mass literacy campaigns pursued in many developing countries during the period of postcolonial nation-building.

At the same time, many countries emerging from colonialism have, historically, identified literacy also as a central variable to *increase levels of economic growth through societal modernisation*, as an integral part of their project for nation-building. Literacy located within the framework of modernisation theory has been allocated both a productive and exchange value; it is seen as increasing levels of productivity, providing better job opportunities, improving income levels and thus facilitating social mobility. These claims remain unproven. Indeed, as we have seen, the links established between literacy and societal development in the modernisation framework have been fractured in terms of the disparities of literacy levels within different societies as well as between regions and subregions. Some of these issues are explored further in the examples of the Tanzanian and Ethiopian mass literacy campaigns.

The Tanzanian mass literacy campaign

In postcolonial Tanzania, Kiswahili which was the second language during colonial times, replaced English as both the national and official language. Underlying the choice of Kiswahili as both national and official language was the fact that it was already a *lingua franca* during the colonial period, 'that it possessed a literature, [and] was the language of trade throughout the country' (Ryan, 1987: 162). Kiswahili also represented the first language of the elite group working in the colonial administration and had gained currency over and above other minority languages in the public school system. In other words, Kiswahili had already become part of the infrastructure. However, although the language was widely used, 'isolated population groups had only an exposure to Swahili and not a knowledge of it' (Ryan, 1987). Large sections of the population, particularly those living in rural areas were, in effect, forced to acquire literacy in a language, which although they had some knowledge of it, was not necessarily intrinsic to everyday community or cultural life.

The incorporation of Kiswahili into the educational system meant that it devalued other vernacular languages of tribal and nomadic groups. These languages were relegated to a domain-specific use including religion, village administration, to a limited extent in court in rural areas and in a supporting role in some primary schools (Rubagumya, 1990). This has contributed to uneven patterns of language development within different regions in the country. For example, there are still people in rural areas, particularly those of older generations, who cannot speak Kiswahili. Rubagumya (1990) goes on to argue that it is likely that the use of vernacular languages in official contexts will disappear in the future and become confined mainly to the informal domain. Further, Kiswahili as a stand-ardised language features most prominently in regions where it is the official language and shows variations in indigenous regions (Ryan, 1987).

Adopting a single-language policy had formed an integral part of Tanzania's national development plans. Following a dual strategy of increasing economic output and mass education, the first development plan identified the need to produce skilled workers for increased production. It stated that 'the nation cannot wait until the children have become educated for development to begin' (quoted in Unsicker, 1987: 231), and that 'the supply of trained manpower is the first development of Education Training' (Annual Report of 1964: 6, quoted in Zuengler, 1985: 245).

President Nyerere played a key role in the articulation of the country's development needs and the shaping of the national language's policy approach. In his speech introducing the First Five Year Plan he fore-grounded the importance attached to increasing levels of adult literacy. He argued:

First we must educate adults. Our children will not have an impact on our economic development for five, ten, or even twenty years. The attitudes of the adults . . . on the other hand, have an impact now. The people must understand the plans for development of this country; they must be able to participate in changes which are necessary. Only if they are willing and able to do this will this plan succeed. (Quoted in Bhola, 1984: 141)

Literacy classes were subsequently arranged through the Division of Community Development in order to 'win the people's commitment to development'. Organised by field assistants, these classes rapidly expanded from 32 to over 400 during the next five years (Unsicker, 1987).

In 1967, the Nyerere government issued the Arusha Declaration which committed the new nation to the principles of *ujamaa* socialism (Unsicker, 1987). This referred to the adoption of a Fabian-style socialism through which it was hoped to link Tanzania with the communalism of pre-colonial Africa. In a post-Arusha policy statement entitled 'Education for Self-Reliance', President Nyerere argued for a re-orientation of the educational system and called for education to cater for the needs of the majority of the people. This policy approach prioritised rural development grounded in socialist principles. It was within this context that literacy in Kiswahili was identified as a national development goal and, by the beginning of 1968, it became the medium of instruction in all primary schools (Zuengler, 1985). Pupils had previously been introduced to English as language of instruction at Standard 3 in primary schools. It remained the language of instruction in secondary school and beyond.

By the time of the country's Second Five Year Development Plan (1969) it was envisaged that Kiswahili would replace English as medium of instruction in secondary schools and higher education. The choice of Kiswahili as national language included its educational use in the sense that it was seen as providing an important means of inculcating 'certain political concepts which are central to the task of socialist education' (Court & Kinyanjui, 1978: 51). As was the case with the First Development Plan, adult literacy was seen to play a central role in this process as it was envisaged that:

literate peasants would provide more effective members in the over eight thousand ujamaa villages into which almost all of the rural population relocated during the 1960s and 1970s . . . Nyerere expected the villages to become increasingly productive economic units involved in collective agricultural production, and, as resources permitted, adding small-scale or cottage industries. Self-help would reduce dependence on the government treasury in the construction of roads and schools [and] in the eradication of diseases. The nation would become more self-sufficient in food and less dependent on imports and foreign aid.

Social class differentiation would be halted, and inequalities between urban and rural areas would be reduced. (Unsicker, 1987: 226)

During this time, the country also 'agreed to participate in the United Nations Development Programme (UNDP)/UNESCO Work-Oriented Adult Literacy Pilot Project (WOALPP) in the Lake Regions of the country' (Bhola, 1984 : 138). This formed part of the broader UNESCO funded EWLP which fostered the ideal of functional literacy oriented towards integrating the acquisition of literacy skills with practical skills in the work-place.

Nyerere launched 'Adult Education Year' in his New Year address on 31st December 1969. Underscoring the principles of the adopted self-reliance policy, he argued:

> In many cases the first objective of adult education must be to shake ourselves out of a resignation to the kind of life Tanzanian people have lived for many centuries past. We must become aware of the things that we, as members of our human race, can do for ourselves and for our country. The second objective of adult education is to teach us how to improve our lives. We have to learn how to produce more on our farms and in our factories and offices. We have to learn about better foods, what a balanced diet is and how it can be obtained by our own efforts. The third objective of adult education must be to have everyone understand our national policies of socialism and self-reliance. (Quoted in Bhola, 1984: 141)

By 1970 Nyerere in his New Year Address identified literacy as the 'key to further progress', stressing that illiterates 'will never be able to play their full part in the development of our country' (quoted in Bhola, 1984: 141). Literacy became signified as a national priority in terms of effecting social development, having the aim of eradicating illiteracy in six districts during 1971 and its elimination in the entire nation in just four years (Unsicker, 1987).

Although this may have resonated with the ideal of self-education and self-development that had provided the driving force to the mass literacy campaign at least initially in post-revolutionary USSR, here the idea of self-reliance was being re-defined within a literacy discourse circumscribed by an external funding organisation (in concert with the national government) whose views of literacy were ultimately grounded in modernisation theory. The notion of self-reliance within this framework took on specific economistic meanings as opposed to those associated with individual empowerment and social transformation that featured in the Freirean approach to literacy. These meanings were clearly contradictory in relation to the socialist ideals championed by Nyerere in his quest for *ujamaa* socialism. Indeed whilst, on the one hand, Nyerere was espousing the principles of socialism grounded in rural communalism, on the other, he was collaborating with what was principally a capitalist project grounded in improving the economic and social returns of literacy.

The language issue needs to be located within this framework of modernisation especially since the targeting of special areas, which was central to the EWLP approach, in effect, benefited from a one-language national policy. Skutnabb-Kangas (1990: 25) argues:

> Since the idea of 'modernisation' included rapid spread of new technologies and ideas through education and mass media, a common language for this was considered necessary. This meant that both basic motivating principles behind UPE [universal primary education] [and functional literacy] led away from local and regional mother tongues, because both nation-building and education for development seemed to 'require' common languages with more currency. (Information in brackets added)

Although issues of language standardisation and sufficient reading materials did present initial problems, much of this was overcome by the large scale use of the primers provided by the earlier WOALPP. Indeed, the literacy infrastructure built during the WOALPP was to provide the basis of the mass literacy campaign that was launched in 1971. Adult Education during the time of the WOALPP had become integrated into the country's existing formal education system under the Ministry of National Education — and thus became incorporated into the organisation of party and government (Bhola, 1984). Launched by the ruling party, the mass campaign was popularised in the media and benefited further by building links with popular culture including performance art, visual art and craft.

Culturally, the one-language national policy adopted fundamentally supported the ideological principles of a *laissez faire* assimilation. The differential levels of incorporation, and the fact that Kiswahili featured as an inter-language and belonged to the same language family as many of the vernacular languages, did not result in the complete displacement of minority languages. Nevertheless, the one-language policy did marginalise these languages and, moreover, decreased their economic and political currency. The extent to which the vast majority of rural peoples were linguistically and culturally empowered is therefore debatable. Since many of the rural and nomadic people would still not be literate in their own languages, the much celebrated 'success' of the Tanzanian literacy campaign needs to be problematised in terms of the linguicism that is implicit in its national language policy. Linguicism refers to 'ideologies, structures and practices which are used to legitimate, effectuate and reproduce an unequal division of power and resources (material and immaterial) between groups which are defined on the basis of language' (Skutnabb-Kangas, 1988: 13). The issue of linguicism within the Tanzanian context refers particularly to English which has been retained as language of instruction in secondary school and tertiary education.

English has also retained its high status within the culture despite its displacement as national and official language by the one-language national policy adopted by the postcolonial regime. Phillipson and Skutnabb-Kangas (1995a: 343) argue:

> English is still favoured at secondary school level and above, despite the fact that English is manifestly a foreign language in Tanzania, is used in very few domains and is unable to function effectively as a medium of education . . . . Support for Swahili has been ambivalent and inadequate. The linguistic hierarchy remains, with English dominant vis-a-vis Swahili, and mother tongues below, confined to local and private functions.

In terms of this, Rubagumya (1990: 2) states that

> in Tanzania it is difficult to see how 'Education for Self-Reliance' can be consistent with education which uses English as the medium of instruction. If education is meant to prepare the majority for the type of life they are likely to lead [i.e. rural areas] rather than to favour only a few, it would seem that Kiswahili is better suited to that task . . . Likewise, Education for Self-Reliance cannot be achieved by attaching to the school a token 'shamba' [farm, garden] while the whole system is still geared to the selection of a few who will 'make it' to the top.

Whilst the mass literacy campaign did provide an international focus on Tanzania which helped the country to secure foreign aid, at national level, the campaign was fraught with internal struggles within and around the state as well as between internal bureaucracies and external funding agents. At village level very little empowerment has taken place to transform peasants' lived experience. Unsicker (1987: 228) argues that the 'short-term impact has probably been to solidify the power of the bureaucracy more than it has to liberate the peasants'.

The success of the Tanzanian mass literacy campaign in terms of fulfilling its aim of facilitating national economic growth has also been fractured in the light of political and economic realities. Tanzania has continued to experience economic difficulties, a decrease in national productivity and, in fact, has become more dependent on external donor aid. Unsicker (1987: 226) maintains:

> As is the case with most Third World nations, the oil price increases that began in 1973 and the deteriorating terms of trade between the

products of primarily commodity-producing countries and those of industrial countries, caused Tanzania to experience significant balance-of-trade deficits . . . The negative balance- of- trade appears also to be partially due to reduced export crops upon which the nation depends for earning foreign exchange, and this reportedly paralleled production declines in major domestic food crops.

Some of this is attributed to drought, state-controlled marketing boards and crop authorities, or parastatals that control producer prices and incentives to peasant production, which 'eat up a growing share of the income generated by export' (Unsicker, 1987). These uneven development outcomes highlight the contradictions that were inherent in Nyerere's strategy of building a socialist cultural and political project onto a predominantly capitalist economic base.

But this provides only a partial view of the underlying political reasons for the continued lack of economic growth in that country. Growing poverty in Tanzania despite its mass literacy campaigns, as is the case also with other developing countries, needs to be questioned also in terms of the nature of investment by donor countries and, more importantly, international funding bodies such as the World Bank and the IMF.

In relation to the latter, the method of capital lending short-term stress relief funds at competitive interest rates which Third World economies ultimately cannot sustain has created many problems within these economies. In effect, an economic stranglehold has been put onto borrowing countries through the lending of money at preferential interest rates, which are slightly lower than current market rates, but which are tied in with stringent controls. These 'curative' measures include specific demands for receiving countries to pursue monetarist economic policies (Naylor,1987). The resulting cuts in the social wage, curbs on welfare spending, decreased farming subsidies, increase in taxes demanded by the IMF have thus contributed to *creating* poverty in many borrowing countries. This highlights the fact that the meanings inscribed into mass literacy campaigns within the context of the nation-state can be undermined by broader power interests operating within the international terrain. The impacts and effects of mass literacy campaigns within the context of the nation-state cannot, therefore, be addressed outside an analysis of international economic relations.

Language relations within the Ethiopian mass literacy campaign

Like Tanzania, Ethiopia is a very complex society linguistically and comprises between 70 and 80 different languages of which Amharic, Oromo and Tigrinya predominate. According to Cooper (1989: 21):

as in other African countries, its linguistic diversity is in part a product of imperial conquest, which brought together diverse ethnolinguistic groups within a single political administration. Unlike other African countries, however, its conquerors were not Europeans but Africans.

Historically, linguistic hierarchies have existed in the country with Amharic, Tigrinyan and Oromo occupying high status. Most of the educated political and financial elite were Amharic and Tigrinyan speakers. In a largely semi-feudal system, ethnic hierarchies coincided with class stratification and as a result, the country experienced sporadic ethnic conflict.

This was exacerbated by the preferential status accorded to Amharic in Haile Sillasie's one-language policy. Amharic became the main language of instruction throughout the country, including Eritrea in which, until its annexation in 1962, the main languages were Arabic and Tigrinya (Cooper, 1981).That is to say, Amharic, which essentially was a minority language belonging to the elite group, was the chosen national and official language. According to Foster (1971) this 'simply reflected the political and social dominance of an ethnic minority who constituted some 20 per cent of Ethiopia's population'. Cooper (1989) argues further that the requirement that initial schooling be conducted in Amharic made it more difficult for the non-Amhara majority to acquire a modern education. To enhance literacy levels, Christian missionaries were drafted in to embark on a process of mass Amharisation. This contributed further to religious-ethnic conflict in areas where Muslim parents refused to send their children to missionary schools. Here then, we had a situation where high levels of illiteracy were being created and sustained by the particular elitist national language policy being pursued by the Sillasie regime.

It was within this linguistic context that the country entered the UNDP/UNESCO WOALPP focused on functional literacy (in Amharic), and closely linked with rural development (UNESCO, 1976). Within the WOALPP, 'literacy training was to be supported by, and closely linked with, agricultural extension, farmer training services, assistance to cottage industries, family living education, industrial vocational training, industrial safety and hygiene' (UNESCO, 1976: 34).

In Ethiopia it tied in with regional plans which, in turn, linked with the country's overall national development plan. The programme was systematically organised at regional, district and local level which comprised the Kebele Peasant Association. The Kebele constituted the smallest administrative unit (Mammo, 1985). The WOALPP existed in parallel with other unrelated literacy programmes throughout the country. The lack of coordination between these projects contributed to confusion and resulted in conflict. For example, the UNESCO evaluation report states that in two of the rural projects conducted, Amharic was not widely spoken, 'the major language being Galigna' (UNESCO, 1976: 35). It argued further that, 'language problems of participants were ignored, and the same materials were used both with participants whose native language was the national language and those whose native language was not the national language' (UNESCO, 1976: 40).

Following the deposition of Haile Sillasie in 1974, the Provincial Military Administrative Council, known as the 'Derg', came into power. Embarking on a mass literacy campaign during the early months of the regime, the Derg mobilised approximately 50,000 students who were sent to the countryside to teach literacy skills to the largely illiterate peasant section of the population. Linguistically this signified a major change in policy direction, for rather than Amharic providing the basis of literacy teaching, the student-trainers were encouraged to use the languages of the country-side. Peasants were to be taught to read and write in languages that they could understand and use in their everyday lives (Cooper, 1989).

In 1976 the Programme of the National Democratic Revolution of Ethiopia was formulated which identified strategies for socioeconomic reconstruction and development (Mammo, 1985). In contrast to the one-language policy of the literacy campaigns that took place under the Sillasie regime, in 1979 the Derg launched the Ethiopian National Literacy Campaign in which literacy teaching was to be conducted in five languages including Amharic, Oromo, Tigre, Wolaytigna and Somali. Five more languages were added and it was envisaged that this would extend to 15 'which, together, are spoken and understood by over 90 per cent of Ethiopia's population, either as a first or a second language' (Ryan, 1987: 165). The overall message of the campaign was articulated by the Chairman, Mengisto Haili Mariam, who argued that, 'in order to grasp the laws of nature, to forestall its wrath, and to march forward continuously towards prosperity, our starting point is the liberation of the broad masses from illiteracy' (quoted in Mammo, 1985: 107).

Once again, literacy was emphasised as providing a means of decreasing poverty on a national level, here articulated in the metaphor of humankind overcoming the catastrophes of nature. Cooper (1989) ascribes the multilingual focus of the campaign to the fact that the new regime recognised the political power and legitimacy gained by university students during the 1960 abortive coup. As part of their protest students had articulated their demands in terms of land reform, representative government, and ethnic self-determination which referred to the right of ethnic groups to govern themselves (Cooper, 1989). Language formed another important aspect of their protest and many students from linguistic minority groups had refused to speak Amharic which they regarded as a colonial language. Instead, they had called for English as a 'world language' to become the medium of instruction.

However, in the aftermath of the Derg's rise to power, the students campaigned for a civilian government, a people's democracy, in opposition to the military regime represented by the Derg. The Derg responded by closing the universities and sending the students into the rural areas to become involved in literacy teaching, the construction of schools and roads and to bring the message of revolution to the peasants (Cooper, 1989). By making this obligatory, the Derg ensured that the students were removed from the political terrain which allowed itself the opportunity to consolidate as a ruling power, especially since its control during the early days had not extended far beyond urban areas.

Cooper goes on to argue that the literacy campaign and the students' large scale involvement with it, ultimately constituted a crisis management strategy adopted by the Derg. First, with the students usefully occupied in the countryside, the Derg could continue the process of government without the threat of civil unrest. Second, by acceding to a multilingual literacy campaign, it could be seen to be fulfilling students' demands for ethnic self-determination — whilst continuing its war against the Eritreans who were demanding political independence. Third, the land reform started in 1976 which sought to dismantle the feudal land-tenure system gained the government more legitimacy with peasants and the students. The fact that the Derg was seen to acquiesce to some of their demands made the students more co-operative in carrying out the government's policies. As part of the implementation of the land reform policy, the students were required to organise peasants into rural associations. But the students later used this forum as a means to politicise the peasants and to mobilise them against the government. Within the new revolutionary ethos, the erstwhile fervour for the literacy campaign flagged.

Despite the multilingual policy of the Derg's literacy campaign, Amharic has retained its social and economic status. Moreover, Cooper (1989: 28) states:

> While the rhetoric of the state's rulers has changed, the state's problems have remained. Or rather they have been exacerbated. the tendency towards fragmentation, normally found after the demise of an old regime, is found today. Not only were the new rulers faced with the old problem of separatist rebellions by Tigrés in Eritrea and Somalis in the Ogaden, but they were soon faced with new rebellions among Tigrés in Tigray province and Afars in the Donakil and by the rekindling of Oromo rebelliousness in Balé Province.

Here then we have an example of the ways in which both one-language and multilingual national language literacy campaigns have been exploited for specific political ends. Again, this bears out my previous argument that mass literacy campaigns need to be analysed within a broader framework that takes account of not only the educational and economic benefits attached to these campaigns, but also of the diverse political motivations behind them. It also bears out Arnove and Graff's (1987) argument that centralised literacy campaigns serve other goals that are, invariably, defined by political power elites.

Both these examples illustrate that, in many instances, common languages used to build particular solidarities, in effect, serve to accentuate linguistic and social differences. Common languages often set up linguistic barriers within institutions and social processes, and through their mediation of selective literary traditions they serve to demarcate the parameters of the culture. This can contribute to the alienation and dissatisfaction of minority social groups which, in turn, can contribute to social instability. Literacy in common languages rather than local or minority group languages in some situations, ultimately underscore real and symbolic social and cultural inequalities.

Mass campaigns and social action in the liberal democracy

The 1960s also heralded a period of change with regard to adult literacy in the developed world. In contrast to the emphasis on nation-building and revolutionary change in the Tanzanian and Ethiopian campaigns, here the rationale for educational intervention was founded on the social construction, the 're-discovery of poverty' particularly within the urban context during the 1960s and early 1970s. In Britain, the social pathology of urban deprivation was articulated within a discourse on the 'seamless web of circumstance' , 'cycles of deprivation', 'areas of special need' and 'twilight zones' consolidated in the Newsom (1963) and Plowden (1967) Reports. In the USA, President Lyndon Johnson's 'War on Poverty Campaign' saw the emergence of social welfare programmes such as 'Operation Head Start' and the 'Right to Read Campaign' targeted at deprived inner-city areas.

Within the general compensatory ethos of the period, the early 1970s had become a particular time for social action which revolved around campaigning around issues of housing and homelessness, and family poverty. The UK saw the introduction of the Urban Aid Programme in 1965, the National Community Development Project, and later, the identification of Educational and Social Priority Areas (1974) which were defined in terms of levels of social deprivation and disadvantage within the inner-city. This provided a natural context in which the adult literacy campaign could find a 'voice'.

Peter Clyne's book *The Disadvantaged Adult* published in 1972 became an influential text. The book articulated the needs of the economy in terms of the perceived needs of individuals living in society which, if remediated, could serve a dual function of social upliftment and also meeting the needs of a 'rapidly developing technological society'. The urgency of the need to improve adult education as a means of social redress was consolidated in the Russell Report *Adult Education: A Plan for Development* (1973). The report called for a comprehensive system of adult education based on an assessment of needs and helped to establish the context for the Adult Literacy Campaign.

The main aim of the adult literacy campaigning lobby in the beginning was to make literacy a popular issue. Thus they sought to conduct a media campaign that would embarrass the government into allocating funds towards the setting up of provision to cater for adult illiterates. They proceeded to produce an estimate of need which was a million people at that time — for which they needed a million pounds to start provision. This was followed by a conference on adult literacy, and subsequently published a pamphlet called *A Right to Read*, a title borrowed from the US campaign. In the words of a campaigner at the time, 'we wanted to get the government to acknowledge that a need existed'. Drawing on existing discourses on the way in which schools had failed a significant number of students allowed them to focus attention on the million adult illiterates. This became an underlying theme of the campaign.

Viewed within the framework of broader struggles taking place in the societal terrain, this implicit criticism of school tied in with the 'moral panic' that was being constructed around 'falling standards in schools', in the polemics of the Black Papers published between 1969–75. This collection of right-wing papers constructed a powerful counter-discourse against the comprehensive school system and its focus on egalitarianism, and child-centred teaching methods. Presented as 'wishy-washy', 'trendy Left' teaching approaches, progressive education was portrayed as serving to undermine and threaten the inherited literary traditions, cultural values and the consensus shaped historically around law and order in society. In addition to their ineffectiveness to produce a functionally literate adult populace, comprehensive education was regarded also as not being cost-effective in terms of labour, time and resources. More importantly, it was presented as lacking an awareness of schools' responsibilities towards society. 'Progressivist' teachers and the curricula that they supported became thus codified as 'subversive' which ultimately served against the 'national interest'.

The media discourse that developed around the neglect of schools to teach pupils adequate reading, spelling, grammar and writing skills served to consolidate the impression of a badly failing schooling system. That is to say, pupils left schools as illiterates because of bad teaching and bad and irresponsible teachers. The notions of 'falling standards' and the 'break down of law and order' became important variables in the structuring of a 'literacy panic' during the early 1970s. Key elements in the Black Papers could now be appropriated and re-positioned into another discourse on welfare rights. The low standards identified in the Adult Literacy Campaign could now be regarded as a 'new' event which could be ascribed to 'recent' causes (Shor, 1980, quoted in Lankshear & Lawler, 1987: 113).

It was within this climate that the British Association of Settlements (BAS) produced the document *A Right to Read*, in which literacy was defined as a civil right from which a vast section of the population had been excluded. Interviewing school failures on television allowed the campaigning lobby to construct literacy as a 'moral' issue on which the government *had* to act. Having diagnosed the problem, the campaign could now be seen as offering a 'solution' to the problem of disaffected illiterates.

The first million pounds allocated for adult literacy came from a pencilled-in increase in the Universities Library Budget under the new Labour Government in 1974. Significantly, it did not come from central government funds. A further development later was the allocation of government funding of Special Development Projects at local education authority level (LEA) in which two-thirds of the annual grant was intended to cover the development of a resource base and working with disadvantaged groups who lacked 'basic skills'.

Attempts to legislate on adult basic education made little impact in Parliament. The Private Member's Bill introduced in May 1974 by Chris Price, the Labour Member of Parliament for Lewisham, did not get beyond the first reading. Instead, the government set up the National Institute of Adult and Continuing Education (NIACE) and ALRA which were organisations that did not require the submission of estimates of literacy needs and plans to meet the established need. Although the campaign talked about eradicating literacy by 1984 — ten years later, the Adult Literacy Resource Agency (ALRA) was funded initially for only one year, later to be extended to three years. Pump-prime funding was to prevail in adult literacy provision for many years, preventing ALRA and its successors, the Adult Literacy Unit (ALU) and the Adult Literacy and Basic Skills Unit (ALBSU), from devising effective long-term development programmes.

ALRA linked with the BBC 'On the Move' programme which was presented in a light-hearted 'tea-for-two' format (Clare, 1985: 24) and focused largely on disseminating information on adult literacy classes held in local areas. The main contribution of the 'On the Move' programmes was the nation-wide publicity that it gave to the campaign. The campaign relied heavily on volunteers and during the period there were about 45,000 volunteers and 4–5000 paid staff. This resulted in some areas having 900 volunteers to 300 students. Most of the staff appointments made at the time were administrative, having the primary aim of spending the million pounds within the year as a basis for future funding.

As a result of the fact that there was no preparation period to allow the formulation of clearly defined policy or practice guidelines, much of the money was spent on buying equipment which was, to a large extent, not used at the time. In an overall sense, however, the campaign of 1974 was judged to have been a success in that the campaigning lobby had achieved what they had set out to do; that is, to force the government to accept that a need existed to provide for adult literacy, and to allocate a million pounds towards the setting up of provision.

Post-campaign developments

With the setting up of ALU in 1978, adult literacy funds became allocated to local government. Money previously allocated to ALRA was now added to the Local Government Rates Support Grant (RSG) and LEAs were given the responsibility for the 'development of basic educational opportunities for adults' (ALU Newsletter, Sept/Oct 1978). On becoming ALBSU in 1980, adult literacy teaching started to incorporate the concept of functional literacy defined in terms of 'basic and vocational skills' into its range of provision. The 1982 ALBSU conference argued that it had to narrow its focus in order to:

> deal more effectively with the needs of those with no immediate prospect of paid work and those who do not seek it, such as women at home and the retired, and to recognise the importance of these basic skills as the first rung on the educational ladder. (ALBSU, Aug/Sept 1982: 2).

Shifting its focus onto the notions of 'self-help', it started to target the rapidly rising number of unemployed, and ethnic minority groups. By 1987, this focus had shifted to include:

> those who may have only recently become unemployed, those who suffer regular short periods without work, those who are early retired or unfit for work, those who do not work and are nor actively seeking a job and those in work but who still have inadequate mastery of reading, writing or basic maths. (ALBSU, Summer 1987)

In adopting these strategies, adult literacy provision became a key terrain in which the state could exercise some measure of control to maintain not only social equilibrium during a period of rising levels of unemployment, but also to re-construct adult training needs to accommodate changes taking place in the labour market. Again, literacy had become defined in terms of the pursuit of other goals.

Mass literacy campaigns and liberationist discourses

In contrast to centralised initiatives elsewhere, the mass literacy campaigns that took place in some South American countries during the 1970s served a different social and political purpose. Here they played an important role in the revolutionary process that prevailed throughout the region during that period. Societal literacy needs were defined in terms of the particular political programme adopted as a means of liberation from oppressive conditions. Within this framework, literacy formed part of a broader counter-hegemonic struggle aimed at changing existing social practices and structures.

Many of the literacy campaigns that took place in South America at the time were influenced by the principles of individual libertarianism espoused by Paulo Freire. As is discussed earlier, his view of 'conscientisation' stressed the importance of intrinsic motivation through the principle of a self-defining learning purpose. Literacy purposes had to arise out of people's own interests which would enable texts to be generated through their own personal and social experiences, as opposed to being externally defined and geared primarily to facilitate economic growth. Meaning production within this framework challenges not only prevailing dominant definitions of literacy but also the structural base of definitions of what should constitute useful cultural knowledge. Further, literacy defined within this framework obtains significant symbolic value: it provides a powerful means of 'naming' the world in terms of people's lived experience, to interpret, understand and contest it — and to aim to transform it. The Nicaraguan literacy campaign presents an interesting example to explore.

The Nicaraguan Literacy Campaign

When the Sandinist National Liberation Front (FSLN) came to power on the deposition of the Samosa dictatorship, it already had its plan for a mass literacy campaign organised. This had taken place already ten years before when the organisation had come into being. Eradicating illiteracy thus had formed part of the revolutionary programme since the beginning, and had been practised amongst the recruits since the early days of the struggle against the Samosa regime. Lankshear and Lawlor (1987: 176) argue that this related to the fact that they needed to recruit and organise:

large numbers of committed people who understood clearly how and why the possibility of a viable future for themselves and their fellows depended entirely upon overthrowing the dictatorship *and* transforming the oppressive structures of daily life. Developing a critical understanding of daily reality among those who suffered most within it was crucial to building and sustaining the struggle. (original emphasis)

The FSLN prioritised the Literacy Crusade (Cruzado National de Alfabetizacion) as a means of building a society free from exploitation and to involve people more actively in the social, political and economic life of the country (Grigsby, 1985). The aims were to eradicate illiteracy throughout the country and to embark on a process of conscientisation with the masses to enable them to 'know and understand the goals and possibilities of the Revolution' (Grigsby, 1985: 66) — and thus to strengthen the democratic base. As part of the same process they sought to establish structures for post-literacy programmes as part of building an ongoing, coherent system of adult education. In order to consolidate this comprehensive approach, a National Literacy Commission was established and this was linked to a National Coordination Committee which formed part of the Ministry of Education. The literacy campaign was thus, from the beginning, linked with state structures which enabled it to operate at different levels and to allocate and coordinate responsibilities for different technical and organisational roles within the campaign.

Under the slogan 'let the people educate the people' the campaign enrolled different sections of the population. The Popular Literacy Army composed of university and secondary students ('*Brigidistas'*) were organised into different sized groups and accompanied by a teacher. This grouping played a significant part in the rural areas and mountain regions where they lived and worked with local people. Groups were also organised to work in urban areas where the focus and approach were different in that they worked in Sandinista Literacy Units which operated in churches, private homes, schools and factories.

Because no adequate literacy figures were available, a census was conducted in order to establish the level of need and, in turn, this information enabled the campaign organisers to strategise regarding effective mobilisation. Advertising in slogans, signs, stickers and banners as well as the media played a significant role in generating popular interest in and enthusiasm for the campaign. This momentum was sustained throughout the campaign in several periodic publications including the bulletin *La Cruzada en Marcha,* the Sandinista Youth publication *El Brigadista,* and several workers newspapers such as *El Machete* of the Association of Agricultural Labourers, *El Troubadour* of the Central Union of Workers, *La Voz de Mujer* of the Women's Association of Nicaragua (Grigsby, 1985).

A multi-levelled training programme which involved all volunteers in an ongoing process of learning through workshop participation was devised. This form of organised learning would provide the basis of inculcating democratic values which could then penetrate society. The curriculum was organised around reading and writing skills, basic mathematics and analytical skills as well as some history and civics. These linked with broader aims which included the need to:

forge a sense of national consensus and of social responsibility; to strengthen channels of economic and political participation; to acquaint people with national development programmes; to record oral histories and recover popular forms of culture; and to conduct research in health and agriculture for future development. (Miller, 1985: 118)

Literacy programmes were conducted in a variety of languages in order to cater for the country's different ethnic minority groups living on the Atlantic coast.

A year after the start of the campaign a systematic development of post-literacy provision commenced. The Popular Basic Education (EPB) operated within a nation-wide network and at national, regional, zonal and individual promoter level which comprised volunteers such as campesinos, housewives, teachers and urban workers (Lankshear and Lawlor, 1987). In rural areas, especially, promoters would support, train and supervise Popular Teachers who had been promoted from within literacy classes. Lankshear & Lawlor argue further that 'the EPB was conceived as a 'special elementary school' for adults; the key weapon in the 'battle for the fourth grade' in Nicaragua' (1987: 194). Teaching took place within the community and the work-place.

The Nicaraguan literacy campaign developed within a context of ongoing dialogue and debate and encouraged the full involvement of its people in the democratic process. These changes were accompanied by broader policy developments including agrarian reforms, free access to health and education, the re-distribution of land and the establishment of a social wage (Lankshear & Lawlor, 1987). The campaign was heralded as a great success, and stimulated much interest within the region and elsewhere.

The campaign's success was to be undermined during the period of war that followed the Reagan/Bush administration's support for the Contra guerrillas throughout the 1980s. In its quest to the rolling back of 'Communism' throughout the world, the American regime sought to overthrow the FSLN using military intervention '[the arming of the mercenary force, the contras], economic [a financial and trade blockade imposed by the US and by institutions like the World Bank], and political [the pressurising of Washington's allies to line up behind US policy]' (Smith, 1991: 59).

The ten-year war impacted on the literacy campaign in several ways as many literacy workers were assassinated, tortured and abducted; literacy workers had to be drafted for military service and there was also a general lack of teaching resources. Economic crisis also meant that people had to engage more in production which diminished the time available for adult education. After a number of years of war, the Nicaraguan economic crisis deepened and both national and international support for the FSLN had been eroded (Borjas, 1989). Ironically, the critical thinking developed in the literacy programme was to rebound during the elections of 1990 in which the FSLN lost to the United National Opposition. Peasants were lobbying for individual ownership of land as opposed to cooperatives, and the country started increasingly to look to foreign investment as a way out of the economic crisis.

Here then we have an example of a well-planned, systematically organised and coordinated literacy campaign which attempted to combine literacy for economic growth as a long-term aim, with literacy as a vehicle for the teaching of democratic sensibilities amongst its populace, accompanied by structural and institutional changes. Thus it sought to cater for a process of change which would systematically revolutionise society as a whole. What it also illustrates, however, is that national literacy programmes can be undermined especially if they subscribe to an ideology that challenges that of a regional super-power. This highlights the fact that, within an increasingly globalised economy, the types of societal change that can take place depend greatly also on the unequal power relations that inhere in geo-politics.

Commonalities and differences: Identifying characteristics

In each example, literacy was regarded as providing a vehicle for a specific set of beliefs, values and behaviours and, moreover, a means of shaping the aspirations, expectations, hopes and desires of people to suit the ultimate social, cultural, religious, economic or political aims pursued. This bears out the view that because literacy cannot be separated from either its knowledge or societal base it is always for something else (Graff, 1987; Oxenham, 1980), and is rarely pursued *en masse* purely for its cognitive and functional value. In terms of this, the powerful symbolic power of literacy provides the means *par excellence* for the maintenance of hegemonic relations.

At the same time, it also confers status, creates scope for active citizenship and provides possibilities for participating in a variety of discourses. The extent to which people may be able to participate as citizens depends on the particular social policy being pursued, the particular political regime in power, the social ethos and the strength of civil society. This supports the argument made earlier that literacy as a social, ideological, cultural and educational practice cannot be discussed outside the social system and the material conditions that prevail within society at a particular moment in its development. For, although there may be similarities in the ways in which the discourses were articulated and popularised, the underlying intentions were quite different. Whether the outcomes were also different and in which ways they differ, are discussed in the next section.

Comparative analysis

Postcolonial nation building provided a common thread in the literacy campaigns that developed in Africa. The issue of language similarly provided a key variable in the process of defining the nation. Whereas a common language was seen to be central to forging nationhood in Tanzania, in Ethiopia the multilingual policy pursued by the Derg served to fracture the hegemony of the one-language policy pursued by Haile Sillasie. Within the context of ujamaa socialism in Tanzania, and the Kebele structures in urban areas in Ethiopia, the literacy campaigns were also supported by strong arguments for de-centralisation and democratisation and literacy was seen as playing a central role in the process of societal modernisation. In reality, however, political expediency prevailed in Ethiopia where use was made of mass literacy campaigning by the Derg as a means of securing a political power base within the country. In both examples, the mass literacy campaigns formed part of specific hegemonic and economic projects pursued by the state.

The mass literacy campaign in Nicaragua illustrated that literacy campaigns generated through grassroots activism within the everyday life of communities have a different cultural and organisational base. Some, including those that form part of a revolutionary or political activist programme, also tend to have a different political and ideological base and often aim for alternative (at least initially) literacy purposes. However, what happens after the revolutionary phase is problematic because of the fact that when revolutionary movements have to make the transition to government, they often find it hard to sustain the level of critique and engagement required during the period of revolution.

In Nicaragua, the critical thinking developed within the literacy campaign and that was encouraged within the social terrain, ultimately worked *against* the political interests of the FSLN. This was evident in the way that political alliances amongst the populace changed in Nicaragua, especially during the period of war with the Contras. The fact that the peasants preferred individual ownership of land as opposed to the collectivism planned for by the FSLN showed the extent that the everyday needs and wants of the peasants did not necessarily coincide with the socialist project at the heart of the FSLN programme. Indeed, the freedom and ability gained to engage in critique of existing social structures enabled them to make alternative choices that served in their own self-defined interests.

The long-term dividends of the EWLP were undermined considerably by the linearity of the functional model of literacy adopted as well as the economic and political crises that ensued in many of the developing nations. Political corruption, financial mis-management, natural disasters, and the inability of countries to repay external debt contributed to growing poverty in many developing countries. Jones (1992: 171) points out:

> Low-income Africa was poorer in 1985 than it was in 1960, with falls per capita output in the 1980s wiping out the gains made in the 1960s and 70s. In many countries between 1980 and 1985, per capita income fell 10 per cent, and up to 30 per cent in countries such as Chad, Niger, Togo and Tanzania. Across the subcontinent, improvements made since independence in health, education and public infrastructure were in real danger of being eradicated.

This highlights the fact that the political framework in which these mass literacy campaigns were conceived can with hindsight, be regarded as having been politically naive and undialectical.

Indeed, UNESCO at its Fifth International Conference on Adult Education recognised some of this. The Conference Report (1997: 2) states:

> It is now agreed that one of the principal reasons for the relative failure of earlier campaigns is that they maintained an evangelical stance to the development of literacy, offering literacy as the royal road to development rather (than) as a key ingredient in the process of development. Earlier programmes failed to determine just how literate activities could be instrumental in the achievements of the participants' own goals.

It argues further that mass campaigns draw few participants and that 'neo-literates relapse into illiteracy because of the lack of opportunities for use' (UNESCO, 1997). It also argues:

> These [mass literacy] programmes are now seen as somewhat superficial both in the concept of literacy as individual competency and in their neglect of the social institutions and practices which would have made such competencies useful. (UNESCO, 1997: 2, information in brackets added)

Moreover, adult literacy provision existed outside the formal education system and was the first casualty in budget cuts in many countries (Hallak, 1990).

Another criticism of the EWLP is the technicist approach adopted to what were, in reality, complex societal problems. Berman (1992: 71) argues that:

> emphasis on technique means that moral, social, or political issues raised by policy choices are avoided and are instead transformed into technical problems to be resolved through the application of the appropriate non-ideological, technical procedures.

The response from the World Bank to the sustained economic crisis in the developing world during the 1980s was to propose three overarching themes, 'adjustment, revitalisation and selective expansion' (Jones, 1990: 172). Included in this was the development of 'basic education, privatisation of educational services, rigorous measures of educational efficiency and concern for equity in educational access' (Jones, 1990: 172) as well as cost reductions effected through staff rationalisation. Further emphasis was placed on job-related training skills and educational quality.

The example of the adult literacy campaign in the UK provided a view of the development of adult literacy provision in a developed country. It illustrated the ways in which social action can work to facilitate educational provision for what previously had been a marginalised minority group. The problem of short-term funding in this instance showed the opportunistic way in which successive governments have used adult literacy to fulfill party political agenda. For example, ALBSU's funding levels were finally increased during the 1980s after it had adapted itself to the evolving needs of the re-structured labour market.

The examples of mass literacy campaigns within the developing world highlight the important role that international economic and political relations play in shaping the nature of social change and, moreover, in regulating the level of social change that can take place within developing countries. The argument that literacy cannot be divorced from social systems and structures, and the ways in which these interact with broader systems of control within an increasingly globalised cultural economy is explored further in Part 3.

Part 3:
Globalisation: The Implications of Technological Development, Social and Cultural Change for Concepts and Definitions of Literacy

The past two decades have been marked by rapid technological changes that have altered fundamentally the way in which we perceive and experience the world. The incorporation of microelectronics technology into diverse industries and, particularly, the communications industry has altered global cultural relations in an organic way — and with it, our expectations of everyday life. Global networks of information provide increasing opportunities for interaction between people, machines and power processes in both 'real time' and 'deferred time'. Moreover, global distribution of film and video, and the ubiquity of satellite television in the world today play a significant role in structuring the aspirations, expectations, dreams and desires of larger groups of people living in different sociocultural and geographic contexts. New, multifaceted, cultural identities are in the process of being shaped.

The rapid transfer of information between countries and continents and, especially the application of information technology in banking and financial markets have also transformed the economic base. This, in turn, has created global networks of power bringing in their wake new social, economic and political inequalities between societies at the 'core' of economic activity, and those existing at the periphery. New economies of space and time made possible by microelectronics technology have transformed not only capital information flows, but also work practices and the labour process within the global terrain. Thus it is argued that 'informational capacity' and, *de facto*, access to information-based technologies provide the new basis of social development.

This section of the book examines the important role that literacy plays in the new informational environment of the late 20th century. In contrast to a linear view of literacy defined in terms of reading and writing print-text, it argues that the concept of 'text', the nature of the literacy process as well as the levels and types of skill and knowledge required to function effectively within the re-defined information-dominated environment have altered in a very fundamental way. The overall discussion is informed by the fact that alongside this dynamic process of technological and global cultural change, we have also witnessed since the 1980s, the rise of the ideology and practice of monetarist economic policy.

The powerful influence of monetarism on national economic policy frameworks, and those of major lenders such as the World Bank's support for national development programmes, has restructured social policy in many countries. The strategy of reducing public expenditure to give free reign to the market as the key, rational, regulatory mechanism within the social sector has contributed to reductions in overall capital spending in education within many countries. This, in turn, has had a major impact on the range of education made available in different societies and, relatedly, levels of societal literacy and the range of skilled employment possibilities. Taking these factors into account the following chapters argue that any analysis of the links between literacy and social development cannot realistically take place outside a consideration of the global re-structuring of economic relations, social policy and sociocultural change.

Chapter 5

Technological and Cultural Transformations

> To understand literacy means that contradictions — oppositions, negations, countervailing factors, or dialectical processes — should be expected to result from the ongoing processes and developments within culture, polity, economy and society. These are neither ironic nor paradoxical, as some call them, but fundamentally historical. (Graff, 1987: 31)

This chapter explores the interaction between technological change, social and economic development, and their collective impact on shaping the social, economic and cultural value attached to particular forms of literacy during periods when societies change from one milieu to another. First, it explores the transformative impact that new technologies during the 'first' and 'second' industrial revolutions have had on (a) social and economic institutions and practices, (b) the nature of work and work practices and (c) the effects of this on the uses and role of literacy in society.

Second, it locates current social, economic and political changes within the context of the ongoing microelectronics-based technological revolution. It problematises prevailing conceptualisations of literacy in terms of the multilevelled changes that are taking place within an increasingly global-ised cultural economy. Contradictions, counter-hegemonic cultural prac-tices as well as development disparities between the developed world and developing countries are highlighted throughout.

Literacy and the First Industrial Revolution

As has been argued in Chapter 3, the emergence of the modern nation-state during the 18th century heralded the transition towards a secular and more complex society. This process according to Anderson (1983) was made possible, largely, by the emergence of print capitalism. This view finds support in the seminal writings of Eisenstein (1979) who argues that the printing press presented 'the supreme turning point in

129

Western history, altering as it did all forms of government, all social and cultural institutions, all ways of thought' (quoted in Smith, 1986: 171). Mass-production facilitated by the steam-press enabled the publication and wider circulation of a range of literature at low cost that secured the basis for the development of a mass reading public. Print technology and the subsequent development of the popular press were to have a major impact on the re-organisation of the economic, cultural and social base. Williams (1961: 200) makes the point that the popular press:

> grew in content and style, from an old popular literature, with three vital transforming factors: first, the vast improvement in productive and distributive methods caused by industrialisation; second, the social chaos and the widening franchise, again caused by industrialisation and the struggle for democracy; third, the institution, as a basis for financing newspapers, of a kind of advertising made necessary by a new kind of economic organization, and a differently organized public.

Typographic print as a means of communication became transformed into an industrial technology (Smith, 1986). Together these made possible *new ways of knowing, new ways of doing* and *new forms of social organisation.*

Industrialisation which followed, brought with it:

> the transformation of the productive forces of society through the application of a machine technology and the factory system; but it also meant urbanisation, secularisation, the 'rationalization' of thought, institutions, and behaviour, the individualisation of consciousness and conduct, and a host of other changes in family life, politics, and culture. (Kumar, 1986: 55)

A change needed to take place also in the 'social character' in order to accommodate the nature of the changes taking place within a modernising society. Literacy was to play a key role in shaping this hegemony.

Literacy and industrialisation

As is argued in Chapter 3, the drive for mass literacy in 19th century England was supported primarily by the need to maintain social equilibrium during a period of rapid rural–urban migration in consequence to new employment possibilities in factories created by the Industrial Revolution. Ball and Kenny (1989: 3) argue:

> The phenomenal growth of urban society in the 19th century literally tore apart the moral fabric of the existing social order. In the experiences and imagination of the landed ruling class and the newly emerging

industrial middle class the city was a focus and a source of political unrest, social disorder, crime and disease.

Within this context literacy became intertwined with education aimed at a moral re-orientation to counter the potential for personal and social deviance. The association of a lack of education with criminality resulted in literacy, as a measurable sign of a lack of education, becoming an integral part of the discourse on universal schooling as a means of 'inculcating restraint, order, discipline, integration: the correct rules for social and economic behaviour in a changing and modernising context' (Graff, 1987: 187). Illiteracy thus became linked with moral deficit.

The transition from craft skills and cottage industries to mass production in factories required a new kind of worker having specific worker awarenesses required by the new industrial mode of production. New labour demands at the time were for increased levels of practical skills, willing and obedient workers having the discipline to produce goods on time (Graff, 1987). The over-riding need was 'to educate the first generation of factory workers to a new factory discipline'(Pollard, 1963, quoted in Graff, 1987: 181).

Thus it was primarily the *symbolic* value of literacy and the ideological framework in which it was embedded, that gained ascendancy during this period. These awarenesses and intentions were inscribed into the particular *form* of literacy that prevailed, namely, decoding skills as well as the *pedagogy* in which it was framed. The latter included drill, repetition, rote-learning and proper codes of behaviour including morality and frugality (Graff, 1987). Significantly, for the popular masses the main emphasis was on reading, not writing, during this period. In other words, rather than being stimulated by the literacy skills-need necessitated by the Industrial Revolution, literacy served primarily in the interests of a *moral* economy.

Lankshear and Lawlor (1987: 56) express the view that:

> it was the achievement of 'moral' development and social control, to be effected through school learning, discipline and order, *mediated by literacy*, that underlay the strong commitment of the school promoters to ensuring universal literacy' (original emphasis).

Literacy as a moral technology thus formed an integral part of societal development goals which, in turn, derived from the specific uses to which new technologies were put in society, and the material benefits associated with it.

Individual literacy purposes

But alongside this were the literacy needs defined by groups and individuals themselves to accommodate the changing social and cultural landscape. Johnson (1983: 10) argues that for many workers:

It was necessary actively to learn new ways because the older common senses were not enough any more; yet customary skills and cultural inheritances seemed all the more precious because they were threatened. Issues around literacy are a case in point. The ability to read was especially valued because its transmission was threatened in communities drastically affected by industrial change, handloom-weaving districts for example. Elementary accomplishments like reading and knowing how to sign your name did decline in some areas in the early Industrial Revolution. Yet the desire to read and write was also very actively stimulated by the new conditions, especially by the great surges of popular political activity, with their extensive presses and expanding reading publics.

These self-defined literacy purposes served the aim of self-empowerment through the development of an alternative, critical literacy in addition to the acquisition of the functional literacies required to operate in everyday life. This highlights Giddens' (1991) view that the fact that oppressive structures which serve to reproduce social inequalities are inherently subject to change through human action. People read and interpret text, and the social context in which it is grounded, within their own frames of reference shaped by their subjective social experiences. These provide them with the terms of reference through which they can re-define their own literacy and skills needs — and, in the process, fracture the hegemony of dominant literacy meanings. These meanings were also reflected in the case-studies discussed by Barton and Hamilton (1998) referred to in Chapter 1.

Changing Realities During the Second Industrial Revolution

The particular uses that new technologies were applied to during the latter part of the Industrial Revolution transformed the whole basis of western capitalist societies. Mechanisation and later, automation, brought with them a new *regime of accumulation* grounded in standardised mass production. They also brought high levels of employment, a rise in income, the development of mass consumption and, relatedly, cultural homogenisation. Mass production which relied on new sets of skills and worker awarenesses also resulted in new forms of control emerging within the work-place. These were consolidated in new *modes of regulation* that revolved around the 'norms, habits, laws, regulating networks . . . that ensure[d] the unity of the process' (Lipietz, 1988: 19).

Already by the late 19th century these conditions had been secured in

the systematic application of science to industrial production; mass production and continuous-process technology [conveyor belt]; the rationalisation of work organisation and management, especially around the conveyor belt and assembly line; the rise of mass 'general labour' unions; the common use of large limited liability companies [instead of the family firm] for the raising of capital; concentration of production and ownership, and control of markets, through cartelisation, trusts, and producers' associations; the separation of ownership and control in the large firms, and the rise of managerialism [scientific management]; a marked increase in the degree of state regulation and control of the economy and society; the global expansion of the industrial economy. (Kumar, 1986: 175, information in brackets added)

This production system, and that of Fordism which followed in 1916, relied primarily on routinised labour which demanded very little craft skills and knowledge, and provided workers with minimal control over the work process. It effectively de-skilled craft workers within some industries such as automobile manufacture.

Again, the specific *uses* to which technologies were put within society during this phase of development, and that which followed the Second World War, resulted in the emergence of new forms of sociotechnical organisation. In most of the developed world,

industrial techniques eclipsed craft work; technologies of modern agribusiness made small scale farming all but impossible; high-speed transportation crowded out slower means of getting about. It is not merely that useful devices and techniques of earlier periods have been rendered extinct, but also that patterns of social existence and individual experience that employed these tools have vanished as living realities. (Winner,1986: 48)

Large-scale plant technology, within this time-frame, became the mechanism through which not only the economic base but society as a whole was to be transformed into a capitalist cultural economy. Within this context, 'the industrial society came to be identified as the distinctive type of *modern* society' (Kumar, 1986: 55). (original emphasis)

Changing forms of labour and skills demands

Developing the industrial base became the principal defining factor in the process of societal *modernisation*. In addition to the transformations brought about in manufacturing and agricultural production by new technologies, this also included the weakening of traditional ties signifying the move towards a secular society, and the rationalisation of authority (Ingham, 1995). Agriculture was to be transformed by mechanisation, becoming just another industry 'with production carried on under industrial conditions in specialised units of production [farms], and entailing no distinctive rural life' (Kumar, 1986: 66).

The subsequent growth of bureaucracy contributed to the development of administrative infrastructures within the state and elsewhere. This included the rise of the bureaucratic firm relying on an:

> office hierarchy ordered in a pyramid of authority; the existence of impersonal, written rules of procedure; strict limits on the means of compulsion at the disposal of each official; the appointment of officials on the basis of their specialist training and qualifications; clearly demarcated specialised tasks demanding full-time employees; and significantly, the separation of officials from ownership of the means of administration. (Held, 1992: 151)

A de-personalised work-place was emerging. Indeed, Weber (1978) saw in the organisational form of the bureaucracy, the replication of the social relations of production that included 'precision, speed, unambiguity, knowledge of the files, continuity, discretion, unity, strict subordination, reduction of friction and of material and personal costs'. The development of new worker skills and awarenesses transcended the requirements of the production process to include also technicist efficiency within other organisational structures such as administration. Commercial enterprise contributed further to the reconstitution of the labour force in the manufacturing industry as well as the development of new occupations including business management and the delivery of services.

With this came the requirement for a range of different functional literacies and skills which were distributed differentially amongst a rigidly stratified work force. A critical appraisal of the role of functional literacy as a means of supporting the modernisation model adopted within the industrial paradigm during the 1970s has already been discussed in Chapters 2 and 3.

The internationalisation of production

During the 1960s a three-levelled division of labour supply emerged, namely:

(1) conception, the organisation of methods and engineering;
(2) qualified manufacturing requiring skilled workers;
(3) de-skilled execution and assembly. (Lipietz, 1988: 30)

These levels were further separated into three labour pools 'differentiated mainly by skills and social conditions' (Lipietz, 1988: 31), with much of the semi-skilled and un-skilled labour transferred to developing countries where labour supply was cheap and largely uncontrolled by unions.

In many instances, this was bolstered by the enforcement of economic policies adopted by autocratic regimes who colluded with transnational economic interests. This was secured later in the development of 'free trade zones' and workshop states mainly in South East Asia. Many of these societies had a 'free climate of investment' that included the ability of investing countries to repatriate profits. Landsberg (1987: 233) describes 'free trade zones' as 'industrial parks, constructed and paid for by Third World nations who turn over their governance and administration to foreign capital engaged in exporting'. But for some countries this provided a route to industrialisation and governments managed to secure the building of an economic and industrial infrastructure which enabled them to emerge as newly industrialised countries (NICs) during the 1980s. The existing (graduated) core–periphery model of international development thus already had its genesis in the early stages of the management of what became known as the crisis of Fordist mass production.

Changing literacy experiences

Alongside these forms of institutional and global developments were other technological, cultural and political changes more directly linked with literacy. For example, the invention of photography and, later, film and television generated new definitions of text and also gave rise to new ways of seeing and experiencing the world. The literacy implications and social effects of these developments are examined in further detail in Chapter 6.

Moreover, the enfranchisement of the working class throughout most of the developed world where the beneficiaries of universal education were making increasing demands on the state for the provision of better services such as health and education, contributed to the development of mass citizenship (Held, 1992). The UK, already during the early years of the century, had a burgeoning industrial unionism 'rooted in the struggle for control in factory or workshop, in the independent shop steward's movement, and in the politics of 'class war' ' (Hall, 1994: 22). As is evident in Johnson's (1983) account of political activism built around literacy, discussed earlier, the working class movement built on older traditions of alternative printing presses producing counter-hegemonic literature.

Multilevelled social changes therefore took place as a consequence of the Industrial Revolution, which, in turn, had a significant impact on the conceptualisation, uses and experience of literacy. This supports the argument that technology is not a separate entity operating autonomously, that it is integral to social process and, as such, interacts discursively with cultural, social, political and economic institutions and practices, transforming them from within — and over time.

The Technological Revolution

As has been argued in earlier chapters, a major section of the world's population is still not yet meeting the literacy demands generated by the printing press, and the skills levels generated by the Industrial Revolution. This is largely a result of the fact that many countries still lack the necessary infrastructure to support universal primary education, and adequate provision for higher education to cater for the complex skills demands of the modern world. Whilst these constraints still prevail in many developing countries, new societal and technological changes taking place are already in the process of re-shaping the mental universes that we can inhabit; creating yet again new possibilities for doing things, and the imperative for new ways of organising life. And, within and through this ongoing process of change, our social roles are once again being re-defined; requiring different sets of awarenesses, knowledges and skills in order to function on an everyday level.

Fordist crisis management

As was the case with mechanisation in the Second Industrial Revolution, the emergence of microelectronic technologies, and their incorporation into new production regimes, signify a new phase in capitalist development. Some writers argue that the technological mode of production signifies a new *historical bloc* that heralds a definitive end to the Fordist crisis of regulation (Bonefeld, 1987; Harvey, 1989). In order to understand the nature of the changes taking place, the Fordist crisis of regulation needs to be contextualised within the broader framework of developments that took place within the international terrain during the late 1970s. In particular, it needs to be analysed within the context of the economic crisis of the 1960s and 70s which, in turn, has to be seen in relation to:

- difficulties generated by the rigidity inherent in the mass production process (Bonefeld, 1987; Jessop, 1988). That is, the production of standardised commodities in a market in which changing consumer trends signified an increasing demand for 'non-standardised, quality, short shelf-life goods' (Amin, 1994: 15).
- the prevalence of a generally stagnant market due to the long recession.
- difficulties encountered in controlling an increasingly dissatisfied and militant workforce.
- the fact that the recession was exacerbated by the OPEC oil crisis of 1973 as well as rapid inflation and price rises.

- rising levels of unemployment which were contributed to, at least in part, by the replacement of traditional forms of labour by new, computer driven, technologies.

In the UK the major impact was on the printing and automobile industries. The economic re-structuring that followed was to contribute to the fracturing of the Fordist paradigm. And, in the process, it created a niche for the consolidation of the new microelectronic technologies. In addition, the rigid bureaucratic powers of control that had developed within the context of the Industrial Revolution, and which matched the hierarchical forms of control inherent in the Fordist paradigm were to be severely challenged and, ultimately, fractured within the economic policy framework of neo-liberalism.

Central to the political project of neo-liberalism was the need to 'roll back' the state, that is, to free capital by decreasing the role of the state within the economy. This would be achieved by exercising cuts in public spending which would boost the private sector, and by reducing taxation and encouraging worker incentive, it would increase productivity. Underlying this was the belief, derived from the economist Friedrich Hayek, that bureaucratic state agencies inhibited individual freedom and that the 'collective good can be properly realised in most cases only by private individuals acting in competitive isolation and pursuing their sectoral aims with minimal state interference' (Held, 1992 : 244). Foregrounding the market as key regulatory mechanism facilitated the development of new flexible accumulation strategies made possible by the microelectronics technology. Indeed, the organic interaction between microelectronics technology, the capital accumulation process and the specific economic policies adopted by western governments were to contribute to the shaping of a new global cultural economy.

The complexity of social relations that are evolving within the global terrain as well as the multi-faceted effects of the new technology on the communication process have created the need to re-appraise literacy within a conceptual framework that takes account of the changes taking place within a world context in which technology has become the *raison d'être* of social development.

A question of flexibility

Technological flexibility

The technological production process itself has been credited as being more flexible than the rigidity inherent in the standard mass production of Fordism (Bonefeld, 1987; Pollert, 1988). This relates to the fact that the new technology can be programmed to produce a variety of products to be used for a range of purposes, with minimal labour requirements. The ability of microelectronics technology to perform multiple tasks, and at great speed, reduces gaps and discontinuities within the production process. This, plus the fact that re-programming a computer to do alternative production tasks takes less time and effort than the re-training of workers, makes the new technology more cost-effective.

Moreover, the fact that it can produce low-cost, quality products allows it to cater more effectively for consumer choice which, in turn, has stimulated the need for constant *innovation* within the design and production process. These factors, combined with the de-regulation of capital transfer within the neo-liberal economic policy framework, and the rapid growth of international markets facilitated by technological development have allowed, to a large extent, to overcome the problem of stagnant markets.

Labour flexibility

Labour flexibility plays a significant role in the restructuring of the capital accumulation process and operates on different levels including:

- the organisation of work practices e.g. multiskilled, cooperative team work which relies on a horizontal dispersal of power controls within the work-place; strategic management; integrated work tasks; and time economies in the management of production outputs;
- flexible workers having transferable, practical skills and knowledges; innovation; entrepreneurism; market awareness; high motivation; engage in ongoing learning; worker efficiency;
- flexible production process, e.g. small batch production, quality control as part of the labour process, quality circles, job rotation, subcontracting. The accent is on reducing wasted time and resources within the production process, and the ability of production to respond effectively and quickly to evolving market needs.

The flexible firm

Work-place flexibility is organised around the concept of *'functional' flexibility* which refers to the division between a multiskilled *core-group* of workers, and a group of low-skilled workers operating at the *periphery*. The latter group has *'numerical' flexibility* in that demand for their labour depends on production demands and thus they are subject to high levels of job insecurity (Pollert, 1988). *Work-time flexibility* is another feature of the flexible firm in that periphery workers tend to be self-employed on short-term contracts, yearly contracts or are subcontracted, which ensure a controlled labour supply.

Moreover, the export of the production of certain commodities to developing countries has resulted in globalised hierarchies of labour. Periphery workers (low-skilled) generally do not benefit from worker protection in the form of pensions and other conditions of service extended to core-group workers. Sivanandan (1989) argues that the production of the micro-chip, which takes place largely in the developing world, relies on repetitive, low-skill tasks requiring only manual dexterity. The 'leaner' firm thus created, allows the existence of smaller production units relying on technical, labour and organisational flexibility to help to reduce production overheads and thus serve to maximise profits.

Collectively, these factors highlight the shift in emphasis from worker skills in the production process itself to the *organisation of work* and *particular worker awarenesses*. The new technology, as will be discussed later in the chapter, can be seen as having transformed manufacturing industry as well as having altered employment patterns.

Flexible accumulation

Computers are described as having been 'designed as the universal machine that could copy any other' (Mulgan, 1988) having the capacity of not only replacing human labour but also reproducing themselves *ad infinitum*. The implications of this for the capital accumulation process is, theoretically, immeasurable — and, again, would depend on the particular applications or uses of the technologies within society. Thus it has been argued that microelectronics constitutes the key technology:

> to drive future growth and to affect the behaviour of the entire economy by raising productivity and lowering output costs in all industries, creating new industries with high levels of demand, and securing a revolutionary onslaught on space and time constraints via electronic networking. Innovation will also involve transformation within pre-vailing managerial best practices, and introduce a new set of inter-sectoral and inter-firm relationships. (Amin, 1994: 17)

Inter-sectoral and inter-firm relationships refer to increasing levels of use of 'out-sourcing' and subcontracting.

Of importance also is the fact that the interactive nature of the new technology involves not only an interplay between individuals and machines but also amongst the technologies themselves. This has already altered conceptions of banking, international capital transfer (on stock exchanges), television, weather forecasting, publishing and warfare. Lyon

(1988: 115) describes the multilevelled influences that the rapid transfer of information has had on the capital accumulation process:

> Manufacturing, office and service productivity increases at a faster rate as communications infrastructures are enhanced . . . capital saving is also facilitated by better telecommunications . . . [t]he SWIFT system [Society for Worldwide International Financial Telecommunications], for instance, makes it possible for finance houses to buy or sell at any time. A kind of stateless currency thus circulates around the globe, twenty four hours a day to the advantage of developed nations.

Clearly, the benefits for multinational corporations are immense, allowing them to exercise considerable power and influence throughout an increasingly globalised economy. The disparities that exist between technological advance and, relatedly, the increased potential for rapid economic growth in the developed world and the multiple constraints that exist in developing countries will be discussed later.

Changing patterns of employment

Whilst, on the one hand, microelectronics technology has *reduced requirements for particular forms of work* or, in some industries, *replaced the requirement for human labour*, on the other hand, it has also created *new areas of employment*. Employment statistics by industry show an average increase of 20% employment in the services sector in developed countries since the 1970s, and at least a 14% increase in services related to information handling (Castells, 1996). Much of this relates to the fact that:

- The centrality of the market to the production process has created new niches in marketing, advertising, sales and market research.
- The growth of the business sector has stimulated demand for personnel catering for different aspects and levels of management and training.
- The synergistic relationship between technology and telecommunications has also resulted in the development of financial and communications services.

Other service sectors have developed around changes in life-styles often brought about by the changing nature of work and leisure. This includes the maintenance of household and other user commodities such as cars; leisure-related employment such as the increase in travel creating jobs in travel centres, hotels and transport; welfare provision including counselling and advisory services; personal services such as beauty therapy, fitness studios, hair dressing; domestic services as well as health services including alternative therapies.

Flexibility in the service sector
Casey (1995: 41) maintains that service workers:

> although low paid and quickly trained, are required to perform a wide range of responsibilities in dealing with customers and operate according to a company masterplan of standardised procedures and principles.

Like their counterparts in technological production industries, they are also subject to multiskilling and flexible work practices. For example, 'in the office, the computer-proficient clerical worker becomes an 'office administrator' performing tasks formerly reserved for specialist accountants, record keepers or receptionists' (Casey, 1995: 43). At a higher level, we have witnessed the development of consultancies in management as well as design and drafting, providing flexible services to business and industry. Although these groups of workers may offer specialist services, the delivery of those services require multiskilling that cater for the overall work process.

Re-structured skills demand
These changes in the nature of work and work practices indicate an increased need for *worker adaptability* and a *willingness to learn new skills*. Moreover, for many workers, especially those operating in high-information industries, the concept of work place itself has become 'de-centred' with knowledge workers, 'symbolic analysts' and specialists 'outsourced' to multinationals and transnationals (Casey, 1995), who are able to access globally networked information via their computers wherever they happen to be working at the time.

The rise in service industries has also spawned the development of new industries requiring new sets of skills and knowledges. Much of this is related to business management and other work-specific practical skills requiring short-term training, some of which are primarily information-based. This has stimulated a general increase in the demand for 'functional' technical skills to access and process data for a variety of purposes, and its dissemination in different forms including print outputs using in-house desktop publishing.

In a broader cultural sense, rather than a diminished demand for print literacy, we have witnessed an increase in the production of information leaflets aimed at developing popular awareness of consumer rights, leisure activities, welfare entitlements and self-help. New literacy purposes are thus in the making, not only in relation to the impacts and effects of the new technology, but also as a response to the evolution of new lifestyles.

As was the case with Fordism before, the centrality of a free-market in the re-structured, flexible, production process has also altered the terrain of cultural relations. In order to explore this argument further, the next two sections will focus on the multilevelled effects and impacts of the new technology on the shaping of new cultural awarenesses, and the discourses in which these have been rationalised in popular consciousness.

Technology, literacy and the social construction of 'reality'

The relative ease with which a diversity of products can be manufactured with the help of new microelectronics technology has increased pressure also for ever-evolving new markets — and, relatedly, the dynamic re-construction of consumer needs and wants aimed at fulfilling market demands. Advertising, product presentation using different forms of imagery, assumes an important position in the social construction, the media packaging of, largely, ephemeral consumer needs (Rassool, 1993). These marketing strategies serve the purpose of mobilising 'desire and fantasy ... as part and parcel of the push to sustain sufficient buoyancy of demands in consumer markets to keep capitalist production profitable' (Harvey, 1989: 61). We live in a world increasingly dominated by the television advert, bill boards and neon-signs defining our consumer needs. Consumerist cultural meanings thus constructed in ever-present, ever-changing media images of designer commodity products serve to refract existing reality and, simultaneously, to produce images of alternative lifestyles replete with their own tastes, desires and standards.

Furthermore, the leisure-use of the new technologies are all pervasive with computer games in homes, arcades and shopping centres; video machines, e-mail, the Internet and CD-Roms in homes and classrooms, and video libraries providing access to a galactic range of different film genres. Dordick and Wang (1993: 117) state that in the developed world:

> Information technologies abound in homes, especially among young families, with or without children. More than 95% of these families have a VCR; more than one-third have a personal computer and, of these, almost one-fifth communicate or access databases remotely; one-third have compact disc players; and there are answering machines in 50% of these households.

Our social reality is also being defined on another level: the commercial use of databanks is reflected in our everyday experience of unsolicited letters, 'special offers' and other 'junk-mail' received from a multiplicity of corporate businesses and manufacturers.

Access to centrally stored personal information raises further questions about the privacy of the individual. Centralised databases allow a free-flow of a range of industry-specific information which can be accessed globally by contracted users in different industries, particularly, banking, libraries, airlines, travel companies, 24 hours a day (Casey, 1995).

At the same time, individuals also define their own reading and learning purposes using information technology. Rogers (1986) gives an account of a Kentucky farmer whose work approach altered radically through his use of information technology. His ability to access information via his home computer about market trends and research findings allowed the farmer to maximise crop production, and also to generate a supplementary income by enabling him to participate in the buying and selling of wheat futures on the Chicago Board of Trade. The farmer expressed the need for the availability of satellite information on weather patterns in other parts of the world producing similar crops. This knowledge, he argued, would enable him to make informed decisions about his crop production output, and would thus provide him with the possibility to generate more profits. Again, this gives some indication of the multiple worlds that people can inhabit through the facilities provided by the new technology.

These technological developments and their relationship with various forms of knowledge and information highlight the problems with prevailing definitions of literacy, common understandings of what constitutes literate behaviour, concepts of text and the frameworks in which these are analysed.

The technological development paradigm

What needs to be emphasised here is the fact that the new technology does not only signify a commodity value. As a social practice, it is also infused with *symbolic* meanings which, in turn, derive from the values attached to it in society, and thus the particular societal development models that they underscore. We have seen in the examples of growing poverty in developing countries discussed in Chapters 2 and 3, that economic growth which is grounded in specific economic outputs, does not necessarily include wider variables associated with social development and therefore does not automatically indicate improvement in living conditions. We have also seen in Chapters 3 and 4 that the adoption of 'functional' literacy as a 'quick-fix' strategy in the process of societal modernisation in developing countries ended in failure. Therefore, before we can address definitions of literacy and the relationship between literacy and development in the technological society, we need to clarify conceptions of 'technological capability' and the ways in which they relate to economic, social, political and cultural practices in different societies, and the discursive ways in which these interact with global processes.

Technological capability

From the discussion so far it is evident that the modernisation model of societal development has been replaced by a new model of development centred on 'technological capability'. Technological *capability* refers to the diverse technological knowledges accumulated within society over time, and the ways in which these are harnessed to stimulate the development of the technological and scientific base. Collectively, these contribute to the development of society's overall technological *capacity* which, in turn, depends on:

> the science base of the production and management process, the R&D [research & development] strength, the human resources necessary for technological innovation, the adequate utilisation of new technologies, and the level of their diffusion into the whole network of economic interaction . . . technological capacity is not simply what results from adding up various elements, but is an attribute of a system . . . the science — technology — industry — society (STIS) system. *It refers to the appropriate articulation of science, technology, management, and production in a system of complementaries, each level being provided, by the educational system, with the necessary human resources in skills and quantity.* (Castells, 1996: 103, emphasis added)

Educational contributions are seen as operating on different levels including the development of (1) the capacity of technologies themselves through innovation (research and development), (2) mastery of the technical skills to use a range of technologies and (3) the worker awarenesses required to operate within the STIS system. However, whilst the first indicates a reliance on high-skills training at tertiary level, realistically, these will be required by a relatively small section of the labour force. The second and third, on the other hand, involve mainly functional skills. And, relatedly, the centrality to the technological production process of learning-by-doing integrated into production tasks, indicates a move to on-the-job training and the need for education to develop close links with industry. Further, the organic relationship that exists between technology and the market also signifies a role for education in providing a knowledge of market processes, business management and functional marketing skills.

As is argued earlier, the new technology represented as the *raison d'être* of the re-defined flexible work force required to facilitate economic growth has become the primary means by which the nature of the economic crisis has been articulated in social discourse. Within this framework, the ongoing economic crisis has become reduced to the lack of an adequately trained work force and the need for rational labour management to facilitate productivity.

Millennial issues: Structuring global inequalities

The notion of technological capability as *the* major criterion by which comparative levels of societal development are judged has also been transferred to the developing world. As is mentioned earlier, newly industrialised countries in South-East Asia, notably, Korea, Singapore and Malaysia have been able to secure an informational infrastructure that has enabled them to compete with growing success in the world market. These countries were able to select appropriate technologies, negotiate favourable terms of transfer and to participate in the design and setting up of production plants which allowed for the subsequent successful adaptation and improvement of technologies (Lall *et al.* 1994).

According to a recent report presented to UNESCO by the International Council for Science Policy Studies (1991), although science and technology capabilities constitute important elements in the development process, their full value lies in 'the extent to which they can be embedded in existing structures and blending with prevailing traditions and cultures' (Salomon, 1993: 37). This is more possible in countries that already have an industrial and scientific base than in others who do not. As we have seen in earlier chapters, the cultural and economic heritage of colonialism and the re-inforcement of inequalities in postcolonial contexts, have contributed to the fact that many developing countries, especially in Africa, still lack the necessary infrastructure to support the development of an adequate industrial base, let alone having the capacity to enter the technological development paradigm as equal competitors in the global market place.

The fact that knowledge and information as well as technological skills are concentrated in the developed world has created huge disparities between the industrialised North and the largely unindustrialised South — with very little scope for the latter to 'catch-up' to compete on an equal basis. Dordick and Wang (1993: 5) summarise the dilemma in their argument that:

> Plagued by barriers of poverty, poor health, low life expectancy, illiteracy, and little access to tertiary education, emerging countries must compete with advanced countries in a highly competitive global market place. What does the information society mean to them? Economic growth in the least developed nations of the world has

stagnated or has been increasing very, very slowly. The gap between the developed and lesser-developed nations continues to widen annually. Can these Third World nations ever catch up?

Within many of these societies, the industrial gap is overlapped by the informational gap thereby creating a cycle of under-development.

Literacy and technological development issues

The argument that literacy, defined in terms of reading, writing and numerate ability, is not sufficient to ensure a high quality work force and that higher education is a pre-requisite highlights the major difficulties still to be overcome by developing countries in order to participate meaningfully in the technological society. Many developing countries do not yet have the necessary educational infrastructure to support the development of their human resources. Contributory factors include mis-government, societal corruption, inadequate social policies and, in some instances, natural disasters which have impacted negatively on levels of societal growth.

But, as is argued in Chapter 4, we also need to take account of the impact of global economic structures such as the IMF and the World Bank, on the levels of national development that can take place in developing countries. Industrialisation within developing countries have been financed, to a significant extent, by external capital borrowing, in many instances, accruing national debt to the level of 38% of their gross national product (GNP) (Peet, 1993).

Of importance is the negative impact that the Structural Adjustment Programme (SAP), imposed on borrowing countries by the IMF during the mid-1980s, has had on educational provision in many developing countries. Adopted as a strategy in the management of the economic crisis that followed the OPEC price rises in 1973, the intention of adjustment policies was to 'reduce imbalances, correct some of the policy biases and establish the basis for sustainable growth' (Stewart, 1994: 128). However, by the late 1970s many of these countries were struggling as a result of the worldwide increase in interest rates. This created difficulties with their ability to meet debt-repayment requirements, and was compounded by a decline in markets for their manufactured goods during a period of world recession (Peet, 1993). The resulting impact on educational provision in developing countries has been catastrophic. The Committee for Academic Freedom in Africa (CAFA) (1992: 52) states:

> Social spending in subSaharan African countries (including on education) fell by 26 percent between 1980 and 1985. Statistics showed that enrolment rates were declining in many countries for the first time in

their history. Books, from school primers to physics texts, became scarce commodities. Cash-strapped governments, pressured by World Bank and IMF officials, cut room and board subsidies for secondary and tertiary level students, who had to end their studies or continue in demoralising living conditions.

Caillods and Postlethwaite (1995), using information gained from the International Institute for Educational Planning (IIEP) surveys conducted in developing countries during the 1980s, similarly argue that teaching resources, especially books, pencils, pupils' slates, chalk, maps, charts and blackboards are in short supply in many countries. They report, for example, that in the Kilosa district of Tanzania, 'pupils had no textbooks at all in 52 per cent of the schools and there was an insufficiency in 79 per cent of them' (Caillods & Postlethwaite, 1995: 6). They argue further that:

> The fact that pupils rarely have any opportunity to read or study from printed material has probably serious consequences for the development of literacy skills. What can pupils learn, seldom reading, listening to a teacher who is not necessarily well trained or motivated, and not always able to exercise or transcribe what they have heard because of lack of exercise books or slates? (Caillods & Postlethwaite, 1995: 7)

These concerns are borne out in World Bank studies. According to Stewart (1994) a 1991 World Bank study found that education had declined in many developing countries as a result of the SAP. This was shown in three educational indicators including the 'education allocation ratio, education per capita and gross primary school enrolment rates — as compared to other countries' (Stewart, 1994: 140).

The main focus of World Bank interest in education in developing countries since the 1980s has been the need to streamline higher education to operate at regional level, expanding primary education and vocational on-the-job and in-service training for those in the middle (Sivanandan, 1989). Underlying this is the belief that developing countries tend to over-produce graduates who cannot be absorbed into the labour market (Delors, 1996). Within the de-centralised framework advocated, primary and secondary schools would be run by 'local communities, religious institutions and private companies taking up the cost of paying for teachers, school equipment and buildings' (Sivanandan, 1989: 54). This development in relation to NGOs was discussed in Chapter 3.

This contrasts with arguments made by developing countries for the re-organisation of educational systems, appropriate curricula and the expansion of the university sector to 'educate the nation on the realities of living in a technological and scientific age' (Porter, 1986: 106). Thus, although the World Bank (1989) frames its educational discourse in terms of the fact that:

> to survive and compete in a competitive world in the twenty-first century, Africa will require not only literate and numerate citizens, but also highly qualified and trained people to perform top-quality research, formulate policies, and implement programs essential to economic growth and development,

the neo-classical market policies that it pursues in developing countries, and the privatisation of the educational base, preclude the possibility of this taking place. Neo-classical market policies include increasing direct costs of education, reducing public sector employment (of which education is part), holding down income levels and reducing government expenditure (Stewart, 1994). These factors and the expanded role envisaged for NGOs discussed in Chapter 3, raise fundamental questions about the re-definition of real power with regard to setting societal development goals in many developing countries.

As we have seen, mass literacy and numeracy do not in themselves provide the basis for economic development. Indeed, Graff (1987: 31) maintains that 'early industrialisation, the evidence from a number of studies agrees, owed little to literacy or the school; its demands upon the labor force were rarely intellectual or cognitive in nature', that it was the ideological role of literacy that was important in shaping new cultural awarenesses and expectations.

Whilst the same argument can be applied to the emerging technological development paradigm, I want to argue that the centrality of knowledge and information to the production process necessitates a systematically organised and coordinated educational provision which includes universal primary education and equality of access to *all* levels of education as the *basis* for the development of a country's technological capability.

Literacy, knowledge and developing technological capability

The centrality of technology in the capital accumulation process and, in particular, the production process has, in the first instance, foregrounded the significance of *technological mastery*, thus emphasising technical skills and knowledge focusing on technological capacity building. In the second instance, as has been indicated earlier, the increased demand for innovation in order to respond to ever-changing market demands as well as market competition, has shifted emphasis onto research and development (R&D), learning by doing, problem-solving and skills adaptation. These are not unproblematic issues since much would depend on the types of technologies chosen for development and the potential uses to which they will be put.

Lall *et al.* (1994) identify a range of capabilities involved in technological mastery:

- Investment capability which requires the skills and knowledge to identify feasible investment projects, purchasing skills to acquire suitable technologies, plant design and managing. This requires technical knowledges and skills, an understanding of technological processes, the merits and suitability of particular technologies for particular purposes, design and planning skills, business knowledge and management skills including finance management.
- Production capabilities which include the skills and knowledge required to operate and maintain production industries; adapting and improving technology; innovation, experimentation; work process management. This requires technical know-how, knowledge of systems and environments, management skills, research skills, knowledge of production processes including quality control.
- Linkage capabilities which include establishing and maintaining 'production and technological links with other firms and institutions' (Lall *et al.*, 1994: 13) which involve setting up networks of cooperative relationships which enable transfer of technological information, skills and plans between enterprises. Adequate levels of communication skills, information gathering and dissemination, analytical and organisation skills are important to this process taking place effectively.

Over and above the need for technical expertise, within a framework geared towards sustainable development, the role of education also extends to the inculcation of an understanding of technological and scientific processes and their potential impacts on society. This derives from the fact that both technological development and the various applications of technologies are subject to human choice exercised within a context where a range of other choices prevail. If we take account of the concept of sustainable development identified by the Brundtland Report, *Our Common Future*, discussed in an earlier chapter, societies must be enabled to make their own choices and decisions on the appropriateness of different technologies to sustain their societies not only economically, but also ecologically, and culturally. This relies on a secured scientific and technological knowledge base as well as an understanding of the potential impacts and effects of particular technologies on cultural ways of life, the ecology as well as social institutions and processes.

North/South technological divide

Whilst industrialised countries are already in the process of addressing some of these issues through educational programmes, this is not yet the case in many developing countries, especially throughout Africa. There are vast disparities between poverty-stricken developing and industrially rich countries. Delors (1996) gives an indication of the inequalities with regard to the levels of investment in R & D in these countries. He argues that 'in 1990, 42.8 per cent of R & D spending was in North America and 23.2 per cent in Europe, as against 0.2 per cent in subSaharan Africa and 0.7 per cent in the Arab States' (Delors, 1996: 72).

Developing countries lack not only the necessary funds to invest in research, but also the scientific and technological expertise, and this is exacerbated by the brain drain to the rich countries. R & D depends on risk-taking and 'presupposes the existence of an environment already adequately provided with scientific resources' (Delors, 1996: 72). Delors goes on to argue that technological transfer from the industrialised world to developing countries 'require a favourable environment that marshals and makes the most of local knowledge, enabling genuine assimilation of the technologies to take place in the context of endogenous development' (Delors, 1996:72). The gaps in knowledge and skills that exist in developing countries therefore pose a major problem in the development of their technological capability.

Malecki (1991) maintains that many developing countries have a major lack of local technological skills, the 'know-how' and 'know-why' of modern technology. In Tanzania, for example, the fact that industrialisation has developed very slowly has impacted negatively on the availability of technological skills in the country. Malecki (1991: 144), in his discussion of the particular situation that exists in Tanzania, argues:

> The level of technological dependence in Tanzania is extreme. In importing technology, the country had too few nationals qualified in branches of engineering, economics, production management, laws of international trade and patent rights, and had very little access to global information on the sources and comparative costs of technology.

This, and the lack of educational resources mentioned earlier, lend a different view to the much celebrated 'success' of the country's 20-year mass literacy campaign discussed in Chapter 4. And, as is argued in Chapter 3, education for 'self-reliance', which formed the basis of President Nyerere's social policy, was to be undermined by budget-deficits, rising inflation and falling investment by debt-burden and, finally, by the controls exercised by the World Bank's Structural Adjustment Programme.

Again, this highlights the importance of the need to rise above the rhetoric of globalisation and to consider the complex ways in which social processes now interact with international structures, institutions and processes, the power relations that traverse this terrain, and the ways in which these factors influence the range of educational and technological choices available to developing countries.

Unless developing countries have their own technical and technological as well as research and development (R&D) expertise, they will be dependent on external technological support provided by multinational and transnational agencies and corporations who then have the power to define national development priorities. Delors (1996: 73) summarises these concerns about unequal development in his argument:

> One of the international community's primary causes of concern must be the risk of total marginalisation facing those who have been excluded from progress in a rapidly changing world economy. Unless a vigorous effort is made to obviate this risk, some countries that lack the wherewithal to join in international tecnological competition are liable to become enclaves of poverty, despair or violence that cannot be eliminated by aid and humanitarian action.

However, Delors' reduction of unequal technological development to 'the uneven distribution of knowledge and skills', ignores broader contributory factors such as the stranglehold placed on social policy within these contexts by the adjustment criteria of the IMF and the World Bank discussed throughout the book. The interdependent nature of life within the global cultural community means that developing the technological capability of these countries cannot be addressed meaningfully outside an analysis of the imposed technocratic principles that underscore the economic and social development of industrialising countries.

Conclusion

The changes currently taking place globally as a result of the applications and uses of the new microelectronics technology, because of the complex and organic ways in which the new technology interacts with both societal and global processes, present unique difficulties to analyses of the nature and scope of the changes taking place. This relates, in part, to the fact that we are part of that process of change that is still taking place. And, therefore, although we can analyse and interpret shifts in terms of skills and knowledge requirements, we cannot provide definitive projections on how these changes will ultimately work out within the life of different societies.

This chapter has explored the multilevelled changes brought about by new technologies in the organisation, structures and institutions of modern society, within three different sociohistorical milieux. What is evident is that technological change, rather than heralding clear breaks with the past, has, historically, *transformed societies from within over a period of time*. As industrial technology did during the late 19th century, the new information technology has effected concrete changes that are reflected in the ways in which organisations and institutions operate on an everyday basis. These, in turn, have impacted on how we work and live within the technological society.

Literacy, both as a set of skills and as a way of knowing, was not a pre-requisite of the different phases of the industrial revolution. It did, however, serve as a powerful *mediating factor* of a particular model of societal development at the time. Thus it served to shape the 'social character' to meet the new cultural and ideological awarenesses of an emergent modern capitalism.

Although the ideological role of literacy is sustained within the current milieu, as a key defining factor of social change, it has been superseded by the concept of *technological capability* within the new development paradigm. We have seen, for example, that changes effected in the production process accentuate the importance of not only functional literacy and technical skills but also new awarenesses within the labour process. The emphasis on both worker and skills flexibility, and the need for learning-by-doing, indicates the necessity for a re-conceptualisation of educational frameworks and processes that lie beyond uniform 'core' knowledges and skills located within borderised disciplines. Indeed, the emergence of 'a new set of worker competencies' (Levin & Rumberger, 1995: 84) identifies further issues, many of which include literacy skills, knowledges and behaviours, to be addressed in educational settings. These are summarised in Table 5.1.

The competencies identified by Levin and Rumberger indicate a strong relationship with particular sets of practical skills, awarenesses as well as adequate levels of both 'analytical' and 'communicative competence' to be acquired through education in order to facilitate individual efficacy in a rapidly changing world. In addition, the multiskilling required increasingly in the production process and service sector jobs as well as other information technology related employment, suggest the need for

> a different kind of worker, one who is not only prepared in terms of cognitive knowledge, but who also has the abilities to take advantage of a work-place requiring greater participation . . . as work-places

Table 5.1 Worker competencies within the technological paradigm

(1)	Initiative, that is, 'the drive and creative ability to think and perform independently' — which suggests independent goal-directed learning experiences.
(2)	Cooperation: 'constructive, goal-directed interaction with others' which suggests interactive, collaborative learning focused on particular outcomes.
(3)	Working in groups: 'interaction in work-groups directed towards both short-term goals of efficient task or activity accomplishment and the long-term goal of group maintenance'.
(4)	Peer-training: learning-by-doing integrated into team tasks, highlighting the importance of engaging learners in 'peer tutoring'.
(5)	Evaluation: 'appraisal, assessment and certification of the quality of a product or service' indicating the importance of building evaluation into learning tasks.
(6)	Communication: 'the appropriate uses of spoken, written and kinetic communication as well as good listening, reading comprehension and interpretive skills for receiving messages'.
(7)	Reasoning: 'evaluation and generation of logical arguments including both inductive and deductive approaches' which suggests experience in open and practical learning tasks structured to develop a range of analytical skills.
(8)	Problem-solving: open learning tasks that allow for hypothesising, generating solutions, implementing plans and evaluating them; organisation skills.
(9)	Decision-making: 'employing the elements of problem-solving on an on-going basis in the workplace' suggesting practice in making informed decisions on the basis of information as well as in relation to evolving situations within a defined framework; research skills.
(10)	Obtaining and using information: media access skills, information retrieval skills, data-processing; data applications — research skills.
(11)	Planning: prioritising activies; goal-directed learning.
(12)	Learning skills: 'cognitive and affective skills that facilitate the acquisition of new knowledge as needed': flexible learning approaches suited to particular learning tasks.
(13)	Multicultural skills: 'understanding how to work with persons from other cultures in terms of language, communication styles and different values' — interpersonal skills.

change over the four decades or so of a working life, workers must have the grounding to learn new tasks and new ways of doing work in response to changes in technology, work organisation, and new products. (Levin & Rumberger, 1995: 86)

These skills, knowledges and awarenesses coincide with Bakhtin's topology of social discourses necessary for functioning in everyday life discussed in Chapter 1. These factors bring to the fore new considerations for the ways in which literacy is conceptualised and defined in the technological development paradigm. I return to this discussion again in Chapter 7.

Chapter 6

Changing Definitions of 'Text' within the Information Society

The previous chapter examined the multilevelled way in which microelectronics technology has transformed our experience of everyday life. It focused on the changes brought about in the labour process and, particularly, the impact of the new technology on the changing nature of work. It suggested that the skills and awarenesses required within the re-structured labour process identify new areas for consideration in the conceptualisation of literacy and, relatedly, knowledge needs within society.

I continue that discussion in this chapter with a specific emphasis on the impact of information technology on conceptualisations of text and, relatedly, literacy within a changing global cultural economy. The underlying argument is that the ongoing debate about literacy and social and individual development becomes more problematic and urgent, if considered against the fact that within a rapidly changing global cultural economy, the literacy goal posts have already been shifted by the multiple facilities offered by new computer technologies. In an era in which information technology is seen as underscoring both cultural and economic development, we need to define the concept of information concretely in terms of its cultural, technological and economic applications — and their relative use to both societal and individual development.

The first section of the chapter explores changing concepts of text in relation to the argument that 'the form of presentation of human thought has a great deal of influence on its content' (Zariski, 1995: 1), and that this frames the range of knowledges and meaning production that are possible. The second section examines the social construction of the 'information society'. It argues that what is 'useful' information, that is, what we all should know and possess in order to function adequately in the information society, needs to be subjected to further scrutiny with regard to the comparative value attached to different forms of knowledge within the culture, the power interests that underscore these meanings as well as the multiple controls exercised over particular forms of knowledge.

Mapping a Typology of 'Texts'

'Textuality' as a concrete expression of thought and knowledge has historically been grounded in institutions such as the academy, archives and libraries that are comprised of producers, compilers and dispensers of information to support scholarship. Primacy has historically been given to the written or printed word as the means by which the concept of 'text' as the basis of theoretical knowledge has been defined. However, the literacy process and our experience of the social world, it is increasingly argued, have been transformed fundamentally by computer technology (Bolter, 1991; Delaney & Landow, 1991; Landow, 1994; Taylor & Saarinen, 1994). These writers, and many others, suggest that, compared to the facilities offered by the computer, both conventional writing and print technology are laborious processes that make the task of composing, organising, revising and presenting ideas a complex experience. The on-screen reading experience, it is argued, has made it possible for readers to access, retrieve and process larger units of information as well as different types of information at any one time than has been possible with conventionally written and print texts.

Indeed, it is claimed that the very concept of text has changed within the technological paradigm and that as a result, 'the idea and ideal of the book will change: print will no longer define the organisation and presentation of knowledge, as it has for the past five centuries' (Bolter, 1990: 2). This would suggest that the concept of 'text' and, relatedly, literacy is undergoing a process of transformation that would make certain forms of literacy experiences obsolete within the foreseeable future. If this is the case, then it would have major implications for provision for educational programmes and also for considerations of literacy and social development.

In order to explore the validity of this claim further, the next section uses different concepts of text, and the technologies that contributed to their development, as the basis of analysis in order to examine changing views and definitions of literacy, knowledge and information. It provides a schematic exposition of a range of historically-specific produced texts, and examines these in terms of:

(1) their organisational aspects including literal and technical features, structures and practices that make for 'readable' texts with regard to access and retrieval of information;
(2) their interpretive frameworks which refer to the range of semantic possibilities inherent in the actual reading of the text; and
(3) the social impacts of different representational texts within particular sociohistorical milieux.

Conventional written and print text

Informational and organisational features

Within print culture, in a literal and technical sense, text is defined in terms of logographic representation which derives its stability from the permanence of the written form or script. Conventionally written and print texts are generally regarded as being linear in their sequential construction; that is, having a beginning, middle and end which signify an order in which they are to be read; thus they are regarded as bounded and fixed. However, this view excludes the fact that association is intrinsic to the writing process in which 'one word echoes another; one sentence or paragraph recalls others earlier in the text and looks forward to still others...[so that] the result is always a network of verbal elements' (Bolter, 1991: 109, information in brackets added). These 'interactive' organisational features include both associations and intra-textual hierarchies that provide the means by which overall textual coherence is secured, and are intrinsic to the process of textual construction. Another externally located nonlinear feature is the practice of classifying written texts into different *genre* that adhere to particular literary and textual conventions, provide specific forms of information, engage in and are embedded in specific discourses and serve different reading purposes. Thus we deal with both various forms and content in different textual genres.

In addition, nonlinear features have been structured into the modern book where hierarchies and association have been incorporated through the use not only of paragraphs, but also headings and subheadings as well as footnotes, tables of content and indices. Bolter (1991: 110) outlines the discursive sets of association made possible by the use of the index:

> An index permits the reader to locate passages that share the same word, phrase, or subject and so associates passages that may be widely separated in the pagination of the book. In one sense the index defines other books that could be constructed from the materials at hand, other themes that the author could have formed into an analytical narrative, and so invites the reader to read the book in alternative ways. An index transforms a book from a tree into a network, offering multiplicity in place of a single order of paragraphs and pages.

Features such as indices provide an inter-textual link with related themes and topics, offer the potential for the production of a range of meanings and also the possibility to construct other texts. Yet, although written texts are situated in a discursive network of textual relations, the print medium keeps most of these out of sight and 'relatively difficult to follow — because the referenced [or linked] material lie spatially distant from the reference mark' (Bolter, 1990 : 5). The task of locating discursive information is made more difficult by the dispersal of locations as well as the time and effort involved in accessing different information sources. Moreover, books also call for huge library stocks as well as the infrastructure and complex management requirements that are thus engendered.

Interpretive framework

Friedman (1995: 73) emphasises the fact that 'no text exists until it is engaged by a subject — textuality is always an interactive, creative process'. Thus, in addition to external and internal structural features, nonlinearity is achieved also through the reading process. Readers bring their own subjective understandings to what they read — linking again with their knowledge of similar, or oppositional texts as well as social and cultural knowledges, their histories and social experiences. Conventional written and print texts therefore allow for *discursive interpretation*. These factors including what has been referred to as the 'metaphysics' of textual interpretation, at least semantically, disrupt the structured stability of the text rendering it more malleable in terms of meaning production.

The metaphysics of the text

The 'metaphysics' of the text, which had its genesis in critical literary theory, identifies additional textual dimensions. I will discuss this in some detail here since, as will become evident later, it has much relevance to textual analysis across different media technologies. Within this analytical framework, texts are seen to signify not only encoded meanings but also as themselves being engaged in a dialogical relationship with other texts; other signifying discourses.

Barthes (1987: 137) states that 'what founds the text is not an internal, closed, accountable structure, but the outlet of the text on to other texts, other codes, other signs; what makes the text is the intertextual'. This is underscored and extended in Todorov's (1984: x) exposition of Bakhtin's concept of *dialogism* in which he posits the view that:

> all discourse is in dialogue with previous discourses on the same subject, as well as with discourses yet to come, whose reactions it foresees and anticipates. A single voice can make itself heard only by blending into the complex choir of other voices already in place. This is true not only of literature but of all discourse.

Polyphony, or multivocality, according to Bakhtin, is an integral feature of all discourse. Materially constituted within specific ideological milieux, texts enter into dialogue with social and political discourses and the institutions, processes and practices in which they are embedded. At the same time, they also engage in dialogue with individual and collective users who, as already argued, bring to them their own subjective meanings. To concretise this point I will focus on the multiple meanings that surround school textbooks. School textbooks are sanctioned overtly, or implicitly, by state policy and thus they mediate dominant or consensual views of knowledge and of learning. Their use and application, however, would depend on teachers' subjective understandings or interpretations of policy meanings. Reading the text is, therefore, not merely a process of assimilation or reception, 'it is an act of production' (Johnson, 1983: 41) which gives rise to the possibility for creating alternative or even oppositional meanings.

In representing selective views of reality, texts also mediate social and cultural 'truths'. According to Foucault (1970: 56):

> there is scarcely a society without its major narratives, which are recounted, repeated, and varied; formulae, texts, and ritualised sets of discourses which are recited in well-defined circumstances; things said once and preserved because it is suspected that behind them there is a secret or a treasure...those which give rise to a certain number of new speech acts which take them up, transform them or speak of them, in short, those discourses which, over and above their formulation, are said indefinitely, remain said, and are to be said again. We know them in our own cultural system: they are religious or juridical texts, but also those texts which are called 'literary'; and to a certain extent, scientific texts.

This view can be seen to coincide with Williams' (1980) notion of the 'selective tradition' through which the making and remaking of a dominant culture is secured within and through institutionalised literary practices. Texts are 'historically linked to a whole world of institutions: the law, the Church, literature, education' (Barthes, 1987: 32), and thus they are imbued with specific ideological values and beliefs that are embedded in specific forms of power.

Texts have authors and also convey messages and meanings in terms of the values and intentions of the writers as well as the particular genre, and the culture within which they are produced (Aarseth, 1994). Meanings, therefore, can be altered not only in interpretation but can also be distorted in the gaps and silences created by censorship of the written word by authors themselves or other external political and cultural agents. In contrast to Barthes' view that there is no closure with regard to the range of meanings that can be produced within and through the text, Said (1984: 48) argues that texts are intrinsically related with 'ownership, authority, power and the imposition of force' which serve to limit the range of meanings that can be produced within particular contexts. I will return to this again later.

At meta-level, texts also represent 'virtual worlds' in which we participate as either spectators in other people's lives or events, or through which we can come to a better understanding of the world in which we live, or through which we can construct other possibilities, other alternative realities in our imaginings .

Collectively, these multilevelled aspects of meaning production broadly identify the dimensions that traditionally have framed textual analysis, most particularly, of literary genres. As will be discussed later, these factors identify areas to be considered in discussions of different literacy practices as well as the discourse structures in which they are grounded.

Social impacts of print-text

The development of written forms and later, print-text, gave rise to the concept of literacy and the development of communication beyond the immediate context of interaction. The possibility that it provided for the processing of larger units of information as well as the opportunity that it offered to reflect on written thought, contributed to the development of systematised forms of knowledge (Goody & Watt, 1968). The development of print also greatly increased the volume of knowledge which, in turn, created the need for organising information.

The social impacts of print or conventional written text and, relatedly, literacy on particular societies; the power/knowledge discourses that have historically framed its dissemination and the forms of literacy made available to different groups of people in different sociohistorical contexts; as well as the political economy of different print-literacy knowledges during different sociohistorical epochs have been discussed in previous chapters. In order to chart the impact of technological developments on conceptions of text and textuality, the next section will provide a brief discussion of different media texts. The concept of media here refers to text production using different technological processes.

Photography

Informational and organisational features

The advent of the image as text, particularly represented in the photograph during the mid-19th century, 'restored gesture to the human technology of recording experience' (McLuhan, 1994: 193). McLuhan goes on to argue that:

> by conferring a means of self-delineation of objects, of 'statement without syntax', photography gave impetus to a delineation of the

inner world. Statement without syntax or verbalisation was really statement by gesture, by mime, and by gestalt. (p. 201)

Although constituted as 'visual language' the photograph is, nevertheless, fundamentally 'invaded with language: in memory, in association, snatches of words and images continually intermingle and alternate' (Burgin, 1984: 226). Indeed, Sontag (1979: 3) views the photograph as 'a grammar and, even more importantly, an ethics of seeing'.

As *textual constructions*, photographs record images of persons, objects, events and places and, as such, constitute reflections of everyday reality. As *artistic compositions* they reflect different interpretations or views of reality. As *informational sources*, they gain meaning and value within the contexts in which they are used, for example, in newspapers, family albums, books, archives, museums, galleries, courts of law, the church, advertising. They are retrieved as informational sources to provide evidence and justification that something happened, exists or did exist.

Interpretive framework

Photography emerged during the printing era of communication (Rogers, 1986), was one-dimensional in its constitution and, like print text, did not allow for interactive communication. The photograph supported print textuality; bringing with it graphic or iconic forms of representation which lay beyond the orthodoxy of literary analysis.

Barthes (1971) identifies three aspects involved in the interpretation of photographic text, namely, the linguistic message, a coded iconic message and an uncoded iconic message. He suggests that:

one way of approaching the apparently uncoded message, that is, the literal image of the photograph, is to start with the linguistic message, then examine the literal message (denotation) and finally examine the overall symbolic meaning of the message (connotation). (Quoted in Bennett, 1986: 99)

Both denotative and connotative interpretation, however, belong to the same process of meaning-making; they cannot, realistically, be separated. Like print text, the production of meaning would take place with the reader drawing discursively on meanings communicated or transferred intertextually, through cultural significations, the ideological meanings that prevail within the institutional and social context as well as the discursive social, cultural and political knowledges brought to the process of interpretation by the reader. Meaning production would, therefore, rely to a significant extent on meta-linguistic or second-order thinking skills including reflection, evaluation and interpretation which generate more textured sets of meaning to those produced in the literal and technical act of communication (denotation).

Presented as reflections of reality, the photograph constitutes a discursive text which is subject to analysis in terms of not only its composition, that is, its framing of content, intentions, purposes, themes and narrative but also its codes, its symbolic meanings or significations; its legitimation of myths drawing on the existing maps of meaning within the culture. Applied to different social practices such as advertising, professional photography and the leisure industries, photographic text enters the terrain of pseudo-reality. It obtains specific meaning from the context in which it is used and the particular use to which it is put, for example, to advertise either commodities or services, or as representations or evidence of real events in newspapers. Thus they can become part of different discourse ensembles. As meta-narratives, photographs also represent 'virtual worlds' in which we participate as connoisseurs of art or as readers of images and as consumers of culture.

Similar issues to those that surround the author of written or print texts surround the photographer's choice and framing of the subject. According to Berger (1972: 10), photographs are not mechanical records of reality; 'the photographer's way of seeing is reflected in his choice of subject' as well as the way in which the subject is framed. Thus they provide selective views of reality, and represent choices exercised over and above other choices available to the photographer. The selection of photographs to support particular written narratives or _vice versa_ plays a key role in the social construction of reality; it serves to construct preferred knowledges, and also preferred readings of the text. Photographs are subject to forms of censorship similar to those that are applied to print text and thus they are constituted in 'power/knowledge discourses' (Foucault, 1980).

Social impacts of the photograph

Photography complemented telegraphically-transferred information. These two media combined to form the basis of a new form of text production, altering further our _ways of seeing_ and _ways of knowing_ the world. Until the advent of telecommunications, first represented in the telegraph, 'information could travel only as fast as the messengers who carried it; communication of information and transportation of people and materials were not separated in meaning' (Rogers, 1986: 29). Telegraphing altered both the range and nature of information that could be made available in newspapers; it 'made possible, indeed demanded, systematic cooperative news gathering by the nation's press' (Czitrom, 1982: 16) and 'transformed the newspaper from a personal journal and party organ into primarily a disseminator of news' (Czitrom, 1982: 18). It made possible the diverse ways in which photographs could be utilised, supported by print text. And, in the process, a new reading public was created. The powerful role that this combination of text media played in the social construction of reality, according to Postman (1986: 74), challenged 'our dominant means for construing, understanding and testing reality'.

Wider uses of photography, for example, radiography and X-ray photography, aerial photography and satellite photography have allowed the gaze of surveillance to penetrate our bodies and almost all aspects of our lives.

Sound and image as text

Informational features

Audio-visual texts such as television, video and film (referred to here as media-text) have transformed previous conceptions of text to incorporate image (visual language) as well as sound, motion and different forms of media language (Corner, 1983). Media language includes the 'literal' which refers to particular linguistic forms, styles and registers used in the construction of media texts as well as the language used by those working with the media, and the 'metaphorical' which relates to the institutional practices, forms and conventions that frame the meanings generated in the production of media texts (Corner, 1983).

Media texts, like print text and the photograph, are classified also into different discourse genres adhering to their own textual and literary conventions. Although two-dimensional in representational form, and interpersonal in presentation, media text is not interactive — it communicates one-to-many and thus constitutes a mass communication practice. In the case of television and video, information is provided on a screen via a network of cables and satellite which emanate in centralised communications centres. The dissemination of information derives from a diverse range of organisational structures and human resources.

Media text follows the narrative structure of written text in that it has a beginning, middle and end that frame the sequential order in which it is to be read. Nonlinearity is derived, technically, from the re-ordering of frames in different genre, for example, flashbacks, inserts or intercuts which provide referential dimensions to the text. This re-ordering of sequence provides a way of studying not only filmic forms but also 'seeing how filmic forms engage concepts and represent ideas' (Turim, 1989: 1). Turim suggests that 'the flashback is a privileged moment in unfolding that juxtaposes different moments of temporal reference' providing a juncture between past and present. Flashbacks provide us with referential information drawing on 'the personal archives of the past' as well as 'images of history, the shared and remembered past' (Turim, 1989: 2). These organisational features also provide the possibility for exploring thought processes, ideas or 'circuitous investigations of enigmas' (Turim, 1989: 6). Flashbacks are often amplified by voice-overs, dialogue or inter-titles which signify shifts in foci, location and time sequencing.

Interpretive framework

Whilst it retains most of the analytic dimensions identified in the interpretive frameworks for print, conventional written text and photography, media text requires additional categories to analyse iconic or visual languages as a system of sign. This refers to the symbolic messages and meanings structured into media texts, inter-textual links, multilevelled sets of interpretive codes including those embedded in culture, society and the institution. It also refers to discourse styles employed within media genre, compositional techniques, programming, selective choice in the dissemination of information, the social construction of preferred meanings or the 'power/knowledge discourses' (Foucault, 1980) that frame text production, subjective and selective reception of messages.

Media texts are constituted in polyphonic discourses, that is to say, they are permeated by different voices. They are also polysemic in that they convey, reflect and signify discursive sets of meaning, not only as texts, but also in relation to their context of production. Represented in different genre, for example, documentary text, news production, or soap operas, their narrative style simultaneously constructs and mediates specific views and aspects of reality.

Social effects

Media text brought with it the power of the mobilised virtual gaze (Friedberg, 1994: 60). Although evident in all forms of visual representation, the virtual gaze was reproduced most in photography. The cinema combined the mobile with the virtual gaze, changing thus in cinematic spectatorship, 'the concepts of the *present* and the *real*' (Friedberg, 1994: 60, original emphases). Discussing its impact on cultural change, Friedberg (1994: 60) goes on to argue:

> During the mid-nineteenth century, the coincident introduction of department store shopping, packaged tourism, and protocinematic entertainment began to transform this gaze into a *commodity*, sold to a consumer-spectator. In postmodernity, the spatial and temporal displacements of a mobilised virtual gaze are now as much a part of the public sphere (in, for example, the shopping mall and multiplex cinema) as they are part of the private (at home, with the television and

the VCR). The boundaries between public and private, already fragile in modernity, have now been more fully eroded. (original emphasis)

Media texts in their content, subjects, process and technique therefore play a central role in the social construction of reality. Its ubiquity has ensured that television provides the primary mass communication medium through which we come to know and vicariously participate in the modern world. 'Reality' is presented in 24 hr cycles of programmes into which consumers dip to satisfy a range of interests and addictions. However, although they seemingly have infinite choice amongst the variety of channels, offering sometimes very much the same fare, depth and substance are rather thinly spread. Children at the age of three are already faithful consumers and connoisseurs of media stylistics, commodities and myths. New multiple identities are in the making.

Underlining the ubiquity of video in our everyday lives, Friedberg (1994: 74) maintains:

> The multiplex cinema and the VCR have taken the flânerie of the mobilised gaze and recast it into a more accessible and repeatable exponent. In this way, the VCR has become a privatised museum of past moments — of different genres, times, and commodities — all reduced to uniform, interchangeable, equally accessible units...The videocassette turns film experience into a book-size, readily available commodity.

The VCR also reconstructs temporal reality in that it allows us:

> to organise a time which is not our own to a *deferred time*, a time which is somewhere else — and to capture it...Time shifting removes the ontology of live television and aligns televisual reception with the elsewhere and elsewhen that have always characterised cinematic spectatorship. (Virilio, 1988, quoted in Friedberg, 1994: 74) (original emphasis)

Computer Text

Arguing that writing is always spatial and that each writing technology has provided the writer, historically, with new spaces to explore, Bolter (1991) maintains that we are still in the process of coming to terms with the new writing space provided by the computer. Thus he argues that 'different computer programs have given us different geometries with which to structure this new writing space' (Bolter, 1991: 105). Electronic publishing includes a variety of textual forms including desktop publishing which involves print-out, 'computer diskettes and CD-ROMs, hypercard stacks, and networked information texts — the dissemination of text over electronic mail networks' (Amiran *et al.*, 1992: 1). Of these, hypertext and hypermedia have recently stimulated much interest and debate amongst scholars.

Hypertext and Hypermedia

Informational and organisational features

Friedman (1995: 74) describes hypertext as:

> software that allows many different texts to be linked, so that simply clicking a mouse on a key word brings up a new related document. It can be used to create fiction with myriad forking paths or to organise concordances and footnotes that do not simply supply page numbers but instantaneously call up whole documents, each of which in turn can be linked with other documents.

Whereas nonlinearity in the printed book features as additional supports to the text in the form of, for example, footnotes and indices, with hypertext, association is made available via electronic links that make it possible for the reader to move between different texts which may include on-screen written-text, graphics, sound and/or moving images. This integration of different forms of data is referred to as *hypermedia* (Gilster, 1996). Gilster underlines the importance of the multifaceted features provided by hypertext and hypermedia in making access to different range of information a much less complicated and burdensome experience than has been the case with the printed book. He states that:

> Rather than noting a footnote number following a sentence, then checking the back of the book for the right reference, you are able to press a key at the marked place and instantly retrieve the linked data. And, instead of setting up a single link, it (is) possible to create a document with numerous connections, each of which opens to other documents containing numerous connections, so that reading this material now loses its sequential nature entirely and becomes a pursuit of ideas through a forest of data. (Gilster, 1996: 12)

Within this environment the reading process is defined by the specific reading purpose. That is to say, readers need only to access the information that is suited to their particular tasks, or that which they are interested in. Hypertext thus transcends the linear, bounded and fixed qualities of conventional written text, and 'unlike the static form of the book, a hypertext can be composed, and read, non-sequentially; it is a variable structure, composed of blocks of text and the electronic links that join them' (Landow & Delaney, 1991: 3). Having progressed from the linearity of word processing and the two-dimensional hierarchies offered by outline process-ing, Bolter (1991: 105) maintains that hypertext has necessitated a redefini-tion of text 'both as a structure of visible elements on the screen and as a structure of signs in the minds of writers and their readers' .

Here then we have a view of a *discursively constructed* text in which networks seemingly can extend indefinitely, using different media forms within a new geometry of writing space that is easily accessible to the reader or information user. Hypertext and hypermedia also provide a means of easy access to information retrieval and note-taking. Barrett (1989: xxi), for example, states:

> It permits the user to assemble an integration of texts partly through dictating structures of meanings [by pathways or windows] and partly through an absence of direction: it offers a suspension of meanings on various levels that the user can string and restring under the impulse of developing an idea.

This indicates a measure of malleability that is not available in the printed book.

At the same time, however, it does not necessarily imply the develop-ment of understanding by the user who could easily be overwhelmed by the 'aggregation of discrete planes of information, rather than [being engaged in] the unique structuring of ideas for a particular purpose' (Barrett, 1989, xx, information in brackets added). Barrett emphasises the fact that the usefulness of hypertext relies on the quality of the database, as well as the opportunity that it provides the user to engage in 'thinking-with' online information which can contribute to the development of knowledge. Without this, he argues, hypertext and hypermedia run the risk of remaining in the realms of 'knowledge representation' (1989: xx).

Interpretative framework

Hypertext and hypermedia in their very constitution demand non-se-quential reading and promote non-sequential thinking in that texts are set up within a discursive network. Whereas in the case of the book, a canonical order is indicated by pagination, Bolter (1991: 112) maintains that:

> a hypertext has no canonical order. Every path defines an equally convincing and appropriate reading, and in that simple fact, the reader's relationship to the text changes radically. A text as a network has no univocal sense; it is a multiplicity without the imposition of a principle of domination.

Again, this subscribes to Bakhtin's view of the multivocality of the text and also gives concrete expression to his view on the diversity of discourses, which become available in very a literal sense, in the hypertext environment.

Computer-generated text and, more specifically, hypertext also share many interpretative features with literary text (Landow, 1994). Electronic linking inherent in the setting up of hypertexts allows users to draw intertextually on a range of other related texts which may be of the same or different genre, as well as different media. Hypertext environments offer the opportunity to contextualise, for example, a literary work within a broader framework consisting of different translations, literary criticism, social history, film, discussion and biographical information. By thus eroding subject boundaries, at least analytically, hypertext could provide a useful means of supporting multidisciplinary inquiry as well as stimulate the pursuit of border pedagogies (see Chapter 8). In this sense we can have 'a single work which may in turn be a web written for reading on line, one adapted from a printed work, or one adapted with such amplification so as to become a hybrid; and a web can also take the form of groupings of such subsets' (Landow, 1994: 14). As such, it can be seen as a textual collage providing layers of representations and interpretations of reality. In addition, we have hypertexts that allow the reader to *add* text and hyperlinks — an interactive process which transforms the role, power and status of the author.

Unlike print, electronic text is not spatially fixed; it is always subject to change depending on the defined literacy purpose. Similarly, meanings are also not fixed, they are subject to alteration depending on not only the reader's subjective interpretation of the text, but also on the range of meanings made available by the discursive sets of other texts that have been electronically linked as subtexts or meta-texts to the main block of text. In terms of this, Delaney and Landow (1991: 10) state:

> The necessary contextualisation and intertextuality produced by situating individual reading units within a network of easily navigable pathways weaves texts, including those by different authors and those in non-verbal media, tightly together. One effect is to weaken and even destroy altogether any sense of textual uniqueness, for what is essential in any text appears intermingled with other texts.

Keep (1995) augments this in his claim:

> Hypertext provides for multiple authorship, a blurring of the author and reader functions, multiple reading paths, and extended works with diffuse boundaries. With the inclusion of sound, graphics, video, and other media as nodes, hypertext expands the world available to the writer. (Quoted in Johnson & Oliva, 1997: 5)

Whilst, on the one hand, hypertext links destroy the hierarchy between text and notes, on the other hand, it can also re-arrange textual hierarchies by allowing centred texts to be shifted to the periphery and *vice versa*, depending on the reading purpose and the nature of the inquiry. With hypertext, 'center is always a transient, decenterable virtual center — one created only by one's act of calling up that particular text — it never tyrannises other aspects of the network in the way a printed text does' (Delaney & Landow, 1991: 11). The boundaries of metatext are blurred in that hypertexts are by definition open-ended, expandable and incomplete — thus creating a montage of textual images in which a diverse range of information is available at once to the reader.

Friedman (1995), however, contests this view and maintains that readers' choices in hypertext are limited by the finite number of links created by the author. Friedman's argument highlights the fact that, at the end of the day, the hypertext is a technical construction which is highly dependent on the subject (and subjective) knowledges and ways of thinking or creativity of the programmers. Theoretically, this level of subjective interpretation leaves room for the manipulation of the range and types of meanings that can be produced through, as is argued earlier, what Williams (1980) refers to as the 'selective tradition' which allows for the construction of preferred meanings.

Another silence or gap in the discourse on hypertext is the fact that computer text has not emerged within a political, economic, cultural and ideological vacuum. Perhaps more than any other texts, they are embodied in technologies that have a material base and are, therefore, as Said (1984) argues regarding print text, subject to ownership, authority and power. Although many of the issues related to authorship, copyright and censorship of computer text still remain unresolved, we cannot address computer-text production without consideration of issues of power and control.

Social effects

Computer-generated text extends the process of writing beyond the mechanical phase of the Second Industrial Revolution. It signifies a new writing technology; a new mode of textual production which, potentially, holds great advantages for improving the learning process. However, the fact that computer texts are so diverse and because the technology is still relatively new, its overall long-term impact on society is hard to quantify, at least in a definitive way.

What *is* evident, though, is the fact that, at least in the developed world, computers have rapidly become a natural feature of everyday life within homes, work-places, shopping malls and arcades. They have transformed our experience of everyday life in a very fundamental way — creating new ways of working, new ways of seeing, new ways of performing particular tasks such as shopping and banking — and, therefore, new ways of participating in the consumer culture of the late 20th century.

Computers transformed the newspaper industry during the 1980s when many of them went online. Computerisation allowed newspapers to be 'written, edited and printed at distance, allowing for simultaneous editions of the same newspaper tailored to several major [geographically dispersed] areas' (Castells, 1996: 337, information in brackets added). Thus they could cater more effectively for differentiated tastes, styles and interests suited to particular social contexts, and also cater for different interests. At the same time, however, computerisation of the printing industry has contributed to large-scale job losses during the past decade.

Cyberspace

The concept of cyberspace originated within the context of science fiction where it provided a means of framing a new technological 'reality' in which human kind had conquered not only the physical environment, but also the more nebulous concepts of space and time. It represented 'a new stage, a new and irresistible development in the elaboration of human culture and business under the sign of technology' (Benedikt, 1994: 1). Transferred to the real world, the concept of cyberspace is seen to describe:

> a new universe created and sustained by the world's computers and communication lines. A world in which the global traffic of knowledge, secrets, measurements, indicators, entertainments, and alter-human agency takes on form: sights, sounds, presences never seen on the surface of the earth blossoming in a vast electronic night. (Benedikt, 1994: 1)

Within cyberspace we read our electronic mail, engage in discussion on computer bulletin boards, exchange information, ideas and knowledge on the Internet. Thus it is argued that we are becoming members of new kinds of 'virtual' communities (Turkle, 1996: 9), and new multiple identities within and through which we can communicate with people in a very direct way across the world, in fractions of seconds. The next section will examine some of these aspects as they relate to concepts of text within what has become commonly known as the 'information society'.

Informational and organisational features

The Internet network developed by the American military with government financial support, provides 'the backbone of global computer-mediated communication (CMC)' (Castells, 1996: 345). The Internet enables instant dissemination of messages from one originating point to an international readership, and 'have impacts far beyond the limits of a traditional face-to-face community and beyond the borders of state-sanctioned public spheres, without the limiting quality of context, community sanctions and the ability of moral arbiters to limit debates and censor topics' (Shields, 1996: 4). The Internet provides open access and allows also for a range of commercial transactions to take place via the computer screen. The World Wide Web (www) comprises a:

> flexible network of networks within the Internet where institutions, businesses, associations, and individuals create their own 'sites' on the basis of which everybody with access can produce his/her/its own 'home page', made of a variable collage of text and images. (Castells, 1996: 355)

Textually, the Internet integrates sound, written text and images and thus is multimodal. Constructed as hypertext, it provides a multilinear path of information dissemination 'which frees the reader from a predetermined sequence, and has been perfectly synthesised in the World Wide Web interface by the point and click action, the essential operation in order to navigate it' (Johnson & Oliva, 1997: 4). It does not have definitive points of closure or any sequence in which it is to be read; the reader can enter or exit at any point — thus 'contributing to the redefinition of the author-reader/artist/viewer relationship' (Johnson & Oliva, 1997: 5). At the same time, however, as with hypertext, the quality of programming and database would circumscribe the range and quality of information made available through hyperlinks. This would depend, to a large extent, on the subject (and subjective) knowledges, ideological 'orientation' and ways of thinking of the programmers.

Bulletin Board Systems (BBS) provide another means of worldwide communication on a diverse range of interests and attractions 'covering the whole spectrum of human communication, from politics and religion to sex and research' (Castells, 1996: 354). Computer Bulletin Boards consist of a host computer to which other computers fitted with special software packages are networked via telephone lines. It provides open access and, like the Internet, it has no social or organisational hierarchy — and no organisational gate-keeping as these can easily be by-passed. According to Rogers (1986: 43) 'in addition to being highly interactive, asynchronous, and de-massified, computer bulletin boards can also be anonymous because most participants use "computer names".' These reflect the multiple identities that now frame the literacy experience within computer-mediated communication.

Electronic mail, commonly referred to as e-mail, provides an increasingly popular form of computer-mediated communication (CMC) allowing instant and direct communication across time and space. Textually, electronic mail also constitutes a form of hypertext allowing messages or information to be sent via a communications network to different individual users or 'newsgroups' that are organised around particular themes or interests. Newsgroups represent virtual worlds and communities on the Internet in which people interact and access information of common interest in virtual libraries within a global context. Electronic mail shares with video the concept of deferred time in that the user may choose to make a print-out of the message to be read at a later time, and within a different context to the one in which it was sent and received. Although largely print-based, electronic mail messages lack permanence, their significance often measured in days (Aycock, 1995). This has been referred to by some writers as constituting 'virtual textuality' (Zariski, 1995: 1). Bolter (1990: 31) posits the following view:

> Electronic text is the first text in which the elements of meaning, of structure, and of visual display are fundamentally unstable. Unlike the printing press or the medieval codex, the computer does not require that any aspect of writing be determined in advance for the whole life of a text... All information, all data, in the computer world is a kind of controlled movement, and so the natural inclination of computer writing is to change, to grow, and finally to disappear ... these constant motions place electronic writing in a kaleidoscope of relationships with the earlier technologies of typewriting, printing, and handwriting.

New 'virtual communities' (Rheingold, 1993) are thus engaged in creating new (global) cultural meanings. Yet, although they are interactive, electronic texts ultimately represent disembodied discourses. Rather than representing a historical break with previous technologies, they have this in common with other technological discourses generated through, for example, the letter, telegraph, telephone and fax in which communication takes place at a distance. What they also have in common with these technologies is the fact that they constitute different forms of social interaction. The difference is the fact that:

> the Internet creates a *crisis of boundaries* between the real and the virtual, between time zones and between spaces, near and distant ... between our sense of self and our sense of our changing roles: the personae we may play or the 'hats we wear' in different situations are altered (Shields, 1996: 7). (original emphasis)

In other words, it enables users to assume different identities.

It is also argued that our sense of 'reality' is being altered by a meta or hyper-reality constructed in computer systems that 'offer visual, auditory, and tactile information about an environment that exists as data in a computer system rather than as physical objects and locations' (Reid, 1995: 164).

Virtual Reality (VR) 'refers to a real time, computer-generated environment, single or multiple users interface with the aid of a Dataglove, full body suit, 3D Eyephones and a simulation of 360 degree sound' (Bukatman, 1995: 1). VR in this form is said to have the potential to produce a state of altered consciousness and a physical sense of disembodiment (Bromberg, 1996).Thus VR technology simulates real or imagined environments giving the viewer a 'real' multisensory experience of that constructed reality. It is seen as providing a 'dizzying phenomenology of direct experience (or the elaborate illusion of it)' (Bukatman, 1995: 1) — and offers the opportunity to explore alternative realities through direct concrete experience (albeit simulated).

Already used in NASA space training, pilot-training and military programmes, it is envisaged that this embryonic technology has great potential for enhancing learning experiences within a variety of contexts. VR is regarded to be potentially of great use in creating 'virtually real' learning environments in which learners can experiment, problem-solve and learn safety aspects of particular jobs before venturing into the real work-place. As such, it constitutes a low-error cost system in that it allows learners to make mistakes without the risk of damage (Crookall & Saunders, 1988). VR programming is also regarded as having major potential in, for example, learning modern languages in simulated 'real' contexts of language use. Furthermore, a recent newspaper article reported that 'archeologists are arranging virtual field trips; doctors are rehearsing surgery with virtual body-parts; engineers are experimenting with virtual wind tunnels, all at a fraction of the real thing, and without anything physical to construct or damage' (Howard, Times Higher Educational Supplement, 3 June 1997). Much of this has been made possible by integrating 3D photography into computer modelling.

A more limited, non-tactile version of VR is also available via the computer screen, of which, the text-based multiuser domains (MUDs) are the most well-known. MUDs first became available in the early 1980s school programme called 'Dungeons and Dragons' which enabled users to participate in role-play situations, to navigate or chart their own way through the programme, and allowing them to re-construct storylines , to build alternative outcomes/realities.

Exploring new forms of reader-text interactions offered by computer games, Friedman (1995: 85) maintains that the virtual reality inherent in computer simulation can optimise the construction of cognitive mapping. He further states:

> Computer simulations bring the tools of narrative to map-making, allowing the individual not simply to observe structures but to become experientially immersed in their logic . . . Playing a simulation means becoming engrossed in a systemic logic that connects a myriad of causes and effects . . . computer simulations provide a radically new quasi-narrative form through which to communicate structures of interconnection. (Friedman, 1995: 86)

This would suggest that VR technologies engender a high level of reliance on meta-linguistic processes involving analysis, hypothesis, interpretation and association that are central to cognitive development.

Other benefits include the fact that the 'anytime–anywhere' mode offered by the new technology means that users can engage with the information available, on their own terms, and in their own time. It provides a powerful direct way of communication with wider audiences, and at different levels of knowledgeability and expertise; it provides scope for peer critique and engagement.

Futhermore, the virtual world of knowledge and information available on the Internet has altered the concept of what a library is in a very fundamental way. At the same time, however, rather than the need for literacy *vis a vis* print-text receding, as is claimed, it is a taken-for-granted aspect of the technological paradigm that users are literate not only in a functional sense, but that they are able to participate in a variety of textual discourses at different levels of engagement. We return to this discussion again later in the chapter as well as in Chapter 7.

Interpretive frameworks

Although virtual reality technology is, in a sense, very literal in that it attempts to represent an integrated multimodal version of reality, the concept of virtual reality is, as has already been suggested, not an entirely new one. We have existed as virtual individuals within the processes of bureaucracy for many years, for example, in records, imprints, photographs, profiles, statistical information (Ovarec, 1996) through which collages of our virtual selves have been constructed to be accessed for specific informational purposes. 'Virtual individuals' also exist within different literary genre such as the novel and biography as well as the performance arts, film and drama. In these textual forms, people, places and events exist as 'real' or 'hyper-real' constructs in our imaginings which, in turn, draw intertextually on memory traces of past experiences, knowledges about social mores, beliefs, behaviours and value systems, whilst at the same time tapping into our dreams, hopes, desires and aspirations. Through this process we can identify, emphasise with and live through the lives, experiences and events with the characters.

What is different in what is offered by virtual reality technologies is the opportunity that they provide in making us able to explore and engage with textual environments in a *tangible* way. Because of this, VR has the potential to enable learners to broaden and deepen their knowledge and understanding and perceptions of the 'real' world and to refine their skills within a non-threatening context, all of which is highly supportive to learning.

Can virtual reality in its full immersion form therefore be regarded as a communication technology, and if so, does it produce 'a text', is it a literacy 'event', is it just a multisensory experience — is it an amalgam of all of these — or, is it something radically different? If it *is* a text, how is this to be defined, how can the information that it offers be coded and classified and how should its interpretive framework be conceptualised? These complex questions have epistemological and ontological implications that lie beyond the scope of what is discussed here. We will limit ourselves to Crookall and Saunders' (1988: 21) suggestion that:

> there are close parallels between simulation (VR) and communication, as both can be considered as forms of reality construction. Communication is a central component in the construction of realities; only in being able to communicate are people able to construct their social realities.

Both communication and simulation involve representation, the creation and negotiation of meaning which, in turn, are integrally linked with language, systems of thought and significations. The concept of simulation thus represents forms of 'textual discourse' traversed by diverse languages, signs, voices — and experiences — it is, like other textual forms, heteroglossic, polysemic and polyphonic.

Since the term 'literacy', with its basis in print-text, becomes problematic in terms of describing the interactive nature of texts produced by information technology, I use the term 'textual discourses' here to describe a broader conceptualisation of meaning production. This includes not only decoding and encoding; denotative and connotative meanings but also the broad range of intra-, inter- and meta-textual meanings in which different texts are constituted — and the processes through which these meanings are reproduced and mediated — and also, deconstructed, altered, re-constituted and subverted. The term 'textual discourses', in other words, incorporates what has been referred to earlier as the metaphysics of text — as well as its political, economic and social materiality. It constitutes an attempt to describe the different texts produced by information technology as communicative practices within and through which discursive meanings are produced within the broader context of society and culture.

Social effects

The multidimensional facilities offered by the new technologies discussed here support the view that a fundamental change has taken place with regard to how we experience text and, relatedly, the 'reading' process. We have moved from being mere readers and spectators to becoming *active participants* in the shaping, deconstruction and re-construction of text, literally, experientially and metaphorically. In this sense, the frontiers of knowledge have been expanded on a global level. At the same time we have also become 'users' of technology in a technical, functional sense. Textual discourses produced by the new microelectronics technologies have, therefore, like print text, both instrumental and symbolic value.

For example, the rapid transfer of information between countries and continents made possible by the new technology provides increasing opportunities for interaction between people, machines and power processes within a global context. The implications of this for both societal and individual development is multifold:

(1) the dynamic process of information exchange as is prevalent, for example, in agriculture, banking, financial transfer and investment, provides scope for social and economic development;

(2) at the level of the individual, information exchange can also, potentially, be empowering in terms of the access that it can provide to information sources on a global level and, also, the range of discussion and exchange that can take place between users located within a global context. New 'communicative fellowships' based on common interests, are being constituted within the networked 'virtual world' of cyberspace. New geometries of space and time in information exchange have been created.

(3) symbolically, information exchange within a global communicative framework also has powerful hegemonic potential with regard to shaping the aspirations, desires, subjectivities, possibilities for social and political action, lifestyles and values of larger groups of people living within different societies.

These discursive dimensions, capacity and multiple capabilities of the new technology identify the need for a different set of literacy and information-related questions to be asked. Combined with the fact that the moral, political and ethical issues raised by print literacy have not yet been resolved, as has been discussed in earlier chapters, they also create the imperative to highlight the ambiguities, dilemmas and problems that inhere in information technology, its links with different 'literacies' and textual discourses, their social applications, and the power/knowledge discourses in which they are grounded globally, as well as within specific societies.

The issues identified here in relation to computer-generated texts bear out Bolter's view discussed at the beginning of the chapter, that a re-definition of text has taken place both as a structure of visible elements on screen as well as a structure of signs in the minds of both writers and readers. However, whilst VR technologies and hypertext, undoubtedly, will influence or shape our ways of seeing, experiencing and knowing the world there is another, more important issue that extends beyond the parameters of textual discourse discussed so far. This refers to the social construction of the 'information society' including the role of information-text and its technologies — as well as the social and institutional practices and power processes in which they are grounded — in shaping common understandings of life, knowledge and experience within it.

Critical Perspectives and Informational Dilemmas

The information society

It is argued that we are entering the third phase of industrial develop-ment which is driven not by 'matter or energy but by information and knowledge' (Kumon & Aizu, 1994: 314). As a result of the new geometries of space and time offered by information technology, we are operating within 'a global economy in which capital, production, management, markets, labor, information, and technology are organised across national boundaries' (Castells, 1993: 18). Information-processing services are seen to play a central role in the new global cultural economy in which 'electronic networks (infrastructure) and a common set of social/human networks (infostructure) will be combined to help create an interconnected global society that will bring people and organisations into closer contact beyond mere economy' (Kumon & Aizu, 1994: 315).

The new technologies, it is argued, are not only centred on informa-tion/data processing but also, in many instances, information/data also constitute the end-product. Together these factors are seen to underscore the power of information — and information as power. The development of new technologies themselves depends to a large extent on the application of new knowledge — and therefore it constitutes the basis of production. In terms of this, the information society is geared towards the accumu-lation of knowledge, and 'towards higher levels in information process-ing' (Castells, 1996: 17). Castells (1996: 17) summarises this in his argument that:

specific to the informational mode of development is the action of knowledge upon knowledge itself as the main source of productivity. Information processing is focused on improving the technology of information processing as a source of productivity, in a virtuous circle of interaction between the knowledge sources of technology and the application of technology to improve knowledge generation and information processing.

This integration of information into design, production and innovation has contributed to the fact that the quality of information, and the level of efficiency in acquiring, processing and applying it 'now constitute the strategic factor in both competitiveness and productivity for firms, regions, and countries' (Castells, 1993: 18). Information is seen as having potent economic currency and, as a result, the pursuit of knowledge and information has become a central part of national development goals.

However, is this the sum-total of information that we need to have access to in order to function adequately in the information society? The importance of this question lies in the fact that in the general discussion about the 'informational needs' of the technological society, there is an assumption that we all understand 'what information is' and what is 'useful information'. Moreover, there is an assumption that our understandings of what 'information' is, is based on consensus. As has been the case with print literacy, information is regarded as inherently 'good' for individuals and for society even though, as a concept, it is not always clarified; it is 'understood' at the level of 'commonsense'. In this sense, information has already become hegemonic cultural capital.

What is information?

Whilst information within the context of computer discourse is defined as data that have been organised and communicated, for Machlup (1962: 15) ' 'information' as the act of informing is designed to produce a state of knowing in someone's mind'. For Machlup, information becomes interpellated with knowledge. Bell (1973: 175) expands on Machlup's concept of knowledge 'as a state of knowing' and argues that knowledge comprises:

> a set of organised statements of facts or ideas, presenting a reasoned judgement or an experimental result, which is transmitted to others through some communication medium in some systematic form. Thus, I distinguish knowledge from news and entertainment.

On the one hand, how these definitions relate to the concept of 'information technology' and the 'literacy' skills and knowledges needed to operate within the 'information society' would, traditionally, depend on the disciplinary framework in which they are articulated. For the economist it would refer to its value as a commodity; for the philosopher it would relate to concepts of knowledge; for the social scientist it would refer to different forms of knowledge grounded in society and culture. For the technologist it would refer to computer data. Each of these definitions would be embedded within a subject-specific discourse, located within the broader framework of subject-disciplines.

On the other hand, the concept of information that features in techno-logical development discourse takes on a particular ideological meaning; not referring to:

> knowledge concerning some particular fact, subject or event', but rather to a kind of intentional substance that is present in the world, a sense that is no longer closely connected to the use of the verb 'inform', anchored in particular speech acts. This is the sense of the word which bears the ideological burden in discussions of the new technologies. (Nunberg, 1996: 110)

Theoretically then the notion of 'information' can be classified into several conceptual frameworks, each having its own terms of reference. These include:

- information as a technology;
- information as a technological discourse;
- information as political discourse;
- information as systems theory (technical, technological, organisa-tional);
- information as an economic, cultural or technical resource;
- information as a product (economic output); and information as a commodity (cultural and economic).

In turn each of these classifications represents a distinctive kind of knowledge serving a specific purpose, or use-value, each constituted within a particular set of significations.

Knowledge versus information

There is also an important distinction to be made between *information-processing* which relies primarily on information access and retrieval skills, and the *organisation of ideas* which involves analysis, evaluation, interpreta-tion, intertextual meanings and reflection; that is, an active engagement with different sets of information (Roszak, 1994). The generation of knowledge depends on the *quality of ideas* that derive from the information input that are subjected to the meta-linguistic processes identified earlier —

becoming abstract thought which is internalised and can be repro-
duced/applied to specific tasks within different contexts. Knowledge is,
therefore, inseparable from content, context (social, political, cultural,
ideological and institutional/situational), language and action. Knowledge
production evolves within a continual and discursive process of making
sense of (politically, socially, economically, ideologically, culturally and
institutionally/situationally) coded information, which require readers/
users/audiences to be critical and knowledgeable enough to make them
discerning users of the information that is available.

Clearly then the generation and acquisition of knowledge depends on
significantly more than just the availability of information. Quality of
thinking and information, in this sense, means more than quantity — which
highlights concerns raised about the vastness of the body/bodies of
information traversing the Internet. Indeed, the Internet has, in many
instances, become a conduit of advertisements for, *inter alia*, books, journals
and the announcement of information events such as conferences. Although the latter provides a useful means of information networking, the
lack of substantive discussion of issues is significant within some areas.

Since the power of information and knowledge ultimately resides in
culture and society, we need to address the social construction of
information and knowledge within and through institutional, social and
political power processes — and especially their role in:

(1) the shaping of preferred cultural knowledges and information;
(2) the role that they play in the range of information made available in
    society;
(3) structuring inequalities with regard to who has access to information
    and knowledge, and who is excluded.

In a world with (metaphorically) flexible frontiers made possible by the
multiple facilities of computer technologies, 'who will be left out, pushed
out, reservationed, in the colonisation of the new frontier'? (Amiran *et al.*,
1992: 5). Who will be denied access to the global information society
through limited availability of computers, telecommunications and networks through lack of the necessary societal infrastructure?

The social construction of information/knowledge as cultural capital
If we take account of Castells' (1996) view discussed earlier, and his
argument that knowledge and information 'now constitute the strategic
factor(s) in both competitiveness and productivity for firms, regions, and
countries' (Castell, 1993: 18), then information as represented in the
technological development paradigm can be seen as constituting, simultaneously, a tool (means), a form of knowledge (technical know-how), a

practical application (artifact/data), a consumer commodity (use value) as well as a commodity with an exchange value. Focused as it is on an input–output model of research and development (R&D) — or production, it represents essentially a utilitarian view of information in which the relentless drive for the accumulation of new and better knowledge as well as higher levels of information processing is underscored, predominantly, by economistic goals. Castells' view, although articulated within a social scientific framework, nevertheless, subscribes primarily to a technology-oriented form of knowledge and information. It signifies an unproblematic acceptance of the hegemonic notion of the information society which silences or marginalises other forms of knowledge and information important to living within a changing global cultural economy.

The ascendancy of the technological paradigm, derived largely from its organic link with the economy, has contributed to the fact that this predominantly economic concept of information now frames the discourse on technology and societal development — as well as individual efficacy in the information society. This is the case despite contrary trends emerging in the labour market which, as was discussed in Chapter 5, indicate a diversification of industries and, particularly, an expansion of low-skilled labour in the service sector, with high-skill technological knowledge workers comprising a relatively small core of designers and programmers.

Informational dilemmas and contradictions

Whilst free access to information provided by the Internet challenges prevailing censorship laws, it has also brought into focus issues of authorship and copyright. Although strong arguments are made in support of preserving our democratic right to information on the Internet, the issue of censorship is by no means clear-cut especially where this involves critical moral and ethical issues related to the protection of minors from certain forms of information, including pornography and cult recruitment.

Censorship also takes many different forms that are applicable not only to different forms of text but also to the active prevention, by governments, of the right of access to information gatherers and knowledge producers such as journalists and researchers within a variety of contexts. In many developing countries with minimal access to Internet and satellite facilities, governments still exercise strong control over different media which they do by controlling ownership of satellite-receiving dishes, and broadcast licences. For example, whilst access to the Internet is open in Ethiopia, the government has only recently rescinded its ban on 'the ownership of private satellite receiving dishes and dropped import controls on facsimile machines and modems' (US Department of State Human Rights Report, 1996: 6). In the case of the Congolese Computer Department (OCI) during the 1980s, powerful gate-keeping within bureaucracies has been a major factor in the marginalisation of information technology training. This is reinforced by the lack of initiatives to diversify the use of information equipment, and the inability to 'chart a consistent information policy for the government' (Franscisco, 1996).

Information and social inequality

Other important exclusionary aspects relate to the lack of (1) adequate institutional, organisational and societal infrastructure to support the development of information technology; (2) network systems; and (3) technological knowledge and skills especially those related to systems design, analysis and programming. Rwanda, for example, has no public, national e-mail or Internet provider and relies on NGOs, and donor agencies such as USAID, UNICEF and UNDP for access. Similarly, Ethiopia has not yet developed its own national communications network and 'for e-mail use depends on the network established by the Pan African Development Information System (PADIS) based at the United Nations Economic Commission for Africa' (UNECA) (Furzey, 1996: 4). The electronic networking project, Capacity Building for Electronic Communication in Africa (CABECA), set up in Lesotho by PADIS failed to take off as a result of the lack of basic infrastructure and adequate technological skills in the institution mandated to implement the project in the country (Chisenga, 1996).

Many developing countries also have a limited culture of information-sharing and dissemination that is the result of a lack of adequate 'library facilities, inadequate resources for journals and books, poor documentation and archive collections, and central resource sites' (Furzey, 1996: 5). In many instances this has contributed to under-utilisation of existing information resources. Under-utilisation of information resources also results from the very low literacy levels in many developing countries, especially in Africa. According to a recent report by the UN Economic Commission For Africa (ECA, (1996: 6)),

> over half of those literate cannot gather information for problem-solving. Most users struggle with everyday life. The availability of hundreds of different local languages without interface to global knowledge resources has made access to information more difficult.

Most of these issues relate to polity discussed in Chapters 2 and 3. This includes the type of regime and model of governance within countries which, together with other factors such as societal poverty, impact on national expenditure priorities. It also includes external economic policy controls exercised by, for example, the IMF and the World Bank discussed earlier, the colonisation of different technologies by transnational information-based industries which serve to widen the divide between information-rich and information-poor societies.

The liberatory claims made about new knowledge frontiers and economic possibilities opened up by information technology clearly need to be questioned on the basis of continuing trends of under-development in many parts of the world.

Chapter 7

Conceptualising Literacy, Knowledge and Power in the Information Society

I have argued in previous chapters that societal discourse meanings are intrinsically linked with social systems, structures and processes and thus they cannot be viewed as being neutral; they represent particular power interests. And, as such, power/knowledge discourses articulated from within power institutions serve an important role in defining the parameters of social debate, that is, what can and should be said on a particular issue (Pecheux, 1982). Although emphases may vary within different contexts, the function of the dominant discourse is to legitimate specific hegemonic projects of (often competing) power interest groups within or beyond the state. This chapter examines the way in which this process is currently being played out in the meanings constructed around the concept of 'technological literacy' within different social and institutional contexts.

As a starting point it explores the meanings attached to the notions of 'technological literacy' and 'technological capability' in the discourse frameworks of key defining sites such as national governments and para-national organisations represented here by the UN and, more specifically, UNESCO. Arguing for clarification of the concept of 'technological literacy' that is being advocated within these contexts, the chapter goes on to examine theoretical perspectives in academic discourse. Drawing on key motifs identified in Chapter 6, it then discusses the implications of new and re-defined literacy demands of the information society as well as the organic nature of the interactions taking place on a global basis, for the way in which we conceptualise, 'read' and interpret meaning within the re-defined 'writing space' (Bolter, 1991) — and the ways in which we interact with the changing cultural landscape in which we live.

The chapter concludes with a schematic set of guidelines to frame a re-conceptualised view of 'technological literacy/capability' that includes the different communicative skills needed (a) to participate effectively in the information society and (b) those required to participate meaningfully in the democratic process within a global cultural economy. Technological, social and economic inequalities between the developed and developing world are highlighted throughout.

The Social Construction of 'Technological Literacy'

Whilst the concept of *'technological literacy'* frames the discourse on education and social change in many national and international defining sites, in the UK and, more particularly, England and Wales, the emphasis has been on the need to develop adequate levels of *'technological capability'*.

England and Wales

The Council for Education and Training (CET) already during the late 1970s forecast that, 'microelectronics itself will be a new industry, and many other or reshaped industries will emerge depending on microelectronics, but their requirements will be for investment capital and for limited numbers of highly qualified staff' (CET, 1978: 5).

Information technology, since the early days then, was seen as constituting a new form of value-production. These meanings did not enter educational discourse until much later. As is indicated earlier, computer literacy, largely defined in terms of keyboard skills, was at the time regarded as forming part of the 'common core of basic skills', a life-skill as important as 'other forms of literacy' (FEU, 1983: 46). Teaching computer literacy relied primarily on word-processing software that was geared to improve reading and writing skills. Computer use in classrooms, at the time, 'served primarily as a way of keeping low ability pupils 'busy' in remedial withdrawal groups' (Rassool, 1993: 230), or teaching word-processing skills on secretarial courses in vocational training programmes.

A major shift took place in the UK discourse in 1989 when the concept of 'key technologies' entered the FEU curriculum framework. The 'key' technologies were defined as 'newly emerging topics in science and engineering which are likely to have a major revolutionary effect on an existing product or process' (FEU, 1989: 7). Computers, having been dissociated from their erstwhile link with 'life-skills' and literacy learning, were to become tied to another discourse focused on technical innovation and enterprise in the production process. Emphasis started to shift from functional computer literacy skills, and concerns about 'knowledge about computers', towards a new approach to the development of technological skills (Rassool, 1993). This included the need to develop technological 'capability' which revolved around computer science, systems design, information technology, engineering and product design. The re-defined FE curriculum also incorporated the Engineering Council/ Society of Education Officers' (1988: 2) recommendation that the key technologies should be combined with 'research, design, development, production, finance, quality, marketing, sales, and service'. The links set up thus between technology, enterprise and production, served to define the concept of 'technological capability' within the framework of market principles. This was justified in the following argument:

> The United Kingdom must learn to operate in a rapidly changing world economy — a world of increasingly competitive markets, rapid technology transfer, and even shorter product life cycles. Certainly, one key to this is technology. (FEU, 1989: 9)

The emphasis now started to shift towards the need to adjust to the requirements of the new technological mode of production in which information technology was to play a significant part, in addition to its enabling role in facilitating capital transfer.

These meanings, shaped within the curriculum framework of the Further Education Unit (FEU), became incorporated also into the discourse on technology in the school curriculum. The letter accompanying the final report of the National Curriculum Design and Technology Task Group, stated that:

> the aim of our proposals for design and technology is to prepare pupils to meet the needs of the 21st Century: to stimulate originality, enterprise, practical capability in designing and making and the adaptability needed to cope with a rapidly changing society. (NCC, 1989: vii).

From the beginning then, the school curriculum framework in England and Wales was defined in terms of addressing the gaps and mismatches between education and the perceived market and labour needs of the evolving technological society.

Most of these meanings were written into the *design* component of Technology as a subject in the National Curriculum. Curriculum *content* centred on 'developing and using artifacts', 'working with materials', 'developing and communicating ideas', 'and satisfying needs and addressing opportunities' (NCC, 1989). These were later modified in the revised curriculum document to focus on developing pupils' designing and making skills, and their knowledge and understanding of 'materials and components', 'systems and control', 'structures, products and applications', 'quality' and 'health and safety' (DfE, 1995).

The curriculum *process* incorporated a problem-solving teaching and learning approach grounded in cooperative team work as well as the development of market awareness and entrepreneural skills. Emphasis was placed on developing three types of activity, namely, 'design and making assignments', 'focused practical tasks', 'investigating, disassembling and evaluating products and applications' (DfE, 1996: 34). In this way, a direct relationship was established between technological learning, and the skills demands of the flexible work-place. As is discussed in Chapter 5, the latter refers to the organisation of work and the re-defined worker skills and awarenesses required within the re-structured, market responsive, labour process.

The concept of 'technological capability' within the Design and Technology component essentially frames a production-oriented view of development within the technological paradigm. Such a framework runs the risk of subordinating technological development to the needs of the market, ignoring the reality that technologies are consciously developed to serve specific social, economic and political purposes. Whilst technologies *do* frame possibilities for development, they do not *in themselves* determine social development in a rational and neutral way. National technological choices, and the uses that technologies are put, are ultimately subject to the exigencies of social policy, and relatedly, the political agenda of a wide range of actors within the policy formulation terrain. Although the concept of 'technological capability' constructed in the *design* component of the National Curriculum in England and Wales does frame the development of a range of technical skills and work process awarenesses, it does not allow a consideration of the discursive way in which technologies impact on different aspects of culture, society and the ecology (see Rassool, 1993).

Information Technology Capability within the National Curriculum is defined in terms of:

- using information sources and IT tools to solve problems;
- using IT tools and information sources, such as computer systems and software packages, to support learning in a variety of contexts;
- understanding the implications of IT for working life and society. (DfE, 1997a: 5)

The development of information technology capability is based on the following criteria:

- communicating information — using IT to present and transmit information in the form of words, numbers, still and motion pictures, and sounds for particular purposes and audiences;
- handling information — selecting, retrieving, collecting, analysing and storing information;

- controlling and monitoring — using IT to control and monitor events;
- modelling — investigating patterns and relationships by using computer models that simulate real or imaginary situations. (DfE, 1997: 5)

Information technology is taught across the curriculum which allows 'technological literacy' to permeate the whole learning experience. This aspect of the National Curriculum does incorporate a multimodal view of 'text' including computer-generated text such as CD-ROM, the Internet and VR textual environments as well as other multimedia texts discussed in Chapter 6.

United States

In contrast, in the USA the over-riding factors justifying the need to teach 'technological literacy' have resided in the broadly stated need to adjust to the technical reading demands of the information society, and the projected impact of information technology on future labour skills requirements. The Education Commission of the States (1982) argued:

> Occupational growth throughout the 1980s is projected to expand most rapidly in the higher-skilled, technical occupations. Tomorrow's workers will likely need improved skills in the selection and communication of information. Many of today's skills considered to be of a 'higher' level are the potential basic skill of tomorrow. (Quoted in Levin & Rumberger, 1984: 2)

These views were underlined ten years later by the Governor of the State of California (1995:1) in his argument that:

> in the Information Age, it is not just what one knows that is so vital, but the ability to think critically and find information when needed. It is the skill of learning that will prepare our children to excel in a world where workers must be as flexible as the companies for which they work.

This has remained a constant theme in the overall information technology discourse despite US labour survey projections that 'high-technology industries employ only a small fraction of the total work force' (Rumberger & Levin, 1984: 18), and that the major challenges to employment lie in the organisation of labour (e.g. the impact of flexible work practices on employment patterns) rather than changes in skills requirements.

A similar theme emerged within the discourse of the Computer Systems Policy Project (CSPP) which argued for the need to provide students with the skills required to 'succeed in the high wage, information-based economy of the future, as well as providing the means for individuals to continue learning and upgrading their skills throughout their lives' (CSPP, 1994: 1). This was supported by the view that:

> success in the knowledge-based society of the future will require a variety of critical skills, including active, self-directed learning, the ability to access, analyse and manipulate remote data, and the ability to communicate across regional and national boundaries. In the job markets of the future, employers will demand workers who can learn new skills to adapt to changing job requirements and new technologies, use knowledge and information to make decisions, and work collaboratively. (CSPP, 1994: 1)

In addition to the emphasis on worker flexibility, and the ability to adapt to evolving change, was a consideration of the impact of information technology on communication and the learning process.

The continuing emphasis placed by the US government on developing students' 'technological literacy' skills is reflected in the enhanced national information infrastructure (NII) focused on building interactive networks in institutions across the country, allowing people to communicate across geographical boundaries. In its 1993 'Agenda for Action for the National Information Infrastructure', the Clinton Administration foregrounded the important role of education in this initiative. It was argued that 'although technology alone cannot fix what is wrong with America's education and training system, the NII can help' (quoted in CSPP, 1994: 1). This was reinforced in President Clinton's support for integrating computer technology into everyday classroom life throughout America. In his 'Call to Action for American Education in the 21st Century' in 1995, the President identified four key principles of his technological literacy agenda. This included the intention to:

(1) connect every school and classroom in America to the information superhighway;
(2) provide access to modern computers for all teachers and students;
(3) develop effective and engaging software and online learning resources as an integral part of the school curriculum;
(4) provide all teachers the training and support they need to help students learn through computers and the information superhighway.

This approach placed emphasis on facilitating access to technology, the value of the computer as a learning tool and the need for students to be able to participate in the information-rich environment of the Internet. Again, in his 1996 State of the Union Address President Clinton consolidated this in his argument that technological literacy 'is a new basic that our students must master' and that 'preparing our children for a lifetime of computer use is now just as essential as teaching them to read and write and do math'.

The NII seeks to fulfil the following *America 2000* goals (CSPP, 1994) set by the Bush Administration in 1990:

(1) *By the year 200, all children will start school ready to learn*: 'through links to the home, the NII can provide parents with the necessary tools to expand their roles in their children's education and better prepare their children to enter schools ready to learn'. The NII would also provide parents with online materials to use with their children and thus aim to develop inter-generational literacy, and to establish early links between teachers and parents through an interactive 'Ask the Experts' computer bulletin board. Child-care information would also be disseminated via the computer.

(2) *By the year 2000, the high school graduation rate will increase to at least 90%*: Links will be established between schools, the private sector and higher education; links between education and the world of work will be enhanced through the NII. Students will be able to liaise directly with experts and professionals and thus be able to observe real-world applications of knowledge and skills. Multimedia and multimodal technologies will be integrated into schools and classrooms.

(3) *By the year 2000, Americans will have competency in challenging subject matter, including English, mathematics, science, history and geography, and be prepared for responsible citizenship, further learning, and productive employment in our modern economy*: Stressing the importance of information access in the knowledge-based society, the CSPP (1994: 4) argues that 'while tools and software will help make the NII easier to use and navigate, information technology-based education techniques will still require readers to conceptualise a problem, use critical thinking skills, access distant resources, and collaborate with fellow students, all while using basic reading and writing skills'. It advocates online, inquiry-driven, interactive learning with access to the Internet allowing students to work within an inter-connected, culturally diverse global environment.

(4) *By the year 2000, US students will be the first in the world in science and mathematics achievement*: The NII will help to facilitate learning in these subjects through provision of network support to simulated 'real learning experiences', computer modelling, and access to the national Academy of Science's Science resource Centre or materials from the Science 2000 project.

(5) *By the year 2000, every adult American will be literate and will possess the knowledge and skills necessary to compete in a global economy and exercise*

rights and responsibilities of citizenship: According to the CSPP (1994: 5), in the information-driven global economy, 'high-wage jobs, quality of life, and competitive advantage will be based on the ability to create, manipulate and deliver information quickly to the right person and place. Literacy or technological fluency, will require the skills to acquire knowledge and to adapt to emerging technologies and work methods'. The Project advocates the setting up of a continuum of networked services drawn from academia, business and the community to facilitate interaction, information sharing and collaboration. It also argues that the NII will provide access to official sources of online information, and that it will 'improve the way in which adult literacy is addressed by providing opportunities to learn in convenient settings — at home, at work, in libraries — at times convenient to the users (1994: 5)'. It argues further that multimedia learning tools will make it easier to acquire literacy skills.

(6) *By the year 2000, every school in America will be free of drugs and violence and will offer a disciplined environment to learning*: Acknowledging the fact that technology cannot cure the problems in society that impede school learning, the CSPP argues that the NII can provide a tool 'to engage students in meaningful, innovative, and interesting learning experiences as well as to directly address specific behavior problems via interactive programs. This could be done by making information on specific problems available, research and development that addresses drug dependency problems, and linking schools and communities with 'the police and other safety agencies to identify trouble spots or issues before they erupt into classroom violence'(1994: 5).

The US approach, based on the information provided here by the CSPP, appears to have been located within a discourse framework centred predominantly on access to information, the importance of communication on the Internet, and projected future skills requirements. Although educational intentions are specified, and means of addressing these are discussed, the concept of 'technological literacy' implicit in the overall discourse lacks pedagogic codification as a form of cultural knowledge. It also does not have a coherent framework for learning and teaching similar to that which inheres in the National Curriculum in England and Wales. Moreover, Lewis (1996: 7) argues that the emphasis in the UK (England and Wales) on *competence* is 'qualitatively different from the goal normally expressed as an end of the teaching of technology in American schools, 'technological literacy', which speaks of *disposition*'. (original emphasis)

Despite this lack of pedagogic clarity, 'technological literacy' has, nevertheless, come to represent that which all Americans 'must have' in order to be personally effective, and a primary means through which national economic growth can be sustained in the information society. This interpellation of the notion of 'technological literacy' with social progress and economic growth has resulted in the former becoming a potent form of hegemonic cultural capital. As such, it is claimed that:

> through new applications of information technologies, the NII will enable unemployed workers to train for new careers and employed workers to upgrade their skills to meet changing workplace demands; it will make learning exciting for students, from preschoolers to graduate students; it will allow teachers to create and customise multimedia curricula on demand; and it will turn community centers into information gateways for a host of network-based resources. This, and broader networking amongst key social institutions would facilitate the process of lifelong learning. (CSPP, 1994: 8–9)

Global perspectives

Within the global terrain, the United Nations has also taken up the theme of information technology in its discourse on social development. As such, it has foregrounded the development of national technological capacity as a priority in developing countries. In its *World Declaration on Education For All* (1990), UNESCO highlighted the importance of information in the world today and especially its relevance to survival and basic well-being. Taking a broader, knowledge-based view of information, the declaration stated that 'this includes information about obtaining more lifeenhancing information — or learning how to learn' (UNESCO, 1990: 1). The importance of information exchange on the Internet was amplified in their argument that 'a synergistic effect occurs when important information is coupled with another modern advance — our new capacity to communicate'(UNESCO, 1990: 2). It stated further that 'sound basic education is fundamental to the strengthening of higher levels of education and of scientific and technological literacy and capacity and thus to self-reliant development'.

The guidelines to the World Declaration, *A Framework for Action: Meeting Basic Learning Needs* (UNESCO, 1990: 7), strengthened these meanings arguing that 'the opportunity exists to harness this force and use it positively, consciously, and with design, in order to contribute to meeting defined learning needs'. The centrality of information technology to social development was similarly re-affirmed in the UN *Paris Declaration and Programme for Action* (1990) which focused on development in the least developed countries (LDCs).

Indeed, the focus on the links between technological literacy and social development permeate the UN discourse, including its Declaration on *Scientific and Technological Literacy for All* (1993). Within this framework the UNESCO-funded *Project 2000+* called on governments, industry, public and private sector interests, education and other authorities in all countries to 'assign priority to the development and introduction of programs leading to scientific and technological literacy for all with the aim of achieving responsible and sustainable development' (UNESCO, 1993: 1).

Gregorio (1995: 2) in a keynote conference address representing the views of Project 2000+, stressed the significance of information in the process of development. She argued:

> Information overload is difficult to contain. One would better understand the growth and advancement of knowledge if I cite you that knowledge grows at the rate of 13% per year. If this is so, then available knowledge would double every 5.5 years, and that in some disciplines, knowledge becomes obsolete in about a year and a half...What do we do with the rapid turn-over of data and information, or with a person who offers less effective solutions to problems because the individual moves within the 'old frame of mind', or who possesses knowledge that is lower than the needed knowledge? Should individuals develop additional skills through continuing education and 'lifelong learning'?

This statement is interesting on two levels: in the first instance, it highlights the interchanges, and 'common sense' assumptions often made in social discourse about the concepts of knowledge, information and data, that were discussed in the previous chapter. In the second instance, knowledge growth is quantified in statistical terms with the purpose of reinforcing the argument about the need for flexibility and for a change in mind-set in order to adapt to the 'inevitability' of a global, information technology-driven, development. The construction of meanings within this discourse framework bears out Pecheux's (1982: 111) argument that, 'words, expressions, propositions obtain their meaning from the discursive formation [e.g. speech, pamphlet] in which they are produced' and moreover, that 'words can change their meaning according to the positions held by those who use them'. Despite the fact that the different claims made may have no empirical validity, the statement obtains legitimacy and global significance within the context in which it is articulated — a keynote address, within a key defining site. As a discursive process, it provided a powerful means of legitimating the concept of technological modernisation — therefore the imperative for developing countries to embrace information technology and, relatedly, the need to identify technological literacy as a primary national development priority.

Outlining the prospects for information technology in Africa, the UN

Economic and Social Council's 'Economic Commission for Africa (ECA)' likewise underlined the interrelated nature of knowledge, information and development. In a report of the conference on 'Prospects for Information Technology in Africa' held in Addis Ababa, in March 1996, the Commission commented that 'well-informed knowledgeable and innovative citizens are causes for human centred development'. It argued further that 'the failure to use information technology is becoming as negative as the refusal to attend school. It is a choice between being left out or benefiting from enormous benefits of information technology' (ECA, 1996: 1). The Commission identified four technologies important in providing access to information in developing countries, namely, desktop publishing, CD-ROM, online access and Internet connection. Desktop publishing is seen as offering a solution to the 'book famine' throughout Africa with regard to both publishing and obtaining books. Networked information via CD-ROM and the Internet, it was argued, would overcome problems of information access posed by geographical location, for example, people living in rural areas. The report suggested that these technologies would also provide an invaluable means of disseminating and harnessing national histories and cultural knowledges. As can be seen later, this is a highly selective view of technology which does not take account of complex realities in many developing countries.

The notion of 'technological literacy' constructed within the overall UN framework, seemingly, assumes the position of a de-ideologised panacea to all development problems. This mirrors the 'quick-fix' ideology that surrounded the production and work-oriented concept of 'functional literacy' which during the 1970s, was widely considered as the means of facilitating societal modernisation. Similarly, the current notion of 'technological literacy' within the UN discourse presents a 'rational' and neutral view of technology which does not take account of the complex historical, political and cultural factors that impinge on levels of social development within many of these societies. Nor does it take account of the cycle of disempowerment, self- or externally imposed, in which they are trapped (some of these issues were discussed in Chapters 3 and 4).

How effectively the rhetoric will translate to the reality in developing countries is therefore highly debatable, especially if we take into account the fact that in the absence of stable and direct telecommunications access in many of these countries, Internet access would remain limited to an economic and intellectual elite. South Africa's deputy prime minister, Thabu Mbeki, stressed these inequalities at the G7 conference in 1994. He commented that half of the world's population has never used a telephone, and that most telephone calls in Southern Africa are still routed via London (Panos Institute, 1995). Highlighting the North/South information technology divide, the Panos Institute argues that 'this colonial pattern of communication means that revenue is drained from Southern telecommunications companies to the North' (1995: 7) — a factor which limits the levels of technological self-reliant development that can take place within these societies. Furthermore, many developing countries still operate without a reliable and well coordinated postal and transport system because of the lack of adequate infrastructure.

This gives some indication of the way in which historical realities have impacted themselves on technological development possibilities in post-colonial societies. It also highlights the level of practical obstacles that these factors present to the process of technologising the economic and cultural base in these societies. In this regard, technology as a UN-defined priority may not coincide with the more immediate and basic needs of national governments. The ECA documents a variety of other problems presented including the fact that:

> information users in Africa have the lowest literacy levels. More than half of Africa's population is illiterate. Over half of those literate cannot gather information for problem-solving. Most users struggle with everyday life. The availability of hundreds of local languages without interface to global knowledge resources has made access to information more difficult. The near absence of information seeking culture has continued to impede progress towards achieving universal success. (ECA, 1996: 6)

The Commission argues that these factors, in addition to financial difficulties, human resource shortages and lack of knowledge, inhibit the diffusion of networking technology in these societies.

Other problems relate to the fact that the language that dominates these textual environments is largely English, although other European languages also feature to a limited extent. This calls into question the extent to which people living in these countries can benefit from equal access to information provided by the Internet, computer bulletin boards and multi-user domains (MUDs). It also has implications for the future maintenance and currency of local literacies. Furzey (1996: 18) identifies some of the difficulties presented by language to technology diffusion in Ethiopia and argues that other than the lack of infrastructure:

> a key factor in promoting information sharing and developing a successful national network in Ethiopia will be the ability to communicate in the Gi'iz alphabet. For most people, English is a second or third language and for ease of communication, the ability to send e-mail or download information in Amharic or Tigrigna is vital.

Stressing the importance of having an Amharic interface for online connectivity, Furzey stresses that it is not yet possible 'to create and sort databases in Sabean alphabets and this hampers data collection and retrieval' (Furzey, 1996: 12). As we saw in Chapter 4, the status of Amharic as official language is not an unproblematic one itself with regard to the language rights of linguistic minority groups in that country. Such questions highlight the fact that the languages used in information technology textual environments, present complex problems regarding equality of access to information within different societies where issues of linguistic minority rights remain unresolved. This is clearly an area that would benefit from further empirical research to inform policy.

Summary

Although the relative emphases in the discourses structured in all three contexts discussed here were different, there were, nevertheless, many commonalities. First, a common theme throughout has been the equation:

information access + technological capacity + technological skills + ongoing learning + conceptual change = societal development.

As a discourse variable, this assumption serves an important ideological function, namely, to shape the 'social character' (Williams, 1961) according to the system of norms, behaviours, values and attitudes defined within the dominant discourse that frames the technological development paradigm. In other words, the notion of 'technological literacy' features as a necessary pre-requisite for the individual to function within the information soci-ety — and for society as a whole to prosper. This particular construction of 'technological' literacy can therefore be seen as constituting a power/knowledge discourse *par excellence* in which technicist meanings frame a, predominantly, economistic approach to social development.

Within this framework, the needs of the economy are presented as best served by the re-structuring and adaptation of industry, and a re-constituted 'flexible' and functionally 'technologically literate' work force inducted into multiskills and ongoing training to meet the evolving needs of the 'information' or 'knowledge-based' society. This articulation of 'techno-logical literacy' and the notion of 'technological capability' can therefore be seen as serving a functional role in the interests of a political economy within the evolving technological development paradigm. Appropriated by dominant power interests, the concepts of 'technological literacy/capa-bility' serve to mediate particular views of social change and, in the process, they also serve to define the frameworks and parameters of knowledge within the culture. Again, comparison here with the meanings historically attached to concepts of conventional print-literacy during periods of social transition is compelling.

Second, despite the fact that there is no general agreement about what 'technological literacy' is in pedagogical terms, the discussion shows that a consensus, nevertheless, does surround the idea that 'technological literacy' is inherently 'good' for the individual and for societal development. Ideologically, it constitutes a powerful hegemonic variable in the 'naturalisation' of the restructured social relations within the technological mode of production. Undefined conceptually, 'technological literacy' as a social construct, has become a strategic ideological device in the management of the transition from the industrial, to the technological development paradigm. In order to address some of these issues, the next section will look at the conceptualisation of technological literacy, and its theoretical underpinnings in academic discourse.

What *is* 'Technological Literacy ?'- Theoretical Perspectives

Ragsdale (1988) discussing the situation in Northern America, highlighted the vague and contradictory views that surrounded the concept of 'computer literacy' at the time. He argued:

> Competing definitions have rendered the term 'computer literacy' almost meaningless. Some proponents of computer literacy emphasise the need to provide students with a complete set of computer skills, information on how they are used, and knowledge of their effects. Others urge a less structured approach, allowing students to learn about computers through writing, drawing, or composing music. Finally, an emphasis on computers as communications media leads to the stressing of applications such as electronic mail, computer conferencing, or the ubiquitous 'bulletin boards'. (Ragsdale, 1988: 160)

The discourse within the US, although now focused on 'technological literacy', had not altered much by the late 1990s. The emphasis is still mainly on access to different forms of information technology.

In the UK during the 1970s and early 1980s, the term 'computer literacy' referred predominantly to developing functional competencies including keyboard and word processing skills. By the late 1980s, as the use value of information technology became more evident in economic terms, the concept of computer literacy became superseded by that of 'technological capability'. This was defined largely in terms of having knowledge and understanding of technology and its uses, technological skills (practical and evaluation) as well as attitudes about new technologies and their application (Steffens, 1986). The focus was on concepts, knowledge, skills and attitudes that frame the process of learning generally. The value of what is being learned would depend very much on the *content* in which the learning process is embedded, the *context* in which learning takes place and the *pedagogical and philosophical principles* that underscore the overall teaching and learning process. Collectively, these would frame the range of literacy meanings that can be produced. In this regard, *information technology* taught across the National Curriculum in England and Wales, would offer a significantly broader scope than the market-oriented content and process inscribed into the *design* component.

Adopting a different perspective, Owen and Heywood (1990) identified three components to technological literacy, namely, the technology of making things; the technology of organisation; and the technology of using information. This provides a classical view of technology as both process and tool, although it excludes a consideration of the symbolic power of technology. For Hayden (1989), on the other hand, it referred to the knowledge and ability to select and apply appropriate technologies within a given context. This view is so broad that it can be applied to all the perspectives that we have discussed so far. Moreover, it does not provide any indication of the pedagogic and philosophical principles that would frame the definition.

Positioning their argument within the framework of development theory, Dordick and Wang (1993: 110) maintain that 'the effective utilisation of information requires a literate population' that goes beyond previous definitions of literacy that referred mainly to people's ability to perform simple reading and writing and numeracy tasks. Higher education, they suggest, is a necessary pre-requisite for the development of 'high-value services and products and high-wage workers (1993: 110)' as the basis of economic development. They advance a view of 'computer literacy' that includes the skills and knowledge to work with information technology but which go beyond programming and technical operating skills. Arguing from Campian (1988), they describe this as the:

> stage in which there would be fundamental innovation in conceptualising and processing information. This would involve a shift in perception about information formats and uses as fundamental as the shift from memory to written records was as the basis for traditional literacy. (Dordick & Wang, 1993: 112)

This view questions prevailing conceptualisations of literacy, and coincides with my earlier argument in Chapter 6, about changing definitions of text as a result of the facilities offered by information technology. At the same time it accepts, implicitly, the rhetoric that surrounds the impact of information technology on future labour demands.

Summary

These definitions, with the exception of those embedded in the National Curriculum in England and Wales, are rather broad and general statements that:

(1) present an incomplete, narrow or functional view of technology;
(2) lack a pedagogic and philosophical framework;
(3) lack criteria for the measurement of 'fluency'/ attainment;
(4) lack a consideration of content, knowledge base and context.

As an *educational practice*, the concept of 'technological literacy' needs to be clarified in terms of both theory and practice. In pedagogical terms, there needs to be clarity about what is being advocated, especially with regard to definitions, a coherent theoretical framework and criteria for measurement.

The perspectives discussed earlier, including the definition of technological capability inherent in the National Curriculum in England and Wales, also project a neutral view of technology without a consideration of the impacts and effects on the re-orientation of social roles, the environment and decision-making processes about the choice of particular technologies adopted within particular societies. Nor do they provide scope for the consideration and interpretation of social and technological inequalities between developed and developing countries, and the practices and processes through which these inequalities are perpetuated. In other words, they do not inherently offer a possibility for the development of critical interpretations, awarenesses and knowledges.

Critical Approaches in Conceptualising 'Technological Literacy'

In an attempt to overcome these difficulties, Croft (1991) identifies a framework that can accommodate at least some of these complexities. He associates the following characteristics with the concept of technological literacy: the ability to make decisions about technology; possession of basic literacy skills required to solve technology problems; the ability to make informed decisions about the uses of technology; the ability to apply knowledge, tools and skills for the benefits of society; and the ability to describe the different technology systems of society. Although still broad in focus this view, unlike the others discussed so far, makes explicit links with the purposes and uses of technology within culture and society. However, it needs clarification with regard to specific sets of criteria to frame the different aspects of 'technological literacy' that he identifies.

Over and above the issues highlighted here, there is the need to evaluate the appropriateness of the very concept of 'technological literacy' to describe meaning production within a context in which the nature of text and the process of communication have altered fundamentally. Although undoubtedly still important in its own right, the question is whether the term 'literacy' with its origins in the written word, *lit(t)era = letter* (OED), can be applied to the 'reading' or interpretation of the different types of media texts that now form part of the computer textual environment. The multimodal and interactive nature of computer text raises further questions about the validity of the term 'technological literacy' to describe the process of communication that inheres in this framework.

Clearly, the concept of 'technological literacy' needs to be analysed concretely in terms of the range of meanings and communication possibilities that it offers, and the types and levels of literacy skills that are involved. This points to the need for a multilevelled approach that addresses the technical, conceptual, analytical, communicative, pedagogic and philosophical frameworks and principles that provide theoretical support to both the literacy and communication process within the technological paradigm. New questions have to be asked about:

- the way in which literacy and communication are linked as part of the process of meaning production within information technology textual environments; and
- computer texts as organic social practices through which discursive individual and cultural meanings are shaped.

Addressing some of these problems, Lankshear *et al.* (1997) focusing on technological literacies within the context of classroom learning, highlight the complexity that surrounds the concept of 'technological literacy'. Emphasising the fact that all literacies are fundamentally embedded in different technologies, for example, 'pens, printing presses, dictionaries, eyes and brains' (1997: 139), these writers identify two aspects to be considered in working towards a definition of 'technological literacy' as this relates to information technology textual environments, and their relationship with the world. The first aspect refers to the need to clarify the relationship between 'technology' and 'literacy'. In doing so, they draw on the distinctions made by Bigum and Green (1992) between 'technology *for* literacy' which refers to the application of various information technologies to literacy (original emphasis); 'literacy *for* technology' which describes 'text-mediated practices that enable people to operate particular technologies' (Lankshear *et al.*, 1997: 140), for example, instructions on how to operate machines; 'literacy *as* technology' which relates to the social technologies in which literacy practices are embedded, 'ways of applying means to ends, tools/techniques to purposes, or applying modes of knowing to goals'; and 'technology *as* literacy' which refers to whether people are 'computer literate', 'information literate', 'audiovisually literate' (1997: 140).

The second aspect that they identify relates to the complexities that surround the concept of 'multiliteracies' discussed earlier in Part 1, including the varying concepts of 'functional literacy', 'cultural literacy', 'critical literacy' etc. and the wider analytical frameworks in which they are grounded. In light of these complexities, Lankshear *et al.* (1997) suggest a broad generic definition that encompasses the discrete technological literacies discussed earlier. Thus they define 'technological literacy' as 'social practices in which texts (i.e. meaningful stretches of language) are constructed, transmitted, received, modified, shared (and otherwise engaged), within processes employing codes which are digitised electronically, primarily, though not exclusively, by means of (micro) computers' (1997: 141). This definition, they argue, can usefully encompass a variety of multimodal texts involving a range of generic practices such as word-, sound- and image-processing, e-mailing, netting and gaming. These variables frame a basic taxonomy of technological literacy skills that are particularly useful to the classification of particular competencies in classroom contexts. Their view of 'critical literacy' incorporates key elements of the general critical literacy paradigm (see Introduction and Chapter 1).

In addition, Lankshear *et al.* foreground the skills of evaluation and analysis as key components in a critical literacy approach that 'engage students and teachers collaboratively in making explicit the socially constructed character of knowledge, language and literacy, and asking in whose interests particular "knowledges" and textual practices are constructed, legitimated and given privileged status within education' (1997: 155). They identify four goals to frame classroom learning including (1) 'enabling learners to render explicit the relationship between 'word' and 'world' ', that is, the relationship between textual practices and larger sociocultural practices, (2) 'providing learners with opportunities to explore the extent to which social practices, ways of doing and being, and forms of knowledge are historical, contingent and transformable, rather than neutral, fixed and immutable' (1997: 156); (3) ' encouraging learners to explore the social implications, for various individuals and groups, of (particular) discursive practices and values being the way they are, and to consider how different forms of practice and different values might produce different outcomes for the individuals and groups in question'; and (4) 'providing learners with opportunities to enhance their appreciation of the vast range of actual and possible ways of doing and being' (1997: 156). These goals identify important underpinnings to the view of 'technological literacy' advanced in Chapter 8 and will be returned to in that discussion.

In the next section I want to return to the point made in the introduction to the book, namely, that the notion of 'technological literacy' needs to be seen within the context of print literacy and the complexities in which it is grounded in society and culture.

Literacy in the Information Society

As I argued in previous chapters, rather than being displaced by computer text, conventional literacy still remains central to the process of societal meaning production. For example, word processing, hypertext, computer bulletin boards and electronic texts depend on the ability of users to be able to read and write. On a functional level, everyday life also still depends on our ability, *inter alia*, to write letters, fill in forms, read printed instructions and sign posts, make lists and to sign official documents. Similarly, despite the ubiquity of television, video and computers, we still live in a print-dominated society that requires the ability not only to decode and encode text but, increasingly, also the ability to participate in a range of textual discourses. Conventional literacy practices therefore remain central variables in the education process.

New literacy challenges

At the same time, in a world increasingly driven by (a) the need for innovation through research and development (R&D), (b) the multilevelled changes brought about in our everyday lives as a result of the nature and speed of technological developments, (c) the volume and range of information available, and its open accessibility, (d) the multimodal features of electronic text as well as (e) its interactive nature, we require significantly *more* than just the ability to read and write in a functional way.

For example, as we saw in Chapter 6, and as is suggested in Lankshear *et al.*'s basic taxonomy discussed earlier, hypertext environments such as the Internet, e-mail and computer bulletin boards are inherently discursive and offer new ways of learning and finding out about a variety of subjects. Similarly, virtual reality 'texts' offer new ways of seeing, hearing and experiencing the world; indeed, they offer an alternative *reality* in which concepts and knowledge can be explored in a simulated environment that offers concrete firsthand, multisensory learning *experiences*. These technologies provide a new means of *actively* knowing the world — through textual environments that represent different forms and modes of information, and also different formats as is argued by Dordick and Wang (1993) — and which can deal with a wide variety of content at the same time. Within these frameworks new conceptual and definitional challenges are presented to conventional literacy by:

(1) the multimodal features of VR and hypertext environments — including sound, image, text and multisensory experience,
(2) the centrality of the knowledge/content base to information retrieval and information processing,
(3) the fact that the author–text–reader relationship has been re-structured in certain hypertext environments, allowing a degree of textual malleability, in terms of both production and interpretation not available with print text. (and, relatedly, the 'historically contingent and consensual nature of information that we interact with at any moment on our screen' [McKie, 1996: 4]);
(4) the flexibility of focus, 'the infinite periphery' that theoretically frames the availability of information;
(5) the immediacy of interaction offered by information technology — and the possibilities that this provides for discussion of issues, and cross-cultural engagement with ideas with users located across different time zones and geographical areas (and, relatedly, the potential that this has for the shaping of trans-national, individual opinions on social, political and cultural issues);
(6) the potential for face-to-face interaction and hands-on learning offered by VR multi-user dimension (MUD) environments that allow participants to speak to and see each other, and jointly manipulate objects within the textual environment — thus integrating orality into the textual environment as well as the context of interaction;
(7) on an elementary level, the centrality of form, content and presentation to the expression of ideas; the ways in which texts can be edited, revised and corrected over time; the manipulability of information;
(8) the fact that texts can be prepared collaboratively within one context as well as within geographically dispersed contexts using, for example, text-based MUDs, or, the attachment facility on the e-mail.

On a *technical* level then, this multidimensional and organic form of interaction calls for a re-conceptualisation of the literacy process and the communication skills needed to function effectively within the new textual environments. The multilinearity structured into these textual environments means that the technical process of accessing information and the interpretation of text is inherently discursive. Moreover, as stated earlier, not only are the texts interactive but users can also interact with each other in a very direct way, involving not only the inner language of thought, but also orality on an overtly interpersonal basis.

Cognitive processes and conceptual issues

These multiple factors highlight the importance of the fact that readers/users of electronic texts operate at a higher level of information-processing than that associated with conventional written and print literacy. It involves the ability to reflect, evaluate, interpret, summarise, re-organise and re-define different sets and modes of information as an integral part of the process of reading. These necessarily involve metalinguistic processes.

Although intertextual associations are set up literally through hyperlinks within the text itself, readers/users also have to make their own classifications and selections to suit particular reading tasks, and to integrate these to be reproduced perhaps in another form and format. Whilst this form of information processing is also required by readers of conventional written/print texts, depending on the particular reading or writing purpose, they do so at a distance in that they have to locate the information texts themselves. To do this they need to have appropriate media access skills. Within the computer textual environment, all the information that is needed can be brought on-screen at the same time, where they form a textual composite made up of collage/ montage. Moreover, readers/users have to be able to cope with the on-screen network of information as well as the networks set up through hyperlinks within the text. This requires the ability to read quickly and also to assimilate different kinds of information; thus making for an intensive and focused reading process.

Multimodality is another factor to consider in the processing of information: image is no longer free of action and words. Seeing and listening and, in the case of VR technology, experiencing textual environments in a multisensory way now become an integral part of information processing. In addition, readers/users also require the ability to analyse the multilevelled interpretive codes that extend beyond the boundaries of the text itself.

These factors signify *conceptual* differences with conventional literacy in that the reading process in the electronic textual environment is inherently discursive. Readers/users therefore need, not only levels of what Bruner and Olson (1978) refer to as 'literate competence' which embraces a 'lower order register', but also 'analytic competence' which involves strategies of ꞏd problem-solving (Bruner, 1975). As is suggested earlier, ꞏnpetence relies on second-order thinking skills and operates at ꞏl of abstraction. Hypertextual and multimodal textual environ- ꞏan play an important role in enhancing the learning process. ꞏges of experiential learning in virtual reality textual environ- ꞏeen discussed in Chapter 6.

Technological literacy and the communication process

Furthermore, the interactive nature of computer bulletin boards, e-mail, MUDs and the Internet highlight the fact that adequate levels of 'communicative competence' also are assumed within the re-defined 'writing space' (Bolter, 1991). The concept of 'communicative competence' here refers to readers'/users' ability to participate adequately in computer-mediated discourse with regard to the appropriateness of contributions to the context of interaction. In order to participate effectively in these environments, readers/users require adequate levels of 'knowledgeability' which is defined by Giddens (1984: 375) as actors' knowledge about 'the circumstances of their action and that of others, drawn upon in the production and reproduction of that action, including tacit as well as discursively available knowledge'. It also includes having discursive knowledge centred on subject-specific, cultural and social knowledges; an understanding of the rules of discourse; and the suitability of utterances to the context of discussion.

The New London Group's (1996) concept of 'designs of meaning' provides a useful means of exploring discourse structure. The concept of 'Design' referred to by the NLG comprises three elements including 'available designs', 'designing' and 'the redesigned' which work together as a dynamic cycle of meaning production. 'Available Designs' refer to the resources involved in textual production and include different 'grammars' such as language, photography, film, or gesture (NLG, 1996: 74). It also includes 'orders of discourse' which refer to:

> the structured set of conventions associated with semiotic activity in a given social space — a particular society, or a particular institution such as a school or workplace, or more loosely structured spaces of ordinary life encapsulated in the notion of different lifeworlds. An order of discourse is a socially produced array of discourses, intermeshing and dynamically interacting.

These, in turn, involve 'particular Design conventions including discourses, styles, genres, dialects and voices' (p. 75). The concept of 'Designing' refers to the transformation of knowledge 'in producing new constructions and representations of reality'(p. 76). This dynamic process of interaction between text and context, it is argued, allows people to transform each other and themselves — and produce 'The Redesigned', that is, they produce new meaning. The NLG argues further that metalanguages are needed to describe different modes of meaning production. This dialogical concept of meaning making provides a useful means of engaging with my argument for the need to 'read the word and the world' in its widest sense discussed in Chapter 8.

Re-conceptualising Technological Literacy

The discussion so far has illustrated the fact that computer text environments rely on significantly more sophisticated skills than those associated with basic literacy defined as the ability to read, write and understand a short piece of written material in the common language of use. Clearly then, whilst conventional literacy is a necessary pre-requisite to access information, it is increasingly no longer _sufficient in itself_ for people to operate in the re-defined textual environment. The multiple facilities offered by information technology and the multilevelled meanings produced by computer text have contributed to the fact that basic literacy _has become a taken-for-granted variable within a broader, multidimensional and organic process of communication._ Conventional literacy therefore should be seen as constituting _one aspect_ of a broader set of communication skills needed to function effectively in the information society.

So far I have highlighted the significance of knowledge competence, information, interaction and a diverse range of textual discourses within the technological paradigm, and the need for a model of 'communicative competence' that integrates conventional literacy skills that operate at a higher level of information processing, functional technological competencies, oracy, discourse genres and a broad range of social and cultural knowledges. Transferred to the broader social terrain, these aspects coincide with the new worker competencies to be addressed in education (Levin & Rumberger 1995) outlined in Chapter 5 (see Table 5.1). Areas specific to the literacy process include:

> (1) their emphasis on communication which, according to Levin & Rumberger (1995: 84), refer to 'the appropriate uses of spoken, written and kinetic communication as well as good listening, reading comprehension and interpretive skills for receiving messages';
> (2) the importance that they attach to higher order thinking skills, for example, 'evaluation and generation of logical arguments including both inductive and deductive approaches';
> (3) the importance of self-evaluation, decision-making and problem-solving that involves lateral thinking, research and organisation skills as well as social knowledges;
> (4) obtaining and using information which includes 'deciding which information is relevant, knowing how to obtain it, obtaining it and putting it into use' (1995: 85).

Implicit in their view of a multilevelled literacy combined with communication skills is the need for a pedagogic framework that emphasises the learning process and creative problem-solving, as opposed to narrow skills acquisition.

Gaps and silences in the technological literacy discourse

However, although these factors are important with regard to providing learners with functional skills to operate in the information society, the power and value of texts ultimately reside in society and culture. An evaluation of the concept of 'technological literacy', therefore, also has to consider its adequacy in addressing what Croft (1991: 3) refers to as 'the ability to make informed decisions about the uses of technology; the ability to apply knowledge, tools and skills for the benefits of society; and the ability to describe the different technology systems of society'. The significance of this perspective lies in the fact that:

> as technologies are being built and put into use, significant alterations in patterns of human activity and human institutions are already taking place. New worlds are being made. The construction of a technical system that involves human beings as operating parts brings a reconstruction of social roles and relationships' (Winner, 1986: 11).

The philosophical framing of the concept of 'technological literacy', in terms of this argument, has to include the fact that technology is insidiously changing not only the way we live but also our positions within society as well as our perceptions and expectations of the world in which we live. This includes the different lifeworlds that we inhabit and the multiidentities that are associated with these.

But it is significantly more than that. Winner (1986: 31) argues further that 'certain devices and systems are almost invariably linked to particular ways of organising power and authority. Of significance in the 'information' society is the increasing role that databases play in constituting us as subjects. Poster (1994; 1996) provides an analysis of the surveillance role of databases in the world today. Comparing it with Bentham's concept of the Panopticon, he argues that 'like the prison, databases work continuously, systematically and surreptitiously, accumulating information about individuals and composing it into profiles . . . instantaneously, across the globe, information from databases flows in cyberspace to keep tabs on people' (Poster, 1994: 184). Databases, he argues, play a significant role in constructing both subjectivities and identities in the postmodern society. Furthermore, highlighting the links between technology and power processes, Winner (1986: 32) maintains that the impacts and effects of technology on society do not relate only to:

how many jobs will be created, how much income generated, how many pollutants added, or how many cancers produced. Rather, the issue has to do with the ways in which choices about the technology have important consequences for the form and quality of human associations.

It follows then that the concept of 'technological literacy' has to cater for the development of the ability to understand and question the nature of the choices made on our behalf in *power institutions*. In order to be effective citizens we need to understand both the 'how' and the 'why' of information technology and its role in society in its broadest sense. As such, it needs to address also the power relations in which it is constituted within society.

Again, this underlines the need for a discursive knowledge-base that is derived from reason and argument rather than commonsense intuition and political rhetoric. In other words, the concept of 'technological literacy' needs to be oriented towards the teaching of the skills and knowledges required to participate effectively in the democratic process. These skills and awarenesses rely on a substantive technological, social and cultural knowledge base, understanding of societal decision-making processes, routes of access to these, and therefore their roles as citizens participating in the building of a strong civil society. But the notion of civil society needs to be qualified in relation to broader developments. As the NLG argues, the very concept of civil society has altered within the context of geo-political change resulting in rising tensions between local diversity and global connectedness. Advocating the notion of 'civic pluralism' the NLG maintains:

> Instead of core culture and national standards, the realm of the civic is a space for the negotiation of a different sort of social order: where differences are actively recognised, where these differences are negotiated in such a way that they complement each other, and where people have the chance to expand their cultural and linguistic repertoires so that they can access a broader range of cultural and institutional resources. (NLG, 1996: 69)

I return to these issues again in Chapter 8, and especially in relation to what this means for people living in developing countries where issues of linguistic human rights remain unresolved.

Technological literacy as a form of discourse

The factors identified earlier highlight the significance of the need for readers/users to be inducted into ways of participation in *different forms of discourse* including meanings produced in face-to-face interaction, at the interface of person and text, with another/others mediated by the computer screen, and cross-cultural discourse. It also includes the ability to analyse the social construction of social and individual 'truths' in power/knowledge discourses. In addition, Fairclough (1989: 198), arguing from Habermas' theory of communicative action, distinguishes between 'strategic' discourse, that is, 'discourse oriented towards instrumental goals, to getting results', and 'communicative' discourse 'which is oriented to reaching understanding between participants'. This links with Verhoeven's reworking of functional literacy discussed in Chapter 1.

Discourse *strategies* used in speaking and writing, constitute another important aspect of the communication process and refers to 'how we make use of linguistic and other kinds of competence in order to achieve our communicative aims, and at the same time, to present a picture of ourselves'(McCarthy & Carter, 1994: 177). Discourse strategies, in terms of this, describe the awareness of the speaker/writer of the overall communicative process, and the ways in which they need to modify their input to suit the context of interaction — thus contributing to the concept of 'communicative competence' discussed earlier. Again, as we saw in Chapter 6, discourse also refers to textual analysis which centres on 'the *description* of the text, *interpretation* of the relationship between text and interaction, and *explanation* of the relationship between interaction and social context' (Fairclough, 1989: 109, original emphasis).

Altogether, these different aspects of the communication process describe the ability to participate in a range of registers suited to particular discourse frameworks. Many of these are included in Bakhtin's typology of discourse frameworks discussed in Chapter 1, but here it includes a specific focus on communication for learning, and a more detailed view of the communication process itself. Also needed is a meta-perspective on the construction of discourse meanings within and through social and communication practices, that is, 'the interpenetration of power and knowledge, and the massive dependence of power upon knowledge' (Fairclough, 1989: 213). Again, this coincides with the NLG's concept of 'metalanguages' previously discussed. These issues are signally important within a global context in which different sets of power relations are embodied in information technology, and legitimated in a discourse centred on the imperative to adjust to the information society. Looked at in this way, a concept of 'technological literacy/capability' that incorporates discourse as a means of communication as well as a means of critical analysis, would provide learners access to what Bruner (1975) refers to as 'the empowering techniques of the culture'.

Towards a re-defined framework for technological literacy

The different literacy and communication skills that are involved in the reading/interpretation of information technology texts highlighted here, reveal a multilevelled, multimodal and organic process of interaction between person and the textual environment. Of significance is:

- the centrality of the higher-order cognitive processes involved in information processing;
- the structural complexity of the textual environment itself;
- the speed required in processing information;
- the need for interaction skills suited to specific discourse frameworks;
- and the importance of having a discursive knowledge base.

Technical and basic literacy skills, within this framework, are taken-for-granted variables — they are necessary pre-requisites to be able to function within the different multimodal textual environments.

The discussion has also highlighted the importance of having a set of broader philosophical and pedagogic principles to frame and underpin the concept of technological literacy within the curriculum, and to provide criteria against which levels technological literacy can be measured. A re-defined framework as a guide to policy consideration, based on the literacy and communication skills and the forms of knowledges identified throughout this chapter, is provided in Table 7.1.

This schematic outline of skills, knowledges and awarenesses associated with the concept of technological literacy, serves to underline the extent to which information technology now defines the learning environment, and also the learning process. Whilst information technology texts may not replace the practical versatility of the book — in that you can carry it with you anywhere, in your pocket, in your bag; you can read it in lying in bed or on the beach; you can handle it — they will become increasingly important as sources of information and as additional learning environments within and beyond the school. Whilst books undoubtedly allow for a more reflective process of reading as is suggested by Eco (1996), reflectivity does form part of the process of learning through the medium of information technology text. Readers/users have to reflect on the information as part of the process of selection, and in applying it to their work task, they assimilate its meanings. Alternatively, they may choose to reject particular forms of information. Since this process is integral to the overall learning process, it has the potential to contribute to a reflexive learning experience, that is, the ability to act upon available sets of information and knowledge. The need for reflexivity is strongly implied in

Table 7.1 guidelines for a technological literacy/capability policy framework

Categories	Knowledge	Skills	Awarenesses
Philosophical framework	Democratic process; impact of technology on society, work, culture; validity and ethics of social uses and applications of technology; alternative solutions	Democratic decision-making; questioning; debate; critical inquiry; problem-solving	Censorship; social inequalities; ecology; technological inequalities; community; global economic, political, cultural awareness including differences, similarities and inequalities
Knowledge base	Different subject registers; different subject knowledges; knowledge of different cultures; understanding the validity and usefulness of particular technological solutions to social problems — and alternatives; how information technology texts are constructed; political processes — technological choices made in social policy;	Skills and knowledge application, knowledge and skills transfer; evaluating information; evaluating VR textual 'experience'	Cause and effect, fact and opinion publishing conventions on Internet; information technology texts as cultural artefacts having both functional and symbolic value; material basis of information technology text
Literacy framework	Data-handling processes; textual environments and how they work; written and graphic formats, metaphysics of different textual modes; different types of information sources including bibliographic databases, library catalogues	Information access; information processing; reading for meaning; skimming, scanning for information; intensive reading; interpreting meanings, analytical competence; writing for different purposes, evaluation; information retrieval; decoding, encoding, textual and meta-textual significations	Multilevelled meanings produced in and through multimedia and electronic texts, alternative interpretations, critical awareness

Categories	Knowledge	Skills	Awarenesses
Communication framework	Oral discourse rules and conventions; discourse strategies; textual discourses; registers suited to context of interaction; hypothesis; contextual meanings	Debate and discussion asking questions listening; presenting an argument; expressing opinions; argumentation negotiating meanings and outcomes in discussion/debate	Respecting different points of view; cause and effect; different discourse outcomes; appropriateness of utterances within specific discourse contexts
Technological framework	Textual environments; technological processes; systems	Technical operating skills: accessing the Internet, using e-mail, computer bulletin boards; desktop publishing, CD ROM, VR textual environments knowledge of different software packages and their usefulness to particular tasks; setting up hypertext environments; creating and working with databases, reasoning	Cause and effect; impacts and effects of information technology on work process
Pedagogic framework	Subject content; learning processes; teaching and learning contexts; peer tutoring; group work	Problem-solving: interactive, textual, practical, cooperative; self-evaluation	Work process; sharing of information; meta-perspective of learning process : goal-oriented or self-directed learning

the use of VR technology textual environments. Thus again, it highlights the significance of the cognitive and affective aspects of learning.

With regard to policy formulation, the framework also underlines the learning process and pedagogic principles suited to a good, balanced education. Considered within this discursive framework, debates about whether technological literacy can comprise a separate discipline based on a shared symbol system (Waetjen, 1993) become questionable.

The framework outlined in Table 7.1 with its emphasis on the learning process, suggests that to be effective and meaningful, technological literacy needs to permeate the curriculum. That is to say, it needs to be interwoven with the content and process of the curriculum to allow the exploration of meaning production at different levels (including its significations) within a variety of contexts. In relation to this, Levin and Rumberger (1983: 11) in their survey report on the implications of technology for education conclude that 'everyone should acquire strong analytic, expressive, communicative, and computational skills as well as extensive knowledge of political, economic, social, and cultural institutions'. They argue further that 'these aptitudes and knowledge are required for understanding daily experiences and for ensuring access to social opportunities' (1983: 12) — and thus provide the basis for a 'good solid basic education rather than narrow vocational preparation' (1983 :13).

Within this context, the knowledge society is defined in relation to not only the 'technological' or 'informational' mode of production as is suggested by Castells (1989; 1996) and Poster (1994; 1996), but also in relation to social and cultural dimensions of information technology. It is also defined with regard to the knowledges, skills and awareness required to take part in informed decision-making at different levels in society, including the complex and increasingly fragmented political process within the global cultural economy.

Technological Literacy/Capability, Power and Inequality

If we take account of the complexity of the literacy and communication skills required to function within the information society, then the inadequacy of the concept of basic literacy/education advocated as a route to social progress in the developing world becomes more evident. It is accepted that the problem of high levels of illiteracy is very real in developing countries and that this impacts on the quality of social life. However, if programmes of basic literacy within the framework of universal primary education remain the basis of educational policy and provision within these societies, it could mean that social and technological inequalities between the developed and developing world would, in fact, be created and sustained — through the model of learning advocated and supported financially within these societies. UNESCO (1997: 6) underscores this in its argument that in the knowledge/information society 'when it comes to both the acquisition of knowledge and the mastery of information technologies, individuals with the necessary threshold of knowledge are in a position to gain more, while others are left out'.

Adopting a different definition and model of literacy to incorporate aspects of technological literacy as outlined in Table 7.1 means that, in policy terms, consideration also has to be given to the organisation of learning contexts, and process-oriented teaching methodologies that allow different forms of inquiry, and therefore different forms of knowledge and skills to be acquired as part of the learning process. Within a global context in which increasingly higher levels of importance are attached to knowledge and information, whether in real or symbolic terms, literacy can no longer be separated from knowledge *content* and learning *context*.

Chapter 8

Towards a 'Communicative Competence' for Democratic Participation in the Information Society

The book has discussed literacy as an organically inter-related social, ideological, cultural and educational practice, within a regionalised field of study. In doing so, it has drawn on categories and terms of reference within a broad range of subject-disciplines, and also on cross-disciplinary perspectives in order to describe literacy as 'a many meaninged thing' (Scribner, 1984). Maintaining that perspective, I return in this chapter to some of the key issues identified throughout the study and, in particular, those related to the changing literacy and communication needs of the information society.

Locating the material basis of the information society, the chapter concretises the social and cultural knowledges identified in Chapter 7 as central to being 'literate' in the technologically suffused world of the new millennium. Taking account of Croft's (1991) perspective of 'technological literacy', and especially its focus on (a) the ability to make decisions about the uses of technology and (b) the ability to apply knowledge, tools and skills for the benefits of society, it examines the concept of 'communicative competence' as a necessary pre-requisite to participating in the democratic process within the information society.

Literacy: Identity, Knowledge and Power

As is argued in Chapter 6, readers bring to the decoding process their knowledge of language and how it works, register, role relationships and statuses as well as tacit and discursive knowledges about culture and society. Together these variables allow readers to encode the text with meanings in terms of their understanding and experience of society and culture. Contextual meanings are also implied in the 'metaphysics of the

215

text' within the broader framework of critical theory which supported the discussion of different textual environments in Chapter 6. Drawing on these frameworks, the dialogical relationship that exists between reading 'text' (language) and 'context' (the world) is explored here in further detail as an important underpinning of the concept of 'communicative competence', and its relationship with democratic participation in the information age.

Arguing within the framework of critical literacy, Freire and Macedo (1987) posit the view that:

> reading does not consist merely of decoding the written word or language; rather, *it is preceded by and intertwined with knowledge of the world*. Language and reality are dynamically interconnected. The understanding attained by critical reading of a text implies perceiving the relationship between text and context. (Freire & Macedo, 1987: 29, emphasis added)

For these writers literacy is regarded an *active* process of interaction with not only the text but also with the materiality of the social world. It constitutes an organic relationship in which reading, writing, oracy, and analysing the semiotics of everyday social life are integrated into the process of learning how to mean. In relation to this it is stated that:

> reading the world always precedes reading the word, and reading the word implies continually reading the world...we can go further and say that reading the word is not preceded merely by reading the world, but by a certain form of *writing* or *rewriting* it, that is, of transforming it by means of conscious, practical work. (Freire & Macedo, 1987: 35)

This view essentially derives from Gramsci's perspective on literacy as a social practice rooted in social action. The organic process of interaction between person, text and context grounded in an ongoing critical interrogation of social life, according to Gramsci, provides the possibility for disempowered groups and individuals to refract and challenge hegemonic meanings within the culture, and to put into place oppositional and culturally 'empowering' discourses on language, knowledge and learning within the context of people's everyday lives. In other words, the positioning of social actors in relation to the social world, the questioning of constructed norms and inequalities, would allow them to produce theories about the world in which they live — and, ultimately, to act on them. Literacy conceptualised within this framework is seen as being integrally linked with a project of social critique.

The view of meaning production subscribed to by Gramsci, and developed by Freire and Macedo, emphasises human agency and *reflexivity* (Giddens, 1991), that is, the possibility for people to engage in a process of defining their own self-identity. Self-identity refers to 'the capacity to experience oneself as an active and relatively coherent *participant* in a social world' (Weir, 1995: 264, original emphasis). Giddens (1991: 52) maintains that self-identity 'is not something that is just given, as a result of the continuities of the individual's action-system, but something that has to be routinely created and sustained in the reflexive activities of the individual'. As part of the process of self-identification, people draw on their discursive and practical knowledges of the social world to define themselves in relation to their specific social experiences. This perspective accords with the New London Group's (NLG) concept of 'Designing' discussed in Chapter 7, which involves learners in a dialogical process of meaning-making through which 'configurations of subjects, social relations, and knowledges are worked upon and transformed' (NLG, 1996: 76). Literacy within this context features as a form of transformative individual and cultural power. I return to this concept of self-identity later. First in order to map the terrain of literacy within the age of information, I want to revisit the discussion of changing views and definitions of text within the information society.

Textuality: Crossing Conceptual Borders

The previous two chapters examined the ways in which the conventional concept of text has altered to include a variety of multi-media and multimodal texts, and also prevailing definitions of 'technological literacy'. I argued that the ubiquity of computers and multimedia technology in society, and their inherently interactive nature have contributed to the omnipresence of textuality and, relatedly, reading and interpreting texts in our daily lives. The all-pervasiveness of television, multi-media and computers has contributed to the fact that information technology also plays a central role in structuring different social realities and identities. This, combined with the organic relationship that exists between information technology and diverse power networks such as manufacturing industry, finance capital and the communications industry, have contributed to the fact that reading the 'word' is no longer a sufficient prerequisite to being 'literate' in the information society.

I have suggested that in order to operate effectively within these textual environments requires a more sophisticated range of knowledges, literacy and communication skills than the linear and functional skills traditionally associated with 'basic' literacy. The incorporation of information technology into social, economic and political processes and practices highlights the importance of interpreting also the sociopolitical and cultural contexts in which information technology is grounded, as an integral part of learning how to mean in the information society.

Using the dialogical process of interaction between text, people and 'society', the next section explores the important role of *context* and, more particularly, *social context* in the literacy and communication process within the information society. I take as my starting point Castells' (1996: 17) argument that whereas:

> industrialism is oriented towards economic growth, that is, toward maximising output; informationalism is oriented towards technological development, that is, towards the accumulation of knowledge and towards higher levels of complexity in information processing. While higher levels of knowledge may normally result in higher levels of output per unit of input, *it is the pursuit of knowledge and information that characterises the technological production function under informationalism.*
> (emphasis added)

This gives some indication of the extent to which information and knowledge are now seen as defining the technological development paradigm on a global scale. The technological skills, knowledges and awarenesses needed to operate within this redefined textual environment have been discussed throughout Part 3 and have been summarised in Table 7.1.

Continuing that discussion, I want to argue that in addition to developing functional technological literacy skills, the idea of 'reading the word and the world' emphasises also the *materiality* of information technology and its effects on changing 'the patterns of human activity and human institutions' (Winner, 1986: 11) within society. Our ability to influence the nature of technology and social change depends on our understanding of how society is constituted politically, socially, culturally and economically, the power relations in, and through which it operates, and the ways and means through which it reproduces itself. In addition, within an increasingly global cultural economy we also need to understand the inter-locking structures and processes through which discursive forms of power construct the social world.

These dynamic sets of interaction and, therefore, meaning production taking place within the broad terrain raise questions about the positioning of social actors in relation to the objective (existing world constituted in social norms) and social (intersubjectively shared by all members of the community) worlds (Habermas, 1997), and the ways in which they engage with these as part of the process of self-identification. I want to argue that within the information society adequate levels of 'communicative competence' and cultural knowledges provide the basis of participation and, at the same time, define the possibilities for social action. In order to maintain overall analytical coherence, the discussion will be framed by the categories used to analyse the different types of text discussed in Chapter 6.

Conceptualising reading the 'word and the world'

Informational and organisational features

Clarifying my particular use of the Freirean notion of 'reading the word and the world' (Freire & Macedo, 1987) demands that the concept of society as a representation of reality be codified at meta-level. In order to explore the dynamic interaction and multi-dimensional meanings suggested in the concept of 'reading the word and the world', I draw on Habermas's argument for a theory of society which combines 'the internalist perspective of the participant with the externalist perspective of the observer, of hermeneutic and structuralist analysis with systems-theoretic and functionalist analysis, of the study of social integration with the study of system integration' (McCarthy, 1997: xxviii). Taking account of these multilayered analytic dimensions, I adopt a perspective that focuses on the *systemic aspects* of society which are integrally linked with power processes, and the *discursive* and *interactive relationship* that exists between these and social actors. This derives from Habermas's (1997) conceptualisation of society as an integration of 'system' and 'lifeworld'. First, to clarify the concept of 'society as system', the social context will be described here in relation to its *organising principles*. These are summarised in Table 8.1.

The organising principles identified in Table 8.1 have to be viewed in relation to the complex ways in which they intersect and interact with one another, and also with peoples' lived experience as gendered, racialised and class subjects, workers, citizens, consumers, individuals, community and pressure groups. That is to say, the different lifeworlds inhabited by people on an everyday basis. Society can thus be seen, on the one hand, as being constituted in relational networks that sustain and exert power to control (and the struggles and tensions thus generated), and, on the other hand, having the potential through the goal-directed intervention of social actors, to be transformed. We can argue then that society derives its materiality from its organising principles, the social relations in which they are embedded, and the network of interactions that traverse its terrain. Ideology defined as a systematised set of norms, ideas, beliefs and values permeates the systems, structures, practices, processes and institutions that comprise the social world — and provides the significations of everyday life through which social meanings are produced.

Table 8.1 The social context: A view of its organising principles

Systems	e.g. economic system, production system, polity, social relations, sociocultural relationships and kinships, community, values, beliefs, social principles, management, systems of control; social rights and entitlements
Structures	e.g. social policy including development policy, language policy, social, political, economic, cultural and communications infrastructure, resources, trade unions, discourse, power interests, self-identity, stocks of knowledge, technologies,trade agreements, race, gender, class subjectivities, collective, institutional and individual strategies, communities
Practices	e.g. media, education, religion, culture; social group, race and gender relations, language and communication, forms of control including censorship, discourse
Processes	e.g. legal, economic, political, technological, social networks, power networks, social relationships, communication within and between individuals/groups, interaction between individuals/groups and social practices, production and consumption of goods and services, individual/community/ interest group action, distribution of resources, strategic actions
Institutions	e.g. cultural, juridical, religious, industrial, political, economic, work organisations; financial; health and social welfare; military, telecommunications, mass communications industry — and the frameworks of power in which they are grounded

As a *field of discourse* the lifeworld can be interpreted in terms of what is going on within the social terrain. That is, the nature of the social action taking place, the activities that social actors are engaged in, their roles and statuses and how these interact with societal structures, processes and practices. Collectively, these principles describe the discursive meanings that intersect within the social terrain, and, which are in a constant state of flux. Within this organic context of interaction, meanings are inherently subject to change according to particular sets of circumstances and interactions as well as through intentional (or unintentional) human action, and thus meanings are constantly made and re-made. This discursive network of social interaction represents the textuality of everyday life in which, as is argued by Freire and Macedo (1987), meanings produced in different sets of interaction between people, institutions, social processes and practices are analysed, reflected upon and 'rewritten' as an integral part of the reflexive process of self-identification.

Interpretive framework

Interpretation of the organic interaction between people, structures, institutions and processes can be regarded as part of the process of 'reading the world' — of understanding the complex, interwoven tapestry of relationships that comprise the objective and social world. It also involves 'learning how to mean' as multiple subjects, citizens, consumers, workers, individuals and communities in relation to that world as well as one another, and thus it incorporates the intersubjective world. In other words, people need to be able to decode not only different kinds of representational texts, but also their experiences of living and working in society, and to encode these with meanings derived from their discursive and practical knowledges of the multiple lifeworlds that they inhabit as genderised and racialised subjects, workers, consumers, parents and children. To do so, people require as is suggested by the NLG, a 'metalanguage that describes meaning in various realms' (NLG, 1996: 77). This view inheres also in Habermas's theory of 'communicative action' which requires a 'method-ological objectification of the lifeworld' (McCarthy, 1997: xxix). For Habermas (1997: 77) this involves:

> an objectivating view of the lifeworld as a system..(requiring) a functional integration of the lifeworld that takes effect in and through the symbolic structures of the lifeworld and cannot be grasped directly from the perspectives of participants. It calls instead for a counterintuitive analysis from the standpoint of an observer who objectivates the lifeworld. Information in brackets added)

This indicates the taking up of a meta-position from which meanings can be analysed and interpreted, then to be reworked to produce new meanings.

Also to be emphasised is the diversity of human relations including different cultural traditions and practices, social activism, social movements, minority and other interest groups that comprise the social context. Dewey (1966: 82) accentuates the complex interests that make up 'society'. He argues:

> Within every larger social organisation there are numerous minor groups; not only political subdivisions, but industrial, scientific, religious, associations. There are political parties with differing aims, social sets, cliques, gangs, corporations, partnerships. Groups bound closely together by ties of blood, and so on in endless variety. In many modern states and in some ancient, there is great diversity of populations, of varying languages, religions, moral codes, and traditions. From this standpoint, many a minor political unit, one of our

large cities, for example, is a congeries of loosely associated societies, rather than an inclusive and permeating community of action and thought.

'Reading' the textual meanings of the world, in this sense, would rely on having categories and conceptions that enable social actors to understand their lived realities as both observable and lived 'phenomena' in which meanings are constituted in conflict, contradictions, ambiguity and struggle. Again, this emphasises the importance of 'meta-languages' and, therefore, the ability to engage with 'society as text' at higher cognitive levels.

We participate in the world also in terms of the meanings that we bring to it. That is to say, our identities and understandings of the world are constructed through our participation in communities, institutions and systems of meaning which frame our interactions and, in turn, influence how we interpret our interactions with the world, ourselves and others (Weir, 1995). Halliday (1978: 139) discussing text as a sociosemiotic process maintains that:

> text is a sociological event, a semiotic encounter through which the meanings that constitute the social system are *exchanged*. The individual member is, by virtue of his membership a 'meaner', one who means. By his acts of meaning, and those of other individual meaners, the social reality is created, maintained in good order, and continuously shaped and modified. (Original emphasis)

The centrality of 'storiedness' in decoding and encoding 'social reality' is reinforced by Kvale's (1990) analysis of the interpenetration of language, power and subjectivity. Kvale argues that 'a narrative is not merely a transmission of information, in the very act of telling a story the position of the storyteller and of the listener is constituted, and their place in the social order, the story creating and maintaining a social bond' (Kvale, 1990: 38). Narrative, including social narrative, as a social semiotic provides 'a string of signifiers that illuminate our past, that reveal our future, that provide us with a heritage for our own times' (Aronowitz & Giroux, 1988: 183).

Meanings are shaped and negotiated not only at an interpersonal level, or between person and different representational texts but also, as I suggested earlier, between social actors and the sociocultural, political and economic processes, structures and practices that collectively make up the social context. Moreover, at meta-level, the social context constitutes a signifying practice, that is to say, it both represents and signifies selected aspects of everyday life, conveying meanings that shape commonsense understandings and conceptions of the world in people's consciousness.

People, therefore, need to be able to interpret and encode the primary significations that give coherence to the social world.

For example, communication technologies play a key role in structuring cultural values, beliefs, expectation, aspirations, dreams and desires of people in the context and process of their everyday lives — and language as mediating variable plays a central role in the social construction of reality. Of importance is the central role that television, radio, billboards, magazines (and increasingly the Internet) advertising plays in shaping the aspirations of consumers towards 'designer-living'. This highlights the extent to which culture has become integrated into commodity production (Harvey, 1989). Consumerist cultural meanings constructed in ever-present, ever-changing media images of designer commodity products serve to refract existing reality and, simultaneously, produce images of alternative lifestyles replete with their own tastes, desires, and standards. The mediation of a fragmented, kaleidoscopic reality serves to consolidate the ideological basis of the postmodern commodified consumer culture (Rassool, 1993). It is therefore not sufficient to be able to analyse the representations and significations of multimedia text but also to understand the roles and functions of the institutions in which they are produced and, in turn, their relationship with specific ideological, political, economic and cultural interests that underscore the social milieu.

The interpretive framework suggested here includes taking account of *structural* inequalities, that is, those inherent in the social system — the differential social, and therefore, power positions in society, the social division of labour, levels of poverty; as well as *structured* social inequalities. These include inequalities generated by policy, for example, the social exclusion or marginalisation of particular social, cultural and linguistic groups, gendered and racialised subjectivities, levels of unemployment, working conditions, availability and distribution of technological resources, and the sociopolitical applications of technology. It also includes access to, and the distribution of leisure and cultural facilities, structured and lived social roles, access to information and decision-making processes, as well as differential levels of participation in societal decision-making processes.

It also underlines the need to understand the process of social change; how society has come to be constituted in this way, and how society has come to 'mean' in a particular way during a specific epoch. People's ability to interpret and analyse these sociocultural and ideological meanings form an integral part of the process of 'reading the world' and, in a Gramscian or Freirean sense, through this process of codification to find ways of countering the hegemony of consumerism. In a broader sense, therefore, people need to be able to understand polity and have the ability to interpret *social trends and patterns of social change*, which refer to the ways in which specific forms of alterations take place in the social, economic and political order. Again, this places emphasis on the interpretation of the *nature* of particular processes of social change, how they inter-relate and what their impact and effects are on social life. Of significance to our discussion is the question of what the real and symbolic impacts and effects of information technology are on the quality of social life. This includes its enabling as well as controlling aspects.

Learning to understand social change within the present milieu requires an understanding of the cultural, economic, political and technological influences that underpin particular transformations and thus how power is constituted and distributed within society. This is particularly important if we consider the relationship between technological innovation and the global need for 'sustainable development'. Within this framework it calls into question the institutions, practices and processes including the social network of relationships and roles that sustain particular forms of technological innovation as part of the broader process of societal development. Technology is deeply implicated in the ways that societies sustain themselves including how people live and work, in health and agriculture. Thus it is argued:

> When looking at technology in sustainable development we have to ask, who developed or introduced it? Who owns and controls and maintains it? Who makes management decisions? Technology cannot be said to contribute to sustainable development, whatever its direct environmental impact and application, unless it also contributes to the social and cultural autonomy, the local-management, and the social infrastructure required for long-term sustainable development. (Wilk, 1995: 212)

In other words, technology is integrally linked with social process, and decisions about technological choices can only take place effectively if they are based on an understanding of how particular societies operate, and the sociocultural relations that frame the lives of all the people living in them.

Other complexities include the fact that societies are constituted in historical relations, and that different processes and practices operating within them provide for their distinctiveness. At the same time, within an increasingly globalised cultural economy, we can no longer talk about culturally homogeneous societies; most societies today comprise a rich tapestry of different cultures and lifestyles. In this regard we have looked in Part 1, at the implications of different types of migration have for the conceptualisation of societal literacy levels, especially as this involves language-state relations in different societies. In relation to this, it explored the view that societies are also differently constituted across space and time as has been the case, for example, with colonial and postcolonial countries which have historically existed in relations of domination and subordination — as well as in struggle and contestation. We have seen throughout the book, the complex ways in which these historical variables have impacted on current technological, social and economic realities within many of these societies.

To summarise, the concept of reading the 'word and the world' adopted here places emphasis on the dynamic interaction between people, social structures, processes, institutions and practices — and the social system in which they are grounded — as well as historical relations.

Social impacts and effects of information technology

Castells (1996: 18) argues that:

> because informationalism is based on the technology of knowledge and information, there is a specially close link between culture and productive forces . . . It follows that we should expect the emergence of historically new forms of social interaction, social control, and social change.

As could be seen in Chapter 5, some of this is already evident in the impact that the social and political uses of information technology have had on the structuring of new, or re-defined social roles, new opportunities and also new, or restructured, inequalities within the work-place and in the labour market. Inequalities have been created between high-skilled labour employed at the 'core' of the technological production process, and those employed intermittently at the 'periphery' within the restructured labour process.

Ideologically, the re-definition of the labour process and the evolution of new work practices have legitimated the concept of structural unemployment as the new hegemony of the technological production process. People often are said to be unemployed or under-employed primarily because they lack the requisite skills and knowledge to operate in the changing skills environment of the work-place. This situation places the onus on people to adjust to and accommodate the needs of the information society, with the role of education and, *de facto*, literacy seen as filling skills gaps and mismatches within the labour market.

The incorporation of these meanings into national economic and social policy frameworks as well as macro-level discourses articulated within key international defining sites such as UNESCO, the OECD and the World Bank have resulted in information technology becoming the primary mediating agent of social change. Thus the informational paradigm provides the conceptual framework as well as the criteria against which both social and individual development are measured.

This period of transition from the industrial to the technological model of development is marked not only by social and cultural re-adjustments, also by *systemic* transformations. Fundamental changes are taking place in the way that political power is organised within both the national and global terrain. At micro-level, these have impacted on institutional organ-isation especially with regard to management structures, the organisation of power networks and the work process itself. Whilst for some workers this has meant an increase in relative power and status, for others it has contributed to marginalisation and a decrease of rights within the work-place and also in terms of their collective bargaining power as members (or enforced non-members) of the labour force.

According to Castells (1996: 374, original emphases), 'who are the *interacting* and who are the *interacted* in the new system, largely frames the system of domination and the processes of liberation in the informational society'. Chapters 6 and 7 discussed the different ways in which multicen-sorships, and forms of social and political exclusion secured through limited access to information and information technology in developing countries, have resulted in the emergence of information-rich and informa-tion-poor societies. I have argued that these inequalities are not the 'natural' outcomes of the technological production process; they result from national development priorities, models and forms of governance, systemic and structural differences between countries and also the conscious and selective social application of different technologies for particular purposes within different societies. These issues highlight the discursive ways in which power operates within the information society, and within the global terrain.

We are still living through this period of transition and, as such, it is difficult to predict what future outcomes will be. As part of the process of shaping our self-identities within this changing milieu, we need to be able to interpret the nature of the changes taking place in society and to assess what our roles are as citizens, workers, consumers, individuals and agents of cultural change within this process of transformation.

What powers do we have in shaping and influencing technological, ecological and social development goals? What are the skills, knowledges and awarenesses needed to participate actively in the democratic process within the information society — and within the global cultural economy? If as is argued in earlier chapters, new realities are in the process of being constructed, and as is maintained by Winner (1986), new worlds are being made and, at the same time, possibilities are created for new ways of seeing, experiencing and knowing the world, then it also requires new ways of engaging critically with that world. In order to do so, we need to have the necessary skills, knowledges and understanding as well as opportunities to participate in the discussion about the nature of the society in which we will live in the future.

Literacy, Communicative Competence and Social Change

Central to the concept of 'technological literacy' discussed in Chapter 7 is the argument that within a global context in which information, knowledge and communication increasingly define our social experience, both personal efficacy and social development are now more than ever, reliant on having a substantive basis of social, cultural, technological, scientific and political knowledges. The dynamic nature of the interaction taking place through the multiple and multimodal facilities offered by information technology and, in addition, its embeddedness in social, political, cultural and economic institutions also require flexibility to adjust to different discourses. People's levels of communicative competence increasingly influence their relative ability to participate in the democratic process.

Defining the democratic process in the information society

Democracy based on the notion of the 'ideal citizen' participating in effecting rational decisions based on reason and deliberation, for the common good, fundamentally belongs to the nation-state grounded in the principles of the Enlightenment. Held (1995: 145) suggests that:

> the idea of democracy derives its power and significance from the idea of self-determination; that is, from the notion that members of a political community — citizens — should be able to choose freely the conditions of their own association, and that their choices should constitute the ultimate legitimation of the form and direction of their polity. A 'fair framework' for the regulation of a community is one that is freely chosen.

Using this ideal-typical, popular-autonomous view of democracy as the basis of discussion, I will examine the ways in which social life has altered, and the impacts of these changes on how we conceptualise the democratic process within the information society.

I have indicated earlier that systemic changes are taking place in society in consequence to globalising processes, of which, information technology constitutes a significant part. The interactive nature of information technology exemplified in electronic mail and the Internet, the widespread application of microelectronics in capital transfer, banking, financial markets; and the expansion of the communications industry — especially the varied use of satellite information — have resulted in a world which is rapidly becoming smaller. The impact and effects of these facilities have generally been positive and enabling in that the rapid transfer of information between countries and continents provides increasing opportunities for interaction between people, machines and power processes within a global context.

Whilst globalising processes are exerting external pressures on the rigid boundaries of nation-states, they are also in the process of re-ordering and re-defining the democratic process from within. The hegemony of the nation-state which has historically provided the basis of citizenship, national identity, nationhood and party-political interests has been fractured by trans-national flows and 'networks of wealth, information and power' (Castells, 1997: 342) undermining, fundamentally, the sovereignty and political legitimacy of the nation-state.

As we saw in Chapter 3, trans-national centres of power, such as the European Union, the IMF and World Bank — as well as para-national NGOs, have redefined the concept of national political accountability, and extended governance beyond the boundaries of the nation-state. This places the democratic concept of the 'will of the people-nation' in juxtaposition with the 'will of the individual' or that of the 'international community' — which may not necessarily coincide. These developments have important implications for conceptions of citizenship and the political process in the information society. Whilst some aspects may be oppressive, others are potentially enabling and transformative.

For example, the internationalisation of production, the emergence of new forms of control within the work-place, and the undermining of the collective bargaining role of trade unions have eroded the rights of workers. Yet, at the same time, with the free-flow of information on the Internet undermining national censorships, the 'fixedness' of documentation replaced by the unboundedness of cyberspace and the emergence of new forms of social movements organised around minority-group interests, feminism, racism, human rights and the ecology have the potential of transforming the terrain of democratic engagement.

There is a burgeoning literature on the emergence of 'informational politics' (Castells, 1997) engendered by the political spaces created by electronic media including television, radio and the Internet — contributing to the emergence of the concept of a 'global civil society'. Several networks centred on social activism have developed including Conflictnet, Peacenet and Econet in the US which address issues related to conflict resolution, human rights and environmental preservation, GreenNet in the UK and several others in countries including Sweden, Canada, Brazil, Nicaragua and Australia (Frederick, 1994: 289). In the UK, LabourNet has emerged as a new means of building alliances amongst workers within the international terrain, allowing them to lobby support within workers movements across the globe. LabourNet evolved within the context of the recently resolved Liverpool dock workers' dispute. With web space provided by GreenNet, LabourNet managed to organise two days of world-wide action in support of their struggle, reaching beyond the confines of the UK Trade Union Council and the International Trade Union Federation. LabourNets are being started in Spain, Germany and Canada (Bailey, 1997). These networks can be seen as constituting new social movements engaged in social activism around topics and issues that concern particular groups within different societies, and in the global terrain. This leaves scope for the development of a variety of alliances across national boundaries and the involvement of people from different spheres of life. Again, this highlights the significance of 'multiidentities' in relation to literacy within computer-mediated textual environments discussed in earlier chapters.

Global information networks clearly have great potential to individuals and groups to explore issues of common interest, if they have access to these technologies. This would suggest that we are living in an era celebrating the free-flow of information which has vast potential for meaningful, interactive political engagement. However, such a claim would need to be balanced against the management of information by corporate and other power interests. For example, we have witnessed in recent years the ascendancy of media politics, scandal politics, the manufacturing of information events and the shaping of public opinion through agenda-setting (Castells, 1996). These developments have served to commodify political knowledge and have brought the notion of democratic participation into the realm of competition in the market place. This and the increasing distance between the state and the people have contributed to large-scale alienation amongst citizen voters and a sharp increase in party-protest votes; a form of option-taking that is not necessarily based on political deliberation. Much of this was illustrated in the recent general elections in the UK and the US. Castells (1996: 349) argues that:

> as a consequence to these developments, we do not witness, in general terms, people's withdrawal from the political scene, but the penetration of the political system by symbolic politics, single-issue mobilisations, localism, referendum politics, and, above all, *ad hoc* support for personalised leadership. With political parties fading away, it is the time for saviors. This introduces systemic unpredictability.

Although not all of these factors are inherently disabling to the political process, they nevertheless present fundamental challenges to conventional understandings of democratic participation. New concepts of community, political identity, self-identification and social action emerging in the information society are in the process of restructuring our common understandings of civil society and the role of the citizen.

Participatory democracy in the information society

For Pateman (1970) the essence of democracy lies in the act of participation. The participatory model, she argues, requires maximum input (participation) and 'output includes not just policies (decisions) but also the development of the social and political capacities of each individual, so that there is 'feedback' from output to input' (p. 43). This suggests the active involvement of every citizen in decision-making processes grounded in a critical knowledge-base, the existence of a democratic polity, dynamic interaction between institutions and citizens as well as freedom of information and freedom of speech. According to Held (1995: 146):

> If democracy means 'rule by the people', the determination of public decision-making by equally free members of the political community, then the basis of its justification lies in the promotion and enhancement of autonomy, both for individuals as citizens and for the collectivity. In this context, the concept of 'autonomy' connotes the capacity of human beings to reason self-consciously, to be self-reflective and to be self-determining. It involves the ability to deliberate, judge, choose and act (or not act as the case may be) upon different possible courses of action in private as well as public life bearing the democratic good or, in Rousseau's terms, the 'common good' in mind.

I quote this at length because, although not entirely unproblematic in terms of relative levels of individual capability, this view is central to the arguments made thus far, and to the concept of 'communicative competence' discussed later. Held's position is reflected, for example, in Giddens' view of self-identity based on reflexivity as well as Freire's view of praxis described earlier. Focused on agency, it requires the ability of people first to be able to read and interpret the social world and, second, to act (or not) on the basis of their knowledge and understanding of specific issues and events.

Giddens' view of 'knowledgeability' grounded in active participation is also central to Pateman's view of participatory democracy. She argues:

> The existence of representative institutions at national level is not sufficient for democracy; for maximum participation by all the people at that level socialisation, or 'social training', for democracy must take

place in other spheres in order that the necessary individual attitudes and psychological qualities can be developed. This development takes place through the process of participation itself. (Pateman, 1970: 42)

Pateman emphasises the importance of education in providing participants with the necessary psychological qualities and practice in the skills and procedures required to participate in the democratic process. Focusing on the cognitive and affective aspects as well as the experiential *process* of learning, she argues that 'participation develops and fosters the very qualities necessary for it; the more individuals participate the better able they become to do so' (Pateman, 1970: 33). Pateman also stresses the importance of socialisation in structuring individual subjectivities, the need to develop self-esteem, self-confidence and confidence in interpersonal relationships, and highlights the absence of these in the authority structure of the work-place. 'Political efficacy', self-governance, people educated in decision-making and having the confidence to participate in decision-making are central elements in her view of participatory democracy in the work-place.

However, participation in the complex social environment of the modern world requires additional knowledges including, as I have suggested earlier, knowledge of how society works, and specific influences on the nature of social change. In other words, people need to be politically educated. Pateman acknowledges in her later work (1985, 1989), that her earlier unproblematic view of participation excluded a consideration of the complexities that surround class, genderised and racialised subjectivities, and systematic exclusion of already disempowered social groups from active participation in societal decision-making. Indeed, analyses of democratic participation have generally:

> failed to explore systematically the ways asymmetries of power and resources impinge upon the meaning of liberty and equality in daily relations... massive numbers of individuals are restricted systematically — for want of a complex mix of resources and opportunities — from participating actively in political and civil life. (Held, 1992: 255)

These issues feature in a recent UNESCO report on social exclusion which states that:

> peoples, groups or individuals may be pushed out of the productive sphere because they have been excluded from the environment that gives one access to it, having been deprived of education and medical care. Entire portions of a society may be excluded from the enjoyment of effective citizenship and, *a fortiori*, from participation in those areas where decisions are made. (Bessis, 1995: 6)

Examples of this taking place have been discussed in Parts 1 and 2, especially as this relates to the high levels of illiteracy amongst women in 'developing' societies, and the role that patriarchal and cultural beliefs and values play in this exclusionary process. It has also been illustrated in the major disparities that exist in the distribution of 'informational' power as a result of inadequate development priorities and technological infrastructure, social and political instability and continued high poverty levels in 'developing' countries. Not only do 'race', class and gender inequalities 'hinder the extent to which it can legitimately be claimed that individuals are free and equal' (Held, 1992: 256), but also the unequal distribution of cultural (linguistic and educational) as well as cultural and economic resources between urban and rural areas. These aspects were explored in the discussions of mass literacy campaigns in Ethiopia and Kenya in Chapter 4.

At the same time, within a global context in which rigid cultural, economic and political boundaries are being fractured by technology and migration we need to have a more flexible view of citizenship and civic engagement. The NLG (1996), for instance, supports the idea of civic pluralism that acknowledges differences in which:

> instead of core culture and national standards, the realm of the civic is a space for the negotiation of a different social order: where differences are actively recognised, where these differences are negotiated in such a way that they complement each other, and where people have the chance to expand their cultural and institutional resources so that they can access a broader range of cultural and linguistic resources.

How these issues are to be resolved in many countries where there is a great divide between a minority elite group and a majority having no or limited opportunity to participate in societal decision-making, or where new nationalisms are articulated around language and culture remains problematic.

On a different level, effective participation in decision-making processes within social and political institutions is dependent on significantly more than a knowledge of democratic procedures, and confidence as is suggested in Pateman's (1970) analysis. In today's world, knowledge is dispersed in both formal and informal setting or locales and, in terms of this, knowledge of community and culture is as important as knowledge of society. Doyle McCarthy (1996: 24) underlines the fact that:

> today's social realities are communicated to us in the forms of newspapers and popular press, the official reports of commissions, data provided by census bureaus, social scientists, political hacks —

texts are produced and witnessed by the members of government organisations, administrative agencies, and such professional organisations as the American Medical Association. The growth and dissemination of these texts is both a mark of what knowledge is today and what *counts* as knowledge today.

In itself, knowledge is not value-free. Making sense of the knowledges made available within and through these defining sites requires the ability to be discerning of what is 'knowledge', 'fact' or 'opinion', or what is ideology. This is particularly pertinent in a world where corporate interests and the media often define the sites, nature and parameters of struggle and debate. For example, making a substantive case or argument to counter decisions made by large corporate firms or powerful political interests requires the ability to debate, analyse and engage in rational discussion. It also requires adequate levels of subject or 'expert' knowledges, understanding and knowledge of power frameworks, knowledge of citizens, workers, consumers and human rights, the legal process and organisational cultures. Some of this has been illustrated in the recent case in the UK in the action brought by two citizens against the fast-food MacDonald chain.

An informed public relies also on having access to and the ability to use specific information on particular issues. How accessible are societal and global information flows in reality? The widely peddalled idea of a free-flow of information on the Internet belies other, more encompassing national and corporate controls of information within the global terrain. Other than the surveillance function of databases, and the technological disparities that exist between the developed and developing world discussed in earlier chapters, control is also exercised by the privatisation of information wealth. Organisations and countries that own and command technological resources are placed in the position where they can dominate:

> the information marketplace whatever the future may bring in new information systems. Greater availability of communications apparatus (whether in developed or less developed nations) can only increase their domination of the information economy and their control over the form and context of the information that is offered. (Bailey, 1987: 397)

US domination of the Internet as well as the virtual monopolies internationally of particular software companies are cases in question. Bailey goes on to argue that the consolidation of the hegemony of information in post-industrial societies will 'constrain the information available, the technology by which value is added to it, and the access to power and authority that information enables' (p. 397). Thus he suggests that 'evolving literacy, therefore, will surely parallel evolving stratification of economic functions and the distribution of wealth. In such a world, democratic ideals will be difficult to maintain' (p. 398). The language of facilities such as the Internet and software packages will have an impact on levels of personal access to information in countries where English is not an official language.

Furthermore, the foregrounding in societal development programmes of economic output, in many instances, contribute to the neglect of emphasis on the social development of human resources. In these circumstances, literacy, education and health-care provision often become casualties of development priorities, catapulting under-developed countries into a spiral of disempowerment. In this sense, asymmetries in information access and technological capacity will reflect asymmetries in power.

There is also the issue of the instrumentality of information, its commodification as a saleable resource, and the interesting question raised by Melody (1994) of whether having increased quantities will necessarily contribute to increased knowledge — or whether instrumental knowledges will instead come to substitute for knowledge. These are key issues to be considered in discussions of concepts such as 'technological literacy' and 'technological capability' as a basis of social development in the era of informationalism outlined by Castells (1996). They are also important variables to consider in our conceptualisation of citizenship within the present milieu, that in turn impact on the levels of participation in decision-making which, as is argued earlier, is central to the concept of sustainable development.

Conceptualising citizenship in the information society

Mouffe (1992: 231) regards citizenship 'not as a legal status but as a form of identification, a type of political identity' forged within a discursive framework in which the social agent is conceived of 'not as a unitary subject but as the articulation of an ensemble of subject positions, constructed within specific discourses and always precariously and temporarily sutured at the intersection of those subject positions' (Mouffe, 1992: 237).

This view takes account of different subjectivities and the discourses in which they are situated, and underscores the plurality of identities which may include ethno-cultural identity, identity as a woman, as a worker, and as an eco-activist. As such, it coincides with Gee's view of 'multiidentities' discussed earlier (see Introduction and Chapter 1). Castells (1997: 7) on the other hand, problematises this view arguing that identity should not be confused with social roles, which he maintains 'are defined by norms structured by the institutions and organisations of society'. Arguing from Giddens he suggests that identities 'are sources of meaning for the actors themselves, and by themselves, constructed through a process of individuation'. Within this framework, 'identities are not 'fixed states of 'being'; they are continually being shaped in their everyday interaction with the social world and thus they are flexible and engaged in a constant, reflexive, process of 'becoming' ' (Rassool, 1997: 189).

The views from Giddens and Mouffe are important in relation to having a conception of active citizenship grounded in democratic participation. The key combining element is the fact that they all emphasise agency, that is to say, they describe a process of interaction between the subjected 'self', the constructed 'self' and the social world. Self-definition is central to this process as it involves the affective and describes the process of 'de-subjec-tification' as individual subjects engage in an ongoing dialogue, critique, negotiation, self-affirmation and validation of themselves in relation to their social experiences (Rassool, 1997). The construction of citizenship as political identities would therefore involve different levels of engagement between the self, society and the institutions and processes that impose particular identities/subjectivities on different groups of people. Again, this process of self-definition relies on the knowledgeability of social actors, that is, drawing on their discursive and practical consciousness (Giddens, 1984), their ability to 'read' the social context and to integrate those meanings into their understanding of the world in which they live — and in the process — to re-define their position in relation to that world. Citizenship based on these principles suggests being involved reflexively in the *process* of civil society. Weir (1995: 265) maintains:

> Essential to an individual's capacity to problematise and define her own identity are cognitive and practical capacities for self-knowledge, self-realisation, and self-direction, which involve cognitive capacities for learning, for critique, and for organisation, and practical capacities for expression, engagement, commitment, and flexibility.

This construction of self-narrative, this 'story-ing' involves people in making conscious decisions about themselves in relation to the social world.

Education for citizenship in the information society

What is the role of education and, more particularly, literacy in providing social actors with the skills, knowledges and awarenesses to participate in the democratic process within this re-defined social and political terrain? Giroux's (1993: 28) concept of border pedagogies grounded in the idea of 'developing a democratic public philosophy that respects the notion of difference as part of a common struggle to extend the quality of public life' provides a useful means of exploring some of these issues further.

For Giroux (1993: 29) border pedagogy 'stresses the political by examining how institutions, knowledge, and social relations are inscribed in power differently'. He argues that it points to 'the need for conditions that allow students to write, speak, and listen in a language in which meaning becomes multiaccentual and dispersed and resists permanent closure'. Literacy within this framework is grounded in critical citizenship based on finding a voice, reclaiming power and a sense of worth. Giroux suggests that 'literacy means making one's self present as part of a moral and political project that links the production of meaning to the possibility for human agency, democratic community, and transformative action' (p. 245). Thus he argues:

> As a pedagogical process intent on challenging existing boundaries of knowledge and creating new ones, border pedagogy offers the opportunity for students to engage the multiple references that constitute different cultural codes, experiences, and languages. This means educating students to both read these codes historically and critically whilst simultaneously learning the limits of such codes, including the ones they use to construct their own narratives and histories. (Giroux, 1993: 29)

Thus they need to be able to read the constructed norms and, in the process, to fracture and then to re-write them in terms of a project of possibility for change. In teaching for democratic engagement, this form of critical literacy can be seen to provide the philosophical principles that frame the whole educational process.

However, to arrive at a set of guidelines for practice we need to take account also of the pedagogical and communicative categories and criteria discussed above and throughout the previous chapters. Not to do so, would be to relegate critical literacy discourse to the realms of rhetoric. Taking these factors into account, the next section will examine the types and levels of communicative skills, knowledge and competence needed to participate in the democratic process in the information society.

On Communicative Competence for Democratic Participation

Conceptual framework

Both Pateman's and Held's analysis, discussed earlier, support the importance of communication in engendering effective participation in the democratic process. Central to the 'self-production' concept advanced by Giroux is the imperative to give 'voice' to students as part of the process of decoding and encoding their experiences and relationships with and in the social world. In addition to reasoning and deliberation stressed by these writers, participation in decision-making and making informed decisions rely also on having appropriate knowledge, information and the ability to articulate ideas and points of view. These skills and knowledges rely on a social ethos that engenders participation. As is argued by London (1995: 33) 'the freedom to speak, to engage in political conversation, to discuss public issues, and to deliberate about the common good is the hallmark of democracy'. The skills of debate, the articulation of ideas and the ability to engage in critical discussion are therefore seen as forming the basis of effective democratic participation. These need to be supported by a strong and healthy civil society that systematically 'promotes discussion, debate and competition among often divergent views — a system encompassing the formation of movements, pressure groups and/or political parties with leaderships to help press their cases' (Held, 1992: 280).

Moreover, oracy in itself needs to be examined in relation to the nature and quality of interaction. In this regard, the structuring of learning interaction within the context of the curriculum has to be examined in relation to the overall view of communication that it represents and, relatedly, the social, cognitive and linguistic opportunities that it provides learners to develop their ability to engage meaningfully in the democratic process. The forms of discussion, the content of what is being discussed as well as the broader communicative process in which learning interaction is grounded, are all important aspects of meaning production. Within this broad framework, I want to emphasise the notion of developing 'communicative competence' as a natural link with the concept of participation.

The discussion in Chapters 6 and 7 of the literacy requirements within the information society has highlighted the need to develop levels of 'communicative competence' with regard to the ability to operate at higher-order linguistic registers suited to the context of interaction. The concept of register refers to the field, tenor and mode of discourse, reasoning patterns, the appropriateness of language use including grammar and vocabulary as well as the rules of discourse and the conventions that frame the interaction. These are inclusive of, *inter alia*, technical, scientific, institutional, political, social, and cultural registers. Registers, in this sense, imply the use of different literacies for specific communication purposes. As is argued by Weir (1995: 265):

> The development of self-identity requires the learning of social and linguistic norms, through which the expression or realisation of one's specificity, and the development of a capacity for the critique of norms, becomes possible.

This brings into focus the need to develop levels of competence in engaging in different discourse genres centring on transactional, expository, informational, critical and exploratory frameworks suited to particular forms and contexts of interaction. At a meta-level these aspects are framed by Hymes' (1974) view of 'communicative competence' which is grounded in the systemic potential (whether communication is formally possible), appropriateness, occurrence (the event taking place or production) and the feasibility of the communication act. Collectively these different elements add up to linguistic and communicative 'knowledgeability', the tacit knowledge that speakers bring to the context of interaction — and, relatedly, of participation. These knowledge, skills and awarenesses are as important in face-to-face interaction as they are in the computer-mediated communication environment.

In teaching for democracy, as is highlighted in the discussion of critical literacy framed by the Kingman Report (1988, see Introduction), the notion of communicative competence includes the development of higher-order thinking skills such as reflection, analysis, the ability to talk discursively on a range of issues — including social issues, negotiation, argumentation from text as well as debate and criticism. Learners need to be able to engage actively in critical reflection beyond the immediate context of interaction, and also have an awareness of themselves as speakers located within a particular speech, religious, cultural and political community. The possibilities offered by the multimodal textual environments for different sets of dynamic interaction between person and text, person and wider audiences also emphasise the significance of not only competence but also flexibility to adjust to different discourse genres.

At a more sophisticated level it also includes the ability to decode the primary significations that have served to provide a hegemonic coherence to the notion of the 'hi-tech' global world. Ultimately, communicative competence within this framework refers to the interactive process in which meanings are produced dynamically between information technology and the world in which we live — and the effects of these on structuring people's social experiences, the ecology and social life, the ability to interpret and articulate these meanings — and to act on them in terms of informed understanding, through existing structures. Thus our levels of communicative competence influence our levels of participation in the democratic society.

The importance of finding a 'voice' lies in the fact that policy-making derives from complex sets of interaction amongst different interest groups operating within a discursively constituted social context. Learners should therefore be able to participate meaningfully in those aspects of decision-making that will have profound effects on life as it is lived now and in the future. Again, in order to do so they need to have an informed knowledge base and adequate levels of understanding to inform the choices made on their behalf about the nature of the society in which they live. As we have seen, these meanings feature centrally in the notion of 'sustainable development'.

Pedagogical Framework

The convergence of the concepts of participation and interaction in both democratic theory and in information textual environments highlights the significance of adopting a pedagogical framework that is grounded in cooperation, collaboration and experience. Problem-solving frameworks of learning serve to harness these skills and allow learners the opportunity to develop knowledge based on informed reasoning and analysis. As we could see in Chapter 6, the multiple facilities offered by information technology textual environments can play a significant role in this process, allowing learners to develop skills, knowledge and awarenesses at a higher level of abstraction.

Lankshear *et al.* (1997) outline some of the learning activities that could serve as a means of engaging learners in dynamic learning tasks that extend beyond the classroom, and involve them in an interrogation of the socially constructed world. They suggest, for example, that:

> a class might create alternative Web pages that present information about the school community, local issues etc., and invite feedback, discussion and appropriate contributions from other Internet users. Within these virtual communities, students and teachers together can engage in dialogue across difference, seeking out commonalities, experimenting with identities, tracing borders and moving in and out of discourse communities. (Lankshear *et al.*, 1997: 157)

In this way a variety of linguistic skills and knowledges including different registers and genre, and higher cognitive skills can be developed in a real and meaningful way. Alternatively, Lankshear *et al.* suggest learning tasks involving comparisons of different types of textual production, for example, book versions versus texts produced on the Internet. This they argue, would enable learners to 'interrogate how information and knowledge are constructed, controlled and legitimated, and to undertake "anatomies" of the various social practices within which these texts were produced' (Lankshear *et al.*, 1997: 157).

Similarly, accessing information on the same topic within different websites could also provide a useful basis of analysing text with regard to different emphases, knowledge content, style and voice. The key issue here is the discursive ways in which learners can interact and engage with issues and events in the world, whilst at the same time engaging in multiple discourses and learning to communicate effectively in a range of situations. This, in turn, requires the ability to adopt the role of the observer, in Habermas' terms, to 'objectivate the lifeworld' and in the process to 'rewrite' it, or alternatively, to imagine alternative realities. Moreover, discussion groups via e-mail or the Internet could also provide a powerful vehicle to explore contemporary issues in the world and, specifically, technological, scientific and ethical knowledges implicated in the concept of sustainable development. Here learners can access existing networks such as Econet, Peacenet, Conflictnet, GreenNet and LabourNet discussed earlier, thus keying in to the 'global civil society'.

Multimodal textual environments provide content and the knowledge frameworks that allow for a substantive exploration and interrogation of different modes of information (image, oral, auditory, written) whilst at the same time, as is suggested in the activities above, enabling the development of knowledge that addresses both the 'how' and 'why' of information textual environments and their relationship with social process. Teaching people to participate in the democratic process therefore needs to emphasise the importance of open-ended learning tasks. Exploratory talk and discussion, even if positioned within a problem-solving model of learning, if it is limited to pre-defined, circumscribed, predominantly task-oriented and context-specific tasks, result in the development of the 'how to' of learning, to the exclusion of the 'why' and 'what for'. The pedagogical approach advocated here requires a process of learning that encompasses initial hypothesis, inquiry/research, project planning, evaluation, synthesising and assimilation.

Many of the skills, knowledge and awarenesses involved in the activities described here coincide with the worker competencies identified by Levin and Rumberger , (1995) discussed in Chapter 5 (see Table 5.1), and those identified in Bakhtin's topology of social discourses necessary to function in everyday life (see Chapter 1).

If the activities are framed systematically and coherently to cater for the development of specific aspects of the communication process, they would be actively involved in the development of 'metalanguages' and multiliteracies (NLG, 1996; Gee, 1996) as part of their overall learning. Thus they would cater for the development of both instrumental and discursive knowledges and skills.

The NLG (1996) suggests a model of pedagogy that includes *situated practice* which focuses on 'mastery in practice' or expert learning and involves 'immersion in meaningful practices within a community of learners who are capable of playing multiple and different roles based on their backgrounds and experiences' (1996: 85). This process, the NLG argues, allows learners to draw on their own knowledges of the social world. *Overt instruction* foregrounds the role of the teacher in scaffolding learning activities and providing explicit information, including metalanguages (1996: 86). *Critical framing* allows learners to 'gain the necessary personal and theoretical distance from what they have learned, constructively critique it, account for its cultural location, creatively extend and apply it, and eventually innovate on their own, within old communities and new ones' (1996: 87). *Transformed practice* describes a process of reflective and reflexive learning. This process lends practical relevance to the concept of 'reading the word and the world' described in this chapter.

Ultimately, the notion of 'communicative competence' described here can be seen to subscribe to the view of literacy, simultaneously, as an act of knowing, as a means of doing, and as a necessary part of the process of 'self-identification' and cultural transformation. The multidimensional view of literacy which includes 'metalanguages' (NLG, 1996) that make possible the 'objectivation' (Habermas, 1997) of the social world then becomes a central part of cultural power.

Participatory learning guided by the ethics and ethos of democratic engagement also has the potential to address the psychological aspects of participation identified by Pateman (1970), in that it would provide learners with the necessary support system to try and test ideas and understandings, to apply and resolve problems, and to ask new questions. Again, this has the potential of setting up a cycle of research-based inquiry grounded in deliberation and reasoning.

At the same time, not all learning is transformative; in many instances raising consciousness through critical engagement, or just learning to get things done in a functional way is appropriate to the particular context. This is the case provided that functional and instrumental knowledges and information do not become the *raison d'être* of the whole education process. The range of skills, knowledges and awarenesses linked with the concept of 'communicative competence' referred to here have been provided in Table 7.1 (see Chapter 7).

Conclusion

Paradigm issues

The book has sought to provide a comprehensive overview of the literacy discourse taking account of dominant definitions and societal approaches to literacy provision within different sociohistorical contexts. In examining critically the relationship constructed in dominant discourse between literacy and social development it has also sought to extend the boundaries in which literacy has been conceptualised, highlighting the organic relationship between economics, politics and culture in framing the literacy discourse. Constructing the analysis of literacy within a regionalised field of inquiry has enabled the exploration of complexities by being able to draw on the subject registers of different disciplines. As critical discourse, it has foregrounded human agency and, as such, it is more than a cross-disciplinary inquiry. It constitutes a border pedagogy in that it has sought to create its own language in which to deconstruct old paradigms that often, 'through their use of particular language forms, produce knowledge and social relations that often serve to legitimate specific relations of power' (Giroux, 1993 : 21).

Literacy and development issues

Definitions that frame literacy and development discourse and policy formulation need to take account of the range of texts that now prevail in our social environment, and their organic links with broader social, cultural, economic and political processes and practices. Thus they need to consider the high level of importance attached to knowledge and information within the technological development paradigm and, moreover, their significance to developing adequate levels of communicative competence to participate effectively in the democratic process in the information society. These factors have implications also for the way in which national literacy programmes are constructed in terms of form and content as well as pedagogy.

The discussion of mass literacy campaigns illustrated that as a quick-fix strategy it has failed. This was recognised at the UNESCO Conference in Hamburg (1997). Universal Primary Education (UPE), although broader in scope than the specific functional literacy focus of mass literacy campaigns during the 1970s, nevertheless, still has fundamental limitations in today's sophisticated literacy and communication environment. The information society which is increasingly also engaged in informational politics, relies on a highly literate and knowledgeable citizenry. This suggests having the ability to work with information in a variety of textual environments as well as having a substantive knowledge base to engage with life as it is lived in the information society, and within the global cultural economy.

These factors reinforce the argument made at the start of the book, namely, that the whole terrain of literacy and education has been altered in a very fundamental way. Within a dynamically changing cultural landscape, the lack of adequate technological infrastructure, technologies, training and expertise in the developing world will contribute further to the divide between information-rich and information-poor societies.

Thus it would reinforce social and economic disempowerment. New questions need to be asked, new registers, and new ways of looking at literacy and social development need to emerge in academic and policy discourse.

Bibliography

Aarseth, E. J. (1994) Behind the lines: What is a text, anyway?' In G. P. Landow (ed.) *Hypertext/Text/Theory* (pp.51–86). Baltimore and London: The John Hopkins University Press.

Adelman, I. and Taft Morris, C. (1967) *Society, Politics, and Economic Development.* Baltimore: Johns Hopkins University Press.

Adult Literacy and Basic Skills Unit (1987) *Newsletter* No. 26, (Summer).

Adult Literacy and Basic Skills Unit (1982) *Newsletter* No. 9. (Aug/Sept).

Allsop, T. and Brock, C. (eds) (1993) *Key Issues in Educational Development* (Oxford Studies in Comparative Education). Wallingford: Triangle Books.

Adult Literacy Unit (1978) *Newsletter* (Sept/Oct).

Amin, A. (1994) Post-Fordism: Models, fantasies and phantoms of transition. In A. Amin (ed.) *Post-Fordism: A Reader* (pp. 1–40). Oxford : Blackwell.

Amiran. E., Unsworth, J. and Chaski, C. (1992) Networked academic publishing and the rhetorics of its reception. *Centennial Review* 36 (1, Winter). < http:/jefferson.village.virginia.edu/~jmu2m/centennial.review.36:1.html >

Anderson, B. (1983) *Imagined Communities: Reflections on the Origin and Spread of Nationalism.* London: Verso.

Anderson, C. A. (1966) Literacy and schooling on the development threshold: Some historical cases. In C. A. Anderson and M. Bowman (eds) *Education and Economic Development.* London: Frank Cass.

Appadurai, A. (1993) Disjuncture and difference in the global cultural economy. In P. Williams and L. Chrisman (eds) *Colonial Discourse and Post-Colonial Theory: A Reader* (pp. 324–39). London: Harvester Wheatsheaf .

Apple, M. W. (1982) *Education and Power.* London: Routledge.

Apple, M. W. (1986) National reports and the construction of inequality. *British Journal of Sociology of Education* 7 (2), 171–190.

Apple, M.W. (1987) Mandating computers: The impact of the new technology on the labour process, students and teachers. In S. Walker and L. Barton (eds) *Changing Policies and Changing Teachers.* Milton Keynes: Open University Press.

Apple, M.W. (1993) *Official Knowledge: Democratic Education in a Conservative Age.* London: Routledge.

Archer, D. and Costello, P. (1990) *Literacy and Power: The South American Battleground.* London: Earthscan.

Arnove, R.F. and Graff, H.J. (eds) (1987) *National Literacy Campaigns: Historical and Comparative Perspectives.* London: Plenum Press.

Aronowitz, S. and Giroux, H. (1988) Schooling, culture, and literacy in the age of broken dreams: A review of Bloom and Hirsch. *Harvard Education Review* 58 (2), 172–94.

Aycock, A. and Buchignani, N. (1995) The e-mail murders: Reflections on 'dead' letters. In S. G. Jones (ed.) *Cybersociety: Computer-Mediated Communication and Community* (pp. 184–230). London: Sage.

Bailey, C. (1997) Towards a global LabourNet. Paper delivered at *LaborMedia '97 Conference* in Seoul, Korea, 10–12 November.

Bailey, R.W. (1987) The hegemony of information. In R. Steele and T. Threadgold (eds) *Language Topics: Essays in Honour of Michael Halliday* (Vol. II) (pp. 385–400). Amsterdam and Philadelphia: John Benjamin.

Ball, S.J. (1983) Imperialism, social control and the colonial curriculum in Africa. *Journal of Curriculum Studies* 15 (3), 237–63.

Ball, S. J. (1990) *Politics and Policy Making in Education: Explorations in Policy Sociology.* London: Routledge.

Ball, S.J. and Kenny, A. (1989) Literacy, politics and the teaching of English. Occasional Paper, King's College London.

Barrett, E. (ed.) (1989) *The Society of Text: Hypertext, Hypermedia and the Social Construction of Information.* Cambridge, MA: MIT Press.

Barthes, R. (1971) The rhetoric of the image. *Working Papers in Cultural Studies,* Spring. Birmingham University: Centre for Contemporary Cultural Studies.

Barthes, R. (1987) Textual analysis of Poe's Valdemar. In R. Young (ed.) *Untying the Text: A Post-Structuralist Reader* (pp.133–61). London: Routledge & Kegan Paul.

Barton, D. (1994) *Literacy: An Introduction to the Ecology of Written Language.* Oxford: Blackwell.

Barton, D. and Hamilton, M. (1998) *Local Literacies: Reading and Writing in One Community.* London: Routledge.

Barton, D. and Ivanic, R. (1991) *Writing in the Community.* London: Sage.

Barton, D. and Padmore, S. (1991) Roles, networks and values in everyday writing. In D. Barton and R. Ivanic (eds) *Writing in the Community.* London: Sage.

Bataille, L.(ed.) 1976. *A Turning Point for Literacy: The Spirit and Declaration of Persepolis.* Oxford: Pergamon Press.

Baumann, G. (ed.) (1986) Introduction. *The Written Word: Literacy in Transition.* Wolfson College Lectures 1985 (pp. 1–22). Oxford: Clarendon Press.

Beer, S.H., Ulam, A.B. Wahl, N., Spiro, H.J. and Eckstein, H. (1963) *Patterns of Government: The Major Political Systems of Europe.* New York: Random House.

Beetham, D. (1991) *The Legitimation of Power.* Basingstoke: Macmillan.

Bell, D. (1973) *The Coming of the Post-industrial Society: A Venture in Social Forecasting.* New York: Basic Books.

Benedikt, M. (ed.) (1994) *Cyberspace: First Steps.* Cambridge, MA: The MIT Press.

Bennett, T. (1986) Media, 'reality', signification. In M. Gurevitch, T. Bennett, J. Curran and J. Woollacott (eds) *Culture, Society and the Media* (pp. 287–308). London: Methuen.

Berger, P. (1972) *Ways of Seeing.* Harmondsworth: Penguin.

Berman, E.H. (1992) Donor agencies and third world educational development, 1945–1985. In R.F. Arnove, P.G. Altbach and G.P. Kelly (eds) *Emergent Issues in Education: Comparative Perspectives.* Albany, NY: State University of New York Press.

Bernstein, B. (1996) *Pedagogy, Symbolic Control and Identity: Theory, Research, Critique.* London: Taylor & Francis.

Bessis, S. (1995) *From Social Exclusion to Social Cohesion: A Policy Agenda.* Management of Social Transformations (MOST), UNESCO, Policy Paper 2. Paris: UNESCO.

Bhola, H.S. (1984) *Campaigning for Literacy: Eight National Experiences of the Twentieth Century, with a Memorandum to Decision-makers.* Paris: UNESCO.

Bolter, J.D. (1990) *Writing Space: The Computer, Hypertext, and the History of Writing.* Hillsdale, NJ: Lawrence Erlbaum.

Bolter, J.D. (1991) Topographic writing: Hypertext and the electronic writing space. In P. Delaney and G. P. Landow (eds) *Hypermedia and Literary Studies* (pp.105–18). Cambridge, MA: MIT Press.

Bonefeld, W. (1987) Reformulation of state theory. *Capital & Class* 33, (Winter), 96–127.

Borjas, P.H. (1989) Perspectives on the Central American crisis: 'Reactionary despotism' or monopoly capital? *Capital & Class* 39, (Winter), 51–81.

Britton, J. (1975) *Language and Learning.* Harmondsworth, Middlesex: Penguin Books.

Bromberg, H. (1996) Are MUDs communities? Identity, belonging and consciousness in virtual worlds. In R. Shields (ed.) *Cultures of Internet: Virtual Spaces, Real Histories, Living Bodies* (pp. 143–52). London: Sage.

Bruner, J. S. (1975) Language as an instrument of thought. In A.R. Davies (ed.) *Problems of Language and Learning.* London: Heinemann.

Bruner, J. and Olson, D. (1978) Symbols and Texts as tools of the intellect. *Interchange* 8 (4), 1–15.

Bryant, P. (1994) Reading research update. *Child Education*, (Oct.), 13–19.

Bukatman, (1995) Virtual textuality. Online Paper. http://jefferson.village.virginia.edu/~jmu2m/bukatman.html

Bullivant, B. (1981) *The Pluralist Dilemma in Education: A Cross-cultural Study.* London: Allen and Unwin.

Burgin, V. (1982) Looking at photographs. In V. Burgin (ed.) *Thinking Photography* (pp. 142–53). London: Macmillan.

Burgin, V. (1984) Seeing sense. In H. Davis and P. Walton (eds) *Language, Image, Media* (pp. 226–45). Oxford: Basil Blackwell.

Caillods, F. and Postlethwaite, T. (1995) Teaching/learning conditions in developing countries. In J. Hallak and F. Caillods (eds) *Educational Planning: The International Dimension* (pp. 3–23). Paris: UNESCO Bureau of Education; International Institute for Educational Planning, London: Garland.

Carter, R. (1996) Politics and knowledge about language: The LINC project. R. Hasan and G. Williams (eds) *Literacy in Society* (pp. 1–28). London and New York: Longman.

Casey, C. (1995) *Work, Self and Society: After Industrialism.* London: Routledge.

Castells, M. (1989) *The Informational City: Information Technology, Economic Restructuring, and the Urban-Regional Process.* Oxford: Basil Blackwell.

Castells, M. (1996) *The Information Age: Economy, Society and Culture Volume I: The Rise of the Network Society.* Oxford: Blackwell Publishers.

Castells, M. (1997) *The Information Age: Economy, Society and Culture, Volume II: The Power of Identity.* Oxford: Basil Blackwell.

Chewpechra, T. (1997) Scientific and technological literacy and sustainable development. In *Proceedings of the Third UNESCO-ACEID International Conference on Educational Innovation for Sustainable Development*, Bangkok, Thailand, 1–4 December 1997 (pp. 5.12–5.27). Bangkok: UNESCO.

Chisenga, J. (1996) CABECA Project in Lesotho: a critical review. *FID News Bulletin* (June). The Hague: FID.

Christian National Education (1948) *C.N.O Beleid*. Johannesburg: Instituut vir Christelik-Nasionale Onderwys.

Clare, M. (1985) *The Adult Literacy Campaign: Politics and Practices*. Centre for Contemporary Cultural Studies, University of Birmingham. Special Paper No. 80.

Clark, M. (1991) *Democratizing Development: The Role of Voluntary Organizations*. London: Earthscan.

Cole, M. and Scribner. S. (1981) *The Psychology of Literacy*. Boston, MA: Harvard University Press.

Committee for Academic Freedom in Africa (CAFA) (1992) The World Bank and education in Africa. *Race & Class* 34 (1), 51–60.

Computer Systems Policy Project (CSPP) (1994) *Information Technology's Contribution to Lifelong Learning*. Washington, DC: CSPP Reports.

Cooper, R.L. (1989) *Language Planning and Social Change*. Cambridge: Cambridge University Press.

Corner, J. (1983) Textuality, communication and media power. In H. Davis and H. Walton (eds) *Language, Image, Media* (pp. 266–81).Oxford: Blackwell.

Council for Educational Technology (CET) (1978) *Microelectronics : Their Implications for Education and Training — A Statement*. London: CET.

Court, D. and Kinynajui, K. 1978. *Development Policy and Educational Opportunity: The Experience of Kenya and Tanzania*. International Institute for Educational Planning Working Paper. Paris: UNESCO.

Croft, V. (1991) Technological literacy: Refined for the profession, applications for the classroom. Unpublished paper presented at the 1991 annual conference of the International Technology Education Association, quoted in 'Technological literacy re-considered' by W.B. Waetjen, *Journal of Technology Education* 4 (2, Spring), 1993. < gopher://borg.lib.vt.edu:70/00/jte/v4n2/waetjen.jte-v4n2 >

Crookall, D. and Saunders, D. (1988) Towards an integration of communication and simulation. In D. Crookall and D. Saunders (eds) *Communication and Simulation: From Two Fields to One Theme*. Clevedon: Multilingual Matters.

Czempiel, E.O. (1992) Governance and democratization. In J.N. Rosenau and E.O. Czempiel (eds) *Governance without Government: Order and Change in World Politics* (pp. 250–71). Cambridge: Cambridge University Press.

Czitrom, D. J. (1982) *Media and the American Mind: From Morse to McLuhan*. Chapel Hill, NC: University of North Carolina Press.

De Castell, S., Luke, A. and Luke, C. (1989) *Language, Authority and Criticism: Readings on the School Textbook*. Lewes: The Falmer Press.

Delaney, P. and Landow, G. P. (eds) (1991) *Hypermedia and Literary Studies*. Cambridge, MA: MIT Press.

Delors, J. (1996) *Learning: The Treasure Within*. Report to UNESCO of the International Commission on Education for the Twenty-first Century. Paris: UNESCO.

Department for Education (1995) *Information Technology in the National Curriculum*. London: HMSO

Department for Education (1996) *Expectations for Information Technology in the National Curriculum*. London: HMSO.

Department for Education (1997a) *Information Technology in the National Curriculum*. London: HMSO.

Department for Education (1997b) *Excellence in Schools*. White Paper presented to Parliament by the Secretary of State for Education and Employment by Command of Her Majesty, July. London: HMSO.

Department of Education and Science (1988) *Report of the Committee of Inquiry into the Teaching of English Language,* Appointed by the Secretary of State under the Chairmanship of Sir John Kingman FRS. London: HMSO.

Department of Education and Science (1989) *Design and Technology in the National Curriculum.* London: HMSO.

Dewey, J. (1966) *Democracy and Education.* London: Macmillan.

Dordick, H.S. and Wang, G. (1993) *The Information Society: A Retrospective View.* London: Sage.

Dore, E. (1992) Debt and ecological disaster in Latin America. *Race & Class: The New Conquistadors* 34 (1), 73–88.

Doyle McCarthy, E. (1996) *Knowledge as Culture: The New Sociology of Knowledge.* London: Routledge.

Eco, U. (1996) Afterword. In G. Nunberg (ed.) *The Future of the Book* (pp. 295–306). Berkeley and Los Angeles: University of California Press.

Edwards, J. (1997) The social psychology of reading. In V. Edwards, and D. Corson (eds) *Encyclopedia of Language and Education, Volume 2: Literacy* (pp. 119–26). Amsterdam: Kluwer.

Eisenstein, E. (1979) *The Printing Press as an Agent of Change: Communications and Cultural Transformations in Early-Modern Europe.* Cambridge: Cambridge University Press.

Eklof, B. (1987) Russian literacy campaigns. In R. Arnove and H.J. Graff (eds) *National Literacy Campaigns* (pp. 123–45). London: Plenum Press.

Engineering Council/Society of Education Officers (EC/SEO) (1988) *16–19 Education and Training: A Statement.* London: Engineering Union.

Fairclough, N. (1989) *Language and Power.* London and New York: Longman.

Fairclough, N. (ed.) (1992) *Critical Language Awareness.* London: Longman.

Foster, P.J. (1971) Problems of literacy in sub-Saharan Africa. In T. A. Sebeck (ed.) *Current Trends in Linguistics.* The Hague: Mouton Press.

Foucault, M. (1970) The order of discourse. Inaugural Lecture at the College de France, given 2 December, 1970. In R. Young (ed.) *Untying the Text: A Post-Structuralist Reader* (pp. 48–78). London: Routledge & Kegan Paul (1987).

Foucault, M. (1972) *The Order of Things* (Colin Gordon, trans.) Brighton: The Harvester Press.

Foucault, M. (1980) *Power/Knowledge: Selected Interviews and Other Writings 1972–1977.* (Colin Gordon, Leo Marshall, John Mepham, Kate Soper, trans.) Brighton: The Harvester Press.

Fransisco, M. (1996) A draft survey of information policy in Africa. < http://www.sas.upenn.edu/African_Studies/ECA/nan.1.html >

Frederick, H. (1994) Computer networks and the emergence of global civil society. In L. Harasim (ed.) *Global Networks: Computers and International Communication* (pp. 283–95). Cambridge, MA: The MIT Press.

Freire, P. (1972) *Pedagogy of the Oppressed.* London: Penguin Books.

Freire, P. and Macedo, D. (1987) *Literacy: Reading the Word and the World.* London: Routledge and Kegan Paul.

Friedberg, A. (1994) Cinema and the postmodern condition. In L. Williams (ed.) *Viewing Positions: Ways of Seeing Film* (pp. 59–83). New Jersey: Rutgers University Press.

Friedman, T. (1995) Making sense of software: Computer games and interactive textuality. In S.G. Jones (ed.) *Cybersociety: Computer-Mediated Communication and Community* (pp. 73–89). London: Sage.

Further Education Unit (1983) *Computer Literacy, Part I — A Manager's Guide*. A Staff Development Publication. London: FEU.

Further Education Unit (1989) *The Concept of Key Technologies: An Appraisal of Current Use and Thoughts for Future Implementation in Education and Training*. Project Director, N. Meeke. (Gloucester College of Arts and Technology). London: FEU.

Furzey, J. (1996) *Empowering Socio-Economic Development in Africa Utilizing Information Technology: a Critical Examination of the Social, Economic, Technical and Policy Issues, with Respect to the Expansion or Initiation of Information and Communications Infrastructure in Ethiopia*. A Country Study for the United Nations Economic Commission for Africa High Level Working Group on Information and Communication Technologies in Africa. Addis Ababa: UNECA < http://www.sas.upen.edu/African _Studies/ECA/eca_furzey.html >

Gee, J. P. (1996) *Social Linguistics and Literacies: Ideology in Discourses* (2nd edn). London: Taylor & Francis.

Giddens, A. (1984) *The Constitution of Society: Outline of the Theory of Structuration*. Cambridge: Polity Press in association with Blackwell.

Giddens, A. (1991) *Modernity and Self-Identity: Self and Society in the Late Modern Age*. Cambridge: Polity Press.

Gillette, A. (1987) The Experimental World Literacy Program: A unique international effort revisited. In R.F. Arnove and H.J. Graff (eds) *National Literacy Campaigns: Historical and Comparative Perspectives* (pp. 197–217). London: Plenum Press.

Gilster, P. (1996) *Finding it on the Internet: The Internet Navigator's Guide to Search Tools & Techniques* (2nd edn). New York: John Wiley & Sons.

Giroux, H.A. (1993) *Border Crossings: Cultural Workers and the Politics of Education*. London and New York: Routledge.

Giroux, H.A. and Macedo, D. (1987) *Literacy: Reading the Word and the World*. London: Routledge and Kegan Paul.

Goodman, K. (1986) *What's Whole in Whole Language?* London: Scholastic.

Goody, J. (ed.) (1968) *Literacy in Traditional Societies*. Cambridge: Cambridge University Press.

Goody, J. and Watt, I. (1968) The consequences of literacy. In J. Goody (ed.) *Literacy in Traditional Societies* (pp. 27–68). Cambridge: Cambridge University Press.

Goswami, U. and Bryant, P. (1990) *Phonological Skills and Learning to Read*. London: Lawrence Erlbaum.

Gough, P.B. (1995) The New Literacy: caveat emptor. *Journal of Research in Reading* 18 (2), 79–86.

Gould, W.T.S. (1993) *People and Education in the Third World*. Harlow: Longman.

Government Gazette 360, (No. 16494), Republic of South Africa. Pan South African Language Board Draft Bill. 28 June 1995.

Governor of the State of California (1995) *Getting Results: Schools Should Focus on Learning — For a Lifetime*. Report of the Governor's Council on Information Technology < http://www.ca.gov./gov/gcit/it_cal.html >

Govinda, R. (1997) Decentralized planning and management of literacy and basic education programmes. In *Proceedings of the Third UNESCO-ACEID International Conference on Educational Innovation for Sustainable Development, Bangkok, Thailand, 1–4 December* (pp. 5.32–5.43). Bangkok: UNESCO.

Graff, H.J. (1979) *The Literacy Myth: Literacy and Social Structure in Nineteenth Century Canada*. New York and London: Academic Press.

Graff, H.J. (1987) *The Labyrinths of Literacy: Reflections on Literacy Past and Present.* London: The Falmer Press.

Gramsci, A. (1971) *Selections from the Prison Notebooks.* London: Lawrence and Wishart.

Gray-Cowan, L., Connell, J. and Scanlon. G. (1965) *Education and Nation-Building in Africa.* New York: Frederick Praeger.

Gregorio, L.C. (1995) The global challenge for scientific and technological literacy for all: 2000+. Keynote paper presented at CONASTA 44: Science Teaching: An International Perspective, the annual conference of the Australian Science Teachers' Association, held at the University of Queensland, Brisbane, Queensland, Australia, 24–29 September.
< http://owl.qut.edu.au/staq/conasta/papers/LITERACY.TXT >

Grigsby, K. (1985) Strategies for mobilization and participation of volunteers in literacy and post-literacy programmes: The case of Nicaragua. In G. Carron and A. Bordia (eds) *Issues in Planning and Implementing National Literacy Programmes* (pp. 66–80). Paris: UNESCO, International Institute for Educational Planning.

Habermas, J. (1997) *The Theory of Communicative Action: Reason and the Rationalization of Society* (Volume 1). Cambridge: Polity Press.

Hall, J. (1994) *Coercion and Consent.* Cambridge: Cambridge University Press.

Hall, S. (1993) Cultural identity and diaspora. In P. Williams and L. Chrisman *Colonial Discourse and Post-Colonial Theory: A Reader* (pp. 392–403). London: Harvester Wheatsheaf.

Hall, S., Held. D. and McLennan, G. (1992) *Modernity and Its Futures.* Oxford: Polity Press in association with Blackwell and The Open University.

Hallak, J. (1990) *Investing in the Future: Setting Educational Priorities in the Developing World.* UNESCO: International Institute for Educational Planning. Oxford: Pergamon Press.

Halliday, M.A.K. (1978) *Language as Social Semiotic: The Social Interpretation of Language and Meaning.* London: Edward Arnold.

Halliday, M. A. K. (1996) Literacy and linguistics: A functional perspective. In R. Hasan and G. Williams (eds) *Literacy in Society* (pp. 339–76). London and New York: Longman.

Halliday, M.A.K. and Hassan, R. (1989) *Language, Context, and Text: Aspects of Language in a Social-semiotic Perspective.* Oxford: Oxford University Press.

Harvey, D. (1989) *The Condition of Postmodernity: An Enquiry into the Origins of Cultural Change.* Oxford: Blackwell.

Hasan, R. (1996) Literacy, everyday talk and society. In R. Hasan and G. Williams (eds) *Literacy in Society* (pp. 377–424). London and New York: Longman.

Hayden, M. (1989) What is technological literacy? *Bulletin of Science, Technology and Society* 119, 220–33.

Heath, S. B. (1983) *Ways with Words.* Cambridge: Cambridge University Press.

Held, D. (1992) *Models of Democracy.* Oxford: Polity Press.

Held, D. (1995) *Democracy and the Global Order: From the Modern State to Cosmopolitan Governance.* Cambridge: Polity Press.

Hettne, B. (1995) *Development Theory and the Three Worlds: Towards an International Political Economy of Development* (2nd edn). Harlow: Longman.

Hildyard, A. and Olson, D. (1978) Literacy and the specialisation of language. Unpublished MS, Ontario Institute for Studies in Education.

HMSO (1963) *Half our Future (Newsom).* Report of the Central Advisory Council for Education (England). London: HMSO.

HMSO (1967) *Children and their Primary Schools (Plowden Report)*. A Report of the Central Advisory Council for Education (England). London: HMSO.

Hobsbawm, E.J. (1990) *Nations and Nationalism since 1780: Programme, Myth, Reality*. Cambridge: Cambridge University Press.

Hymes, D. (1974) *Foundations in Sociolinguistics*. London: Tavistock.

Ingham, B. (1995) *Economics and Development*. London: McGraw-Hill.

Jessop, B. (1988) Regulation theory, post-Fordism and the state: More than a reply to Werner Bonefeld. *Capital & Class* 34 (Spring), 147–68.

Jessop, B. (1990) *State Theory: Putting the Capitalist State in its Place*. Cambridge: Polity Press in association with Basil Blackwell.

Johnson, J. and Oliva, M. (1997) *Internet Textuality: Toward Interactive Multilinear Narrative*. < http:/italia.hum.utah.edu/~maurizio/pmc/ >

Johnson, R. (1983) What is cultural studies anyway? Stencilled Occasional Paper No. 74. Birmingham: Centre for Contemporary Cultural Studies, The University of Birmingham.

Johnson, R. (1988) Really useful knowledge 1790–1850: Memories for education in the 1980s. In T. Lovett (ed.) *Radical Approaches to Adult Education: A Reader* (pp. 3–34). London : Routledge and Kegan Paul.

Jones, P. W. (1988) *International Policies for Third World Education: Unesco, Literacy and Development*. London: Routledge.

Jones, P. W. (1990) Unesco and the politics of global literacy. *Comparative Education Review*. (Feb.) 34(1), 41–60.

Jones, P.W. (1992) *World Bank Financing of Education: Lending, Learning and Development*. London: Routledge.

Khoo, S. (1999) Envisioning the Malaysian nation: Ethnic nationalism or corporate nationalism? In K. Brehony and N. Rassool (eds) *Nationalisms Old and New* (pp. 216–66). London: Macmillan.

Korten, D. C. (1991) The role of nongovernmental organizations in development: Changing patterns and perspectives. In S. Paul and A. Israel (eds) *Nongovernmental Organizations and the World Bank: Cooperation for Development* (pp. 20–43). Washington: The World Bank.

Kress, G., Leite-Garcia, R and van Leewen, T. (1997) Discourse semiotics. In T. Van Dijk (ed.) *Discourse as Structure and Process* (pp. 257–91). London: Sage.

Kumar, K. (1986) *Prophecy and Progress: The Sociology of Industrial and Post-Industrial Society*. London: Pelican Books.

Kumon, S. and Aizu, I. (1994) Co-emulation: The case for a global hypernetwork society. In L. Harasim (ed.) *Global Networks: Computers and International Communications* (pp. 311–26). Cambridge, MA: The MIT Press.

Labov, W. (1972) *Language in the Inner City: Studies in Black English Vernacular*. Philadelphia: Philadelphia Press.

Lall, S., Navaretti, G.B., Teitel, S. and Wignaraja, G. (1994) *Technology and Enterprise Development: Ghana under Structural Adjustment*. Basingstoke: Macmillan.

Landow, G. P. (1994) *Hypertext/Text/Theory*. Baltimore and London: The Johns Hopkins University Press,

Landsberg, M. (1987) Export-led industrialization in the Third World: Manufacturing imperialism. In R. Peet (ed.) *International Capitalism and Industrial Restructuring: A Critical Analysis* (pp. 216–39). Boston: Allen & Unwin.

Language Plan Task Group (LANTAG) (1996) Towards a National Language Plan for South Africa. Presented to the Minister of Arts, Culture, Science and Technology, Dr B.S. Ngubane, 8 August 1996.

Lankshear, C. and Lawlor, M. (1987) _Literacy, Schooling and Revolution._ London: The Falmer Press.

Lankshear, C. with Gee, J. P., Knobel, M. and Searle, C. (1997) _Changing Literacies._ Buckingham: Open University Press.

Lawrence, J.E. (1992) Literacy and human resources development: An integrated approach. _The Annals, The American Academy of Political and Social Sciences_ 520, 42–53.

Leftwich, A. (1995) Governance, democracy and development in the Third World. In S. Corbridge (ed.) _Development Studies: A Reader_ (pp. 427–47). London: Edward Arnold (1995).

Levin, H. M. and Rumberger, R. W. (1995) Education, work and employment in developed countries: Situation and future challenges. In J. Hallak and F. Caillods (eds) _Educational Planning: The International Dimension_ (pp. 69–88). UNESCO Bureau of Education, International Institute for Educational Planning. London: Garland.

Levine, K. (1994) Functional literacy in a changing world. In L. Verhoeven (ed.) _Functional Literacy: Theoretical Issues and Educational Implications_ (pp.113–31). Amsterdam: John Benjamins.

Lewis, E. G. (1980) _Bilingualism and Bilingual Education: A Comparative Study._ Albuquerque: University of Mexico Press.

Lewis, T. (1996) Accommodating border crossings. _Journal of Industrial Teacher Education_ 33 (2), 7–28.

Lipietz, A. (1988) _Mirages and Miracles: The Crisis of Global Fordism._ London: Verso.

London, S. (1994) Electronic democracy — a literature survey. A paper prepared for the Kettering Foundation, March. < http://www.west.net/~insight/london/ed.htm >

London, S. (1995) Teledemocracy vs. deliberative democracy: A comparative look at two models of public talk. _Journal of Interpersonal Computing and Technology_ 3 (2) April, 33–55.

Luke, A. (1996) Genres of power? Literacy education and the production of capital. In R. Hasan and G. Williams (eds) _Literacy in Society_ (pp. 308–38). London and New York: Longman.

Luria, A. (1979) The making of mind. In M. Cole (ed.) _Soviet Developmental Psychology._ Boston, MA: Harvard University Press.

Lyon, D. (1988) _The Information Society: Issues and Illusions._ Oxford: Basil Blackwell.

Macdonell, D. (1987) _Theories of Discourse: An Introduction._ Oxford: Basil Blackwell.

Machlup, F. (1962) _The Production and Distribution of Knowledge in the United States._ Princeton: Princeton University Press.

Mackay, D., Thompson, B. and Schaub, P. (1978) _Breakthrough to Literacy: The Theory and Practice of Teaching Initial Reading and Writing._ London: Longman for the Schools Council.

Malecki, E. J. (1991) _Technology and Economic Development: The Dynamics of Local, Regional and National Change._ Harlow: Longman Scientific and Technical.

Mammo, G. (1985) Structures and linkages for involvement of political leadership in the Ethiopian mass-literacy campaign. In G. Carron and A. Bordia (eds) _Issues in Planning and Implementing National Literacy Programmes_ (pp. 107–21). Paris: UNESCO, International Institute for Educational Planning.

Mathieson, M. (1975) _The Preachers of Culture: A Study of English and Its Teachers._ London: George Allen and Unwin.

McCarthy, M and Carter, R. (1994) *Language as Discourse: Perspectives for Language Teaching*. London and New York: Longman.

McCarthy, T. (1997) Translator's Introduction. In J. Habermas, *The Theory of Communicative Action: Reason and the Rationalization of Society* (Volume 1) (pp. vii–xliv). Cambridge: Polity Press.

McKie, J. (1996) Is democracy at the heart of IT? Commercial perceptions of technology. *Sociology Online*1(4), 1–14. < http://www.socresonline.org.uk/socresonline/1/4/1.html >

McLaren, P. (1988) Culture or canon? Critical pedagogy and the politics of literacy. *Harvard Educational Review* 58 (2, May), 213–34.

McLaren, P. (1995) *Critical Pedagogy and Predatory Culture: Oppositional Politics in a Postmodern Era*. London: Routledge.

McLuhan, M. *Understanding Media: The Extensions of Man*. London: Routledge.

Melody, W. (1994) Electronic networks, social relations and the changing structure of knowledge. In D. Crowley and D. Mitchell (eds) *Communication Theory Today* (pp. 254–73). Oxford: Polity Press.

Miller, V. (1985) *Between Struggle and Hope: The Nicaraguan Literacy Crusade*. Boulder, CO: Westview Press.

Mouffe, C. (1992) Democratic citizenship and the political community. In C. Mouffe (ed.) *Dimensions of Radical Democracy: Pluralism, Citizenship, Community* (pp. 225–39). London: Verso.

Mulgan, G. (1988) Collapse of the pyramid of power. *The Guardian*, 28 November.

National Curriculum Council/Department of Education and Science (1989) *Design and Technology for Ages 5–16*. Proposals of the Secretary of State for Education and Science and the Secretary of State for Wales. London: HMSO.

Naylor, R.T. (1987) *Hot Money and the Politics of Debt*. New York: Simon and Schuster.

Ngugi wa Thiongo (1993) The language of African literature. In P. Williams and L. Chrisman (eds) *Colonial Discourse and Post-Colonial Theory: A Reader* (pp. 435–55). London: Harvester Wheatsheaf.

Nunberg, G. (1996) Farewell to the information age. In G. Nunberg (ed.) *The Future of the Book* (pp. 103–38). Berkeley, Los Angeles: University of California Press.

Oakhill, J. and Beard, R. (1995) Guest editorial. *Journal of Research in Reading* 18 (2), 69–73.

Olson, D. (1977) From utterance to text: The bias of language in speech and writing. *Harvard Education Review* 47 (3), 257–81.

Ong, W. (1982) *Orality and Literacy: The Technologizing of the Word*. London: Routledge.

Organisation for Economic Cooperation and Development (OECD) (1995) *Literacy, Economy and Society: Results of the First International Adult Literacy Survey*. Paris: OECD.

Ovarec, J.A. (1996) *Virtual Individuals, Virtual Groups: Human Dimensions of Groupware and Computer Networking*. Cambridge: Cambridge University Press.

Owen, S. and Heywood, J. (1990) Transition technology in Ireland: An experimental course. *International Journal of Research in Design and Technology Education* 1 (1), 21–32.

Owens, E. (1987) *The Future of Freedom in the Developing World: Economic Development as Political Reform*. New York: Pergamon.

Oxenham, J. (1980) *Literacy: Writing, Reading and Social Organisation*. London: Routledge and Kegan Paul.

Panos Institute (1995) The Internet and the South: Superhighway or dirt-track? Paris: Panas Institute. < http://www.oneworld.org/panos/panos_internet_press.html#information >

Parry, J. (1982) Popular attitudes towards Hindu religious texts. Unpublished MS.

Pateman, C. (1970) *Participation and Democratic Theory*. Cambridge: Cambridge University Press.

Pecheux, M. (1982) *Language, Semantics and ideology: Stating the Obvious*. (Harbans Nagpal trans.). London: Macmillan.

Peet, R. (1987) *International Capitalism and Industrial Restructuring: A Critical Analysis*. Boston: Allen & Unwin.

Perfetti, C.A. (1995) Cognitive research can inform reading education. *Journal of Research in Reading* 18 (2), 106–15.

Phillipson, R. and Skutnabb-Kangas, T, (1995a) Language rights in postcolonial Africa. In T. Skutnabb-Kangas and R. Phillipson (eds) *Linguistic Human Rights: Overcoming Linguistic Discrimination* (pp. 335–46). Berlin: Mouton de Gruyter.

Phillipson, R. and Skutnabb-Kangas, T. (eds) (1995b) *Linguistic Human Rights: Overcoming Linguistic Discrimination*. Berlin: Mouton de Gruyter.

Pollert, A. (1988) Dismantling flexibility. *Capital & Class* 34, (Spring), 42–75.

Porter, A.T. (1986) Education priorities in Sub-Saharan Africa. In H. Hawes and T. Coombe with C. Coombe and K. Lillis (eds) *Education Priorities and Aid Responses in Sub-Saharan Africa*. Report of a Conference at Cumberland Lodge, Windsor 4–7 December, 1984 (pp. 106–12). London: University of London Institute of Education/Overseas Development Administration.

Poster, M. (1994) The mode of information in postmodernity. In D. Crowley and D. Mitchell (eds) *Communication Theory Today* (pp. 173–92). Oxford: Polity Press.

Poster, M. (1996) Databases as discourse; or, electronic interpellations. In D. Lyon and E. Zureik (eds) *Computers, Surveillance, and Privacy* (pp. 175–92). Minneapolis, London: University of Minnesota Press.

Postman, N. (1986) *Amusing Ourselves to Death: Public Discourse in the Age of Show Business*. London: Heinemann.

President Clinton's call to action for American education in the 21st Century. In *America's Challenge: Background to President Clinton's State of the Union Address to Congress, Jan 1996*. Washington DC. (Press release) http://www1.whitehouse.gov.WH/New/other/challenge.html#education.

Ragsdale, R.G. (1988) *Permissible Computing in Education: Values, Assumptions, and Needs*. New York: Praeger.

Rassool, N. (1993) Post-Fordism? Technology and new forms of control: The case of technology in the curriculum. *British Journal of Sociology of Education* 14 (3), 227–44.

Rassool, N. (1995) Language, cultural pluralism and the silencing of minority discourses in England and Wales. *Journal of Education Policy* 10 (3), 287–302.

Rassool, N. (1997) Fractured or flexible identities? Life histories of 'black' diasporic women in Britain. In H. S. Mirza (ed.) *Black British Feminism: A Reader* (pp. 187–204). London: Routledge.

Rassool, N. (1998) Postmodernity, cultural pluralism and the nation-state: Problems of language rights, human rights identity and power. *Linguistic Sciences* 20 (1), 89–99.

Rassool, N. and Honour, L. (1996) Cultural pluralism and the struggle for democracy in post-communist Bulgaria. *Education Today* 46 (2), 12–23.

Reid, E. (1995) Virtual worlds: Culture and imagination. In S. Jones (ed.) *Cybersociety: Computer Mediated Communication and Community* (pp. 164–83). London: Sage.

Rheingold, (1993) *The Virtual Community: Homesteading on the Electronic Frontier.* Reading, MA: Addison-Wesley.

Rockhill, K. (1987) Gender, language and the politics of literacy. *British Journal of Sociology of Education* 8 (2), 153–67.

Rogers, A. (1993) The world crisis in adult education: A case study from literacy. *Compare* 23 (2), 159–75.

Rogers, E.M. (1986) *Communication Technology: The New Media in Society.* London: Collier Macmillan.

Rostow, W.W. (1960) *The Stages of Economic Growth: A Non-Communist Manifesto.* London: Cambridge University Press.

Roszak, T. (1994) *The Cult of Information.* Berkeley, Los Angeles: University of California Press.

Rubagumya, C.M. (ed.) (1990) *Language in Education in Africa: A Tanzanian Perspective.* Clevedon: Multilingual Matters.

Rumberger, R.W. and Levin, H.M. (1984) *Forecasting the Impact of New Technologies on the Future Job Market.* Project Report No. 84–A4. Institute for Research on Educational Finance and Governance. School of Education, Stanford University.

Ryan, J. (1992) Literacy research, policy and practice: The elusive triangle. *The Annals, the American Academy of Political and Social Science* 520, (Mar.), 36–53.

Ryan, J.W. (1987) Language and literacy: The planning of literacy activities in multilingual states. In G. Carron and A. Bordia (eds) *Issues in Planning and Implementing National Literacy Programmes* (pp.159–175). Paris: UNESCO, International Institute for Educational Planning.

Sached (1986) *The Right to Learn: The Struggle for Education in South Africa.* Prepared for Sached by Pam Christie. Braamfontein: The Sached Trust and Ravan Press.

Said, E. (1984) *The World, The Text, and The Critic.* London: Faber & Faber .

Salomon, J. J. (1993) Policy implications of new and emerging areas in science and technology for development. In C. Brundenius and B. Goransson (eds) *New Technologies and Global Restructuring: The Third World at the Cross-Roads* (pp. 35–51). London: Taylor Graham.

Scollon, R. and Scollon, S. (1979) *Linguistic Convergence: An Ethnography of Speaking at Fort Chipwyan, Alberta.* New York: Academic Press.

Scribner, S. (1984) Literacy in three metaphors. *American Journal of Education* (Nov.), 6–21.

Scribner, S. and Cole, M. (1988) Unpackaging literacy. In N. Mercer (ed.) *Language and Literacy from an Educational Perspective Vol. I: Language Studies* (pp. 241–55). Milton Keynes: Open University Press.

Shields, R. (ed.) (1996) *Cultures of Internet: Virtual Spaces, Real Histories, Living Bodies.* London: Sage.

Shor, I. (1980) *Critical Teaching and Everyday Life.* Boston: South End Press.

Shorish M. M. (1984) Planning by decree: The Soviet language policy in Central Asia. *Language Planning and Language Problems* 8 (1, Spring), 284–301.

Sivanandan, A. (1989) New circuits of imperialism. *Race & Class* 30 (3), 1–19.

Skutnabb-Kangas, T. (1988) Multilingualism and the education of minority children. In T. Skutnabb-Kangas and J. Cummins (eds) *Minority Education: From Shame to Struggle* (pp. 9–44). Clevedon: Multilingual Matters.

Skutnabb-Kangas, T. (1990) _Language, Literacy and Minorities_. London: Minority Rights Group.

Smith, A. (1986) On audio and visual technologies: A future for the printed word? In G. Baumann (ed.) _The Written Word: Literacy in Transition_ (pp. 151–69). Oxford: Clarendon Press.

Smith, A.D (1995) _Nations and Nationalism in a Global Era_. Cambridge: Cambridge University Press in association with Basil Blackwell.

Smith, F. (1971) _Understanding Reading: A Psycholinguistic Analysis of Reading and Learning to Read_. London: Holt, Rinehart & Winston.

Smith, F. (1979) _Reading_. Cambridge: Cambridge University Press.

Smith. H. (1991) Revolutionary diplomacy Sandinista style: Lessons and limits. _Race & Class: Configurations of Racism in the Civil Service_ 33 (1), 57–70.

Sontag, S. (1979) _On Photography_. London: Penguin Books.

Stalin, J. V. (1913) Marxism and the national question. _Prosveshcheniye_, 3–5, (March–May), transcribed for the Internet by Carl Kavanagh, 1996.

Stanovich, K. B. and Stanovich, P. J. (1995) How research might inform the debate about early reading acquisition. _Journal of Research in Reading_ 18 (2), 87–105.

Stanovich, K. E. (1986) Mathew effects in reading: Some consequences of individual differences in the acquisition of literacy. _Reading Research Quarterly_ (Fall), 360–406.

Steffens, H. (1986) Issues in the preparation of teachers for teaching robotics in schools. In J. Heywood and P. Mathews (eds) _Technology, Society and the School Curriculum_. Manchester: Roundthorn.

Stewart, F. (1994) Education and adjustment: The experience of the 1980s and lessons for the 1990s. In R. Prendergast and F. Stewart (eds) _Market Forces and World Development_ (pp. 128–59). Basingstoke: Macmillan.

Stiefel, M and Wolfe, M. (1994) _A Voice for the Excluded: Popular Participation in Development: Utopia or Necessity?_ London: Zed Books.

Street, B.V. (1984) _Literacy in Theory and Practice_. Cambridge: Cambridge University Press.

Street, B. V. (ed.) (1993) Introduction. _Cross-cultural Approaches to Literacy_ (pp. 1–21) Cambridge: Cambridge University Press.

Stromquist, N. P. (1990) Women and illiteracy: The interplay of gender subordination and poverty. _Comparative Education Review_ 34 (1), 95–111.

Stubbs, M. (1980) _Language and Literacy: The Sociolinguistics of Reading and Writing_. London: Routledge.

Tanguaine, S. (1990) _International Yearbook of Education_. Volume XVII (1990), _Literacy and Illiteracy in the World: Situation, Trends and Prospects_. Prepared for the International Bureau of Education. Paris: UNESCO.

Taylor, M. and Saarinen, E. (1994) _Imagologies: Media Philosophy_. London: Routledge.

New London Group (1996) A pedagogy of multiliteracies: Designing social futures. _Harvard Educational Review_ 66 (1, Spring), 60–92.

Todaro, M. P. (1989) _Economic Development in the Third World_. Harlow: Longman.

Todorov, T. (1984) _Mikhail Bakhtin: The Dialogical Principle_. (Wlad Godzich, trans.). Manchester: Manchester University Press.

Tollefson, J.W. (1991) _Planning Language, Planning Inequality: Language Policy in the Community_. London: Longman.

Turim, M. (1989) _Flashbacks in Film: Memory and History_. London: Routledge.

Turkle, S. (1996) _Life on the Screen: Identity in the Age of the Internet_. London: Weidenfeld and Nicolson.

UNESCO (1972) Literacy 1969–71: Progress achieved in literacy throughout the world. Paris: UNESCO.

UNESCO (1976) *The Experimental World Literacy Programme: A Critical Assessment.* Paris: Unesco/UNDP.

UNESCO (1990) *World Declaration on Education For All: Meeting Basic Needs.* Paris: UNESCO. < http://www.education.unesco.org:80/efa/07Apubl.htm >

UNESCO (1993) *Project 2000+ Declaration: Scientific and Technological Literacy for All.* International Council of Associations for Science Education. Paris: UNESCO. < http://sunsite.anu.edu.au/icase/dec.html >

UNESCO (1995a) *Compendium of Statistics on Literacy.* Paris: UNESCO.

UNESCO (1995b) *World Education Report.* Paris: UNESCO.

UNESCO (1997a) *Conference Report: Fifth International Conference on Adult Education, Hamburg, 3–4 July .* Paris: UNESCO.

UNESCO (1997b) *Status and Trends: Adult Education in a Polarizing World.* Report for the International Consultative Forum on Education for All, EFA Forum Secretariat. Paris: UNESCO. < http://www.education.unesco.org:80/efa/03697.htm >

United Nations (1990) *Human Development Report.* Paris: UNDP.

United Nations (1990) *Paris Declaration and Programme of Action of the Second United Nations Conference on the Least Developed Countries.* Excerpt from A/CONF.147/18. Paris: United Nations Department for Policy Coordination and Sustainable Development (DPCSD). < gopher://gopher.un.org:70/00/sec/dpcsd/oscal/paris.txt >

United Nations Economic Commission for Africa (ECA) (1996) *Prospects for Information Technology in Africa.* Report on Ninth Session of the Conference of African Planners, Statisticians, Population and Information Specialists, Addis Ababa, Ethiopia 11–16 March 1996. Paris: UNECA/UNDP < http://www.sas.upenn.edu/African_Studies/ECA/eca_planrs6.html >

Unsicker, J. (1987) Tanzania's literacy campaign in historical-structural perspective. In R.F. Arnove and H.J. Graff (eds) *National Literacy Campaigns: Historical and Comparative Perspectives* (pp. 219–44). London: Plenum Press.

US State Department (1997) *Ethiopia Country Report on Human Rights Practices for 1996.* Released by the Bureau of Democracy, Human Rights, and Labor, 30 January 1997. Washington, DC. < http://www.usis.usemb.se/human/ethiopia.htm >

Van Leewen, T. and Humphrey, S. (1996) On learning to look through a geographer's eyes. In R. Hasan and G. Williams (eds) *Literacy in Society* (pp. 29–49). London and New York: Longman.

Veel, R. and Coffin, C. (1996) Literacy learning across the curriculum: Towards a model of register for secondary school teachers. In R. Hasan and G. Williams *Literacy in Society* (pp. 191–231). London and New York: Longman.

Verhoeven, L. (1994) Modeling and promoting functional literacy. In L. Verhoeven (ed.) *Functional Literacy: Theoretical Issues and Educational Implications* (pp. 3–34). Amsterdam: John Benjamins.

Waetjen, W.B. (1993) Technological literacy reconsidered. *Journal of Technology Education* 4 (2), Spring < gopher://borg.lib.vt.edu:70/00/jte/v4n2/waetjen.jte-v4n2 >

Watson, J.K.P. (1983) Educational policies in Peninsular Malaysia. In C. Kennedy (ed.) *Language Planning and Language Education* (pp. 132–50). London: Allen & Unwin.

Watson, K. (1993) Changing emphases in educational aid. In T. Allsop and C. Brock (eds) _Key Issues in Educational Development_ (pp. 59–86). Oxford Studies in Comparative Education. Wallingford: Triangle Books.

Weaver, C. (1990) _Understanding Whole Language: From Principles to Practice._ Portsmouth, NH: Heinemann.

Weber, M. (1978) _Economy and Society_ (Vol. 1). Berkeley University of California Press.

Weir, A. (1995) Toward a model of self-identity: Habermas and Kristeva. In J. Meehan (ed.) _Feminists Read Habermas: Gendering the Subject of Discourse_ (pp. 263–82). London: Routledge.

Wells, G. (1986) _The Meaning Makers._ London: Hodder & Stoughton.

Wilk, R. R. (1995) Sustainable development: Practical, ethical, and social issues in technology transfer. In K. Ishizuka, S. Hisajima and D. R. J. Macer (eds) _Traditional Technology for Environmental Conservation and Sustainable Development in the Asian-Pacific Region_ (pp. 206–18). Tsukuba: Masters Programme in Environmental Sciences, University of Tsukuba, Japan.

Wilkinson. A. (ed.) (1965) _Spoken English._ With contributions by A. Davies and D. Atkinson. Educational Review Occasional Publications, No. 2, University of Birmingham.

Williams, R. (1961) _The Long Revolution._ Harmondsworth: Penguin Books in association with Chatto & Windus.

Williams, R. (1980) _Problems in Materialism and Culture: Selected Essays._ London: Verso New Left Editions.

Williams, R. (1989) Hegemony and the Selective Tradition. In S. de Castell, A. Luke and C. Luke (eds) _Language, Authority and Criticism: Readings on the School Textbook_ (pp. 56–60). Lewes: The Falmer Press.

Winner, L. (1986) _The Whale and the Reactor: A Search for Limits in an Age of High Technology._ Chicago: The University of Chicago Press.

World Bank (1989) _Sub-Saharan Africa: From Crisis to Sustainable Growth._ Washington, DC: World Bank.

World Bank (1991) _Nongovernmental Organizations and the World Bank; Cooperation for Development._ Washington: The World Bank.

World Bank (1996) _From Plan To Market, World Development Report._ Oxford: Oxford University Press.

Young, M.F.D. _Knowledge and Control: New Directions for the Sociology of Education._ London: Collier Macmillan.

Zabala, G. (1992) The role of literacy NGOs in a post-apartheid South Africa. In _Report on the Proceedings of the Conference on Empowerment of the Oppressed: Taking Literacy to the Grassroots_ (pp. 34–42). Durban: South African Association For Literacy and Adult Education (SAALAE).

Zariski, A. (1995) Virtual textuality and the library. _Law Librarian_ 26 (1, March), 279–81. < http://carmen.murdoch.edu.au/~zariski/virtual.html >

Zuengler, J. (1985) English, Swahili, or other languages? The relationship of educational development goals to language instruction in Kenya and Tanzania. In N. Wolfson and J. Manes (eds) _Language of Inequality_ (pp. 214–54). Berlin: Mouton.

Index